n or before the date below.

The Home Front
in the Great War

The Home Front in the Great War

Aspects of the Conflict
1914-1918

David Bilton

Pen & Sword
MILITARY

Published in 2003 by Leo Cooper
and re-printed in this format in 2013 by

Pen & Sword Military
an imprint of
Pen & Sword Books Ltd
47 Church Street
Barnsley
South Yorkshire
S70 2AS

The right of David Bilton to be identified as author of this work has
been asserted by him in accordance with the Copyright, Designs and
Patents Act 1988.

Copyright © David Bilton, 2003, 2013

ISBN:- 978-1-78346-177-6

Printed and bound in the UK by CPI Group (UK) Ltd, Croydon, CR0 4YY

Pen & Sword Books Ltd incorporates the Imprints of Pen & Sword Aviation,
Pen & Sword Family History, Pen & Sword Maritime, Pen & Sword Military, Pen
& Sword Discovery, Wharncliffe Local History, Wharncliffe True Crime,
Wharncliffe Transport, Pen & Sword Select, Pen & Sword Military Classics, Leo
Cooper, The Praetorian Press, Remember When, Seaforth Publishing
and Frontline Publishing.

For a complete list of Pen & Sword titles please contact
PEN & SWORD BOOKS LIMITED
47 Church Street, Barnsley, South Yorkshire, S70 2AS, England
E-mail: enquiries@pen-and-sword.co.uk
Website: www.pen-and-sword.co.uk

Contents

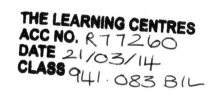

Acknowledgements

'Are you writing another book daddy?' and 'When can I use the computer?' or 'That's not fair,' cried my children. 'Sorry', I replied. Thank you Joshua, Rachel and Esther for allowing me. Heartfelt thanks to my wife for taking over nearly everything (and even providing photographs to use in the book), while I tapped into the night.

As usual, many thanks to Anne Coulson for proof reading and editing the book.

Much of the material used comes from my own archive but especial thanks for the use of photographs and ephemera must go to Ian Anderson.

Researching the book would have been considerably more difficult and a lot more painful without the help of *The Prince Consort's Library* in Aldershot – kind to a fault. The material for the section on the workings of a Prisoner of War Committee were kindly provided by Pam Boyd at the Prince of Wales's Own Regiment of Yorkshire Museum.

Foreword

The history of the Home Front during the Great War has recently featured in a Channel 4 *Secret History* programme. Entitled *Horror on the Home Front* it tried to show that Britain was on the verge of collapse by 1917 and that the experience on the Home Front was essentially horrific. Horror, however, is a relative concept. Nothing that was experienced on the Home Front could truly match the levels of horror and terror of the Western Front. Some of the experiences were clearly horrendous: for example, when listening to my grandparents' recollections of Zeppelin attacks on Hull, one is filled with a sense of fear and foreboding. Similarly, one cannot imagine the 'corrosive anxiety' of the wife left behind to bring up the children, while the father is in the trenches. However, on the whole, life during the period is more accurately described as being grim, and grew grimmer as the war progressed; England was no longer merry. On the other hand, like life in the trenches, there were positive aspects to the whole experience.

In this book I have tried to give an overall impression of the war on the Home Front on a yearly basis, followed by a timeline of the events for the period. There are many good books on the minutiae of daily life, mostly no longer available except through second-hand sources. However, there are many aspects of the conflict that are not generally covered by such works; in the third part of the book I have attempted to cover these areas using the writings of the period and therefore the feelings of the day. *The Times History of the War*, which was published during the period, contains many such articles, written by those who were there; I have used these as the basis of this section in order to show **their experiences** and **their perceptions** of their war. This is not a book full of original research or investigations: it is designed to open up new lines of thought and interest and to stimulate further research into these forgotten aspects of the similarly forgotten Home Front of the Great War. In the final section I have showed how one City, in this case Hull (though its contents are symptomatic of many other towns and cities), felt about its war.

The experience of over forty million people during the War to end all Wars was quickly subsumed by the realities of the returning combatants and the overwhelming grief for their compatriots of the un-returning army. Experienced by so many, the Home Front is not so much a secret history as a forgotten one.

Introduction

The effect of the war on the Home Front was to be profound and long lasting. At the start of the war, everything was swept along on an euphoric wave with a belief in the right of the cause and a rapid end to the war; for the first few months it was a case of 'business as usual'. Civilian life was impinged upon but it was essentially a war for the armed forces to fight and win. As casualties rose and the German Navy bombarded the East Coast the war came to the civilian population. Zeppelins and aeroplanes followed in 1915 causing further death, injury and damage. As the war on the Western Front intensified and the army grew in size, its demands for material put serious strains on the economy and production, necessitating an increasing mobilisation of civilians of both sexes in order to feed the guns. Increasing output meant new factories and a more mobile population that put a further strain on the people.

Old pleasures slowly died out: race meetings disappeared, as did much professional sport. Alcohol was diluted and taxed, and licensing hours were changed. Movement at night became more difficult due to lighting restrictions and healthy young men disappeared from the street as the armed forces' need for men increased with each year of the war to be replaced by those discharged as unsuitable for further service. Rents increased as did food prices and there were food shortages. At the start of the war Britain had been a major food importer, producing only around a third of the population's needs; unrestricted submarine warfare eventually meant food shortages and *ersatz* foods. Food shortages resulted in queues and worker discontent that eventually forced the government to take action, first with price controls and later with rationing.

Increasing war output led to war profits for the factory owner and higher wages for the worker. However, the rising price of food meant that the real value of wages fell by 15%. For workers who before the war had struggled to make ends meet due to the uncertainties of the job market, constant employment did improve their living standards and, for many, the war meant better health.

As the number of volunteers for the armed forces decreased, it was necessary to introduce conscription for those who were deemed to be non-essential to the maintenance of the war effort. Even this did not produce enough men for the Army and as the war casualties increased more and more men were 'combed-out' from essential industries and occupations. As the number of men in employment fell women took their place. This temporarily allowed women to make a greater contribution to the war effort and improved their financial status. However, this was short-lived and upon the return of the men from the war they left industrial employment to such an extent that by 1921 there were fewer female industrial labourers than there had been in 1911.

Mass production in British factories came as a result of the insatiable demands of the army for munitions. Assembly lines were introduced and production was further quickened by electrification. Eventually production was standardised and the government took control of more than 20,000 private factories, one of the largest being the Austin car factory at Longbridge. Before the war this had employed 2,000 workers making 80 cars a week. Under government control production was altered and new workshops built for the 20,000 workers who were to eventually make up the work force. By the end of the war Austin's had made 9 million shells, 650 artillery pieces, 2,000 aeroplanes, 2,500 aircraft engines, 480 armoured cars and 2,000 lorries. There were also National Factories that were government owned; many of these produced artillery shells and around 200 women lost their lives in explosions at these factories.

The standard of literacy before the war was high, with most people able to read. Popular newspapers provided the population with the information they needed but, during the war, this right to know was taken away by the Press Bureau that vetted each story. This was, supposedly, to avoid giving information to the enemy (as had been done by *The Times* during the Crimean War) and to ensure that the public did not panic when things did not run smoothly. Hand in hand with censorship went propaganda, provided by the government, to the people, in the form of posters and film.

The military aspects of the war would also play a part in the everyday life of the Home Front both during and after the war. Advances in medical treatment included blood transfusions and the use of X-rays, while damaged bodies would be repaired with the use of prosthetic limbs and plastic and cosmetic surgery. In the factories, the mass use of electricity resulted in the construction of power stations with powerful generators that would eventually form the 'National Grid' in 1926. The war also gave a boost to air travel. By the end of the war there was a large aircraft industry and over 15,000 airmen looking for some form of employment. It was these men who started the fledgling air passenger services to France, flying converted bombers, that later became airlines. The techniques of mass-production also resulted in cheap cars produced in their thousands by Morris and Austin. As a result of their contribution to the war effort women received the vote; however, it was not until 1928 that this was universal.

On a less consequential level there were other changes. The length of women's skirts went up and some factory women became used to wearing trousers. Gold coins disappeared in 1914 and never returned. War savings certificates continued and are still available today (but under a different name). Twice a year the clock is changed for winter and summer time, and the wristwatch, which had first become popular in the trenches, replaced the pocket watch. And where would civilisation be without the zip fastener that was invented during the war?

1

1914 – The Background

If the war had started a year later, Britain would have been able to celebrate a century of continental peace; the last time its armies had fought in Europe had been the Battle of Waterloo in June 1815. But it was not to be. While across Europe the weather had been very good, for those in Britain who had been following the events in the Balkans, the dark clouds of war could clearly be seen.

The assassination of the Archduke Ferdinand on 28 June set in motion a chain of events, which, while not inevitable, were wanted by many in authority. Even before the assassination, Von Moltke, Chief of the Great General Staff of the German army, had called for a preventative war and, by July, Kaiser Wilhelm was ready to run the risk of a conflict. The plan was to fight an imperialist war of conquest against the Western Powers using the conflict between Austria-Hungary and Serbia as the excuse. The Austria-Hungarian ultimatum of 23 July was made so severe that it would be rejected and a war would follow. Serbia did not want war and acceded to all but one of the demands: unfortunately for the rest of Europe it had not been unconditional and Austria-Hungary declared war. On the same day as the ultimatum, Russia ordered a partial ultimatum and when this had no effect ordered full mobilisation. The German response to this was to declare war on Russia on 1 August.

Even at this point a full-scale European war was not inevitable. But the fate of millions was sealed, when the next day German troops invaded Luxembourg. In Britain, sections of territorial units were recalled from their summer training camps and Naval and army reservists were called back to their units. Mobilisation plans were put into operation and the armed forces waited.

While mobilisation plans went ahead the British government tried in vain to stop the war. King George wired the Tsar that Germany had recommended British proposals to Austria but Russia did not reply to the German ultimatum. The chain of events that led to the war can be briefly stated. At 3.40 pm the French ordered mobilisation and Belgium announced her intention to remain neutral. When German troops invaded Luxembourg they also crossed into French territory and killed a number of French troops. At the same time German troops entered Poland and East Prussia was attacked by Russian troops. In response to the Belgian neutrality statement, Germany demanded that the country remain passive while German troops pass through their nation in order to counter the perceived attack by the French through Belgium. Britain assured France that the Fleet would stop the German Fleet if it attacked French shipping in the Channel. The Belgians were unable to accede to the German demands and asked King George to intervene to safeguard their integrity. The next day, 3

August, Germany declared war on France and the Cabinet authorised the mobilisation of the British Expeditionary Force.

Business as usual

On 4 August, after British protests in Berlin against the possible violation of Belgian territory, Germany invaded Belgium and then declared war; as a result, British forces were mobilised. After Sir Edward Goschen's interview with the German Chancellor, in which the Chancellor queried the need to honour a 'scrap of paper', the Government gave the Germans an ultimatum which expired at midnight Central European time. When the German government did not respond, a state of war existed between Britain and Germany. The war on the Home Front would begin the next day. All that the public could do in the meantime was go to the pub and either celebrate or commiserate.

The next day the Bank Holiday was extended and the banks were closed until the end of the week. Gold sovereigns were called in and replaced by paper money, the one pound and ten shilling notes. The Stock Exchange ceased its dealings and was not allowed to re-open until January 1915.

The first problem to be solved was: who was to be the Secretary of State for War? Asquith had been combining this job with being Prime Minister since the resignation of J E B Seely over the Curragh incident in March of that year. It was obvious to Asquith that this situation could not continue and a new man would have to be found. His first choice was Haldane but he was felt to be too pro-German. A more popular candidate and one that the Cabinet felt would inspire the people was Lord Kitchener of Khartoum. On 5 August, Asquith persuaded him to take the position. The way was now open to some form of direction for the war. The next day Kitchener outlined his plans for a much expanded army based on the regular army system. This was to provide a further 500,000 men but the first appeal, launched on 7 August, asked for an initial 100,000 men.

The first major change that the war would bring was the rapid removal of tens of thousands of men to France, leaving regimental depots all over the

A patriotic postcard showing what the British would do to the Kaiser given the opportunity.

Cheering the King and Queen at Buckingham Palace on the night of the Declaration of War with Germany.

A French postcard of Lord Kitchener, the Secretary of State for War

Recruits taking the Oath of Allegiance before a magistrate at a recruiting office in London.

The older generation as recruiting officers.

country empty. This exodus would rapidly be followed by removal of even more men from their normal place of abode to new parts of the country as units were formed and moved to training grounds far and wide. While many men volunteered for their local army regiment or Corps, some deliberately volunteered, like one Tynesider, who had never been south of Gateshead, for the Rifle

Leicestershire Regiment Territorials being mobilised at the start of the war.

Medical Officer. "SORRY I MUST REJECT YOU ON ACCOUNT OF YOUR TEETH."
Would-be Recruit. "MAN, YE'RE MAKING A GRAN' MISTAKE. I'M NO WANTING TO BITE THE GERMANS, I'M WANTING TO SHOOT 'EM."

Many men were turned down at the recruiting office because of bad teeth. A Punch cartoon on the subject and (opposite) an advertising flyer from a dentist in Grimsby, offering to help would-be recruits overcome this problem.

Corps which was stationed at Winchester; the army even paid his train fare!

This recruiting boom had started on 5 August, when arriving at their recruiting office at Great Scotland Yard after the Bank Holiday, it took the recruiting officer and a police escort twenty minutes to get into the office. It took him and his medical staff all day, working solidly, to process the men. The next day, even though it was raining, there were further crowds. By the end of the first day there were still over 700 men waiting to enlist. On 7 August the crowds were so big that mounted police were needed to hold them back. Initially, the enthusiasm for the war seemed to be almost solely in London where the majority of the recruits came from. However, with the opening of new recruiting offices all over the country the flow of volunteers increased. Pre-war, the average daily intake into the army had been around a 100 per day, now it was in its thousands, overwhelming recruiting stations and the facilities to house them.

What to do with the increasing number of recruits? Accommodating such a large number of men with the available resources was impossible. The first make-shift alternative would be the provision of tents, which was fine while the weather was good but with the coming winter other avenues would need to be investigated. There was insufficient space in existing barracks so buildings were

13

The rapid building of wood and corrugated iron huts helped solve the shortage of accommodation.

requisitioned, both empty and those in use. But even this was insufficient for the number of volunteers, and new camps sprung up across the country. While these camps were constructed many men lodged at home, receiving a daily allowance to cover their costs.

As well as there being a shortage of suitable buildings there was also a severe shortage of equipment and uniforms. For many months men trained in their own clothes, using pieces of wood to imitate rifles, their armbands alone designating them as soldiers. Some received a partial uniform, some received ceremonial uniforms made of red cloth, while for many thousands a special blue uniform was produced. This was detested because it made them look like Post Office employees more than soldiers.

It became a common sight across the country to see men in training on any

Even though huts were being put up as quickly as possible, many men were billeted in tents well into the late autumn.

With insufficient uniforms to go round, many men were issued with a blue uniform that was universally hated because it made them look like GPO workers rather than soldiers.

The 2nd City Battalion of the Liverpool Regiment arriving at Hooton Park racecourse, October 1914.

Any open space could be used for training. In this photograph, the troops in the foreground are probably pre-war Territorials, while those in the background are new recruits, lacking both weapons and uniforms.

On the sea front in southeast England.

available space. Men trained in the local parks, in the grounds of stately homes, marched out into countryside and then marched back into town. Seafronts could be seen covered in men running up and down beaches or doing press-ups on the seafront. The Sheffield City Battalion learned squad drill on Sheffield United's pitch, the Bradford Pals trained in Manningham Park while the Hull Pals trained on Hull Fairground, West Park, Anlaby Road Cricket ground and the playing fields of Hull Grammar school. Everywhere there were men in training.

Initially, the war was expected to have serious effects upon the economy and as a result relief committees were set up and large sums donated by the public. Fortunately, the envisaged level of distress never materialised although there was initially some unemployment in the cotton industry and in some luxury trades. The main cases of hardship were among the families of men joining the armed forces. This applied early on to wives and children of recruits – separation allowances were slow to arrive; over a longer period it applied to other dependants, such as elderly parents, for whom no state provision was made

THE PALS

MANCHESTER'S OWN.

THE CITY EXPECTS AND THE CITY KNOWS THAT EVERY MAN WILL DO HIS DUTY.

Many areas recruited 'Pals' battalions, with each town producing its own postcards of the event.

A church doorway with a notice asking people to say their prayers for the soldiers and sailors.

The Noon Prayer Watch was started shortly after the outbreak of the war.

until late 1915. But in general there was little distress and many industries entered upon a boom. Most of the money raised went to other causes.

Another prophecy that proved incorrect was that of predicted food shortages. Immediately on the outbreak of war, there was panic buying of foodstuffs, mostly by those affluent enough to be able to both buy and store it. Grocers reported eight days' business done in a day with some shops selling out completely. In some cases foodstuffs were withheld to push up prices. There were even reports of angry poor women snatching parcels from the rich. As a result of this, the government began to requisition foodstuffs that were being unreasonably withheld in an attempt to keep prices more stable. But because of the Royal Navy's control of the sea, there was no immediate and desperate threat to food supplies. Two-thirds of Britain's sugar supplies had come from what were now enemy states but the government acted quickly to replace these suppliers. Meat supplies were reduced slightly because of the generous meat allocation given by the rapidly increasing army. There was also a shortage of wheat that was caused by two factors; difficulties in getting supplies from Russia and a generally poor world harvest. Government maximum price fixing stopped

Many men over the military age wanted to help their country but were denied the chance by the army; eventually they were allowed to form Home Defence units (Volunteer Corps) at their own expense. Here, some 1914 'volunteers' are inspected.

the rush to hoard but later prices did rise, partially offsetting any increase in wages brought about by increased employment. By the end of 1914 price-fixing had been abandoned.

All foreigners had to register with the police and were not allowed to venture outdoors between the hours of 9 pm and 5 am unless they had a warrant. They were banned from sensitive areas of the country, and all hotels and guesthouses had to register any alien guests.

In both Britain and Germany the outburst of patriotism was accompanied by a wave of xenophobic spy-mania and the mere presence of large German communities in some towns provided the population with many untrue stories. Many Germans had left at once for Germany; those who remained had to register, many of whom were later interned. The government acted to arrest

Aliens at a London Police Station waiting to be transferred to an internment camp.

There were many
rumours about German
barbers and what they
did to their customers.

Teutonic Barber. "SHAFE, SIR?"
Customer. "YE-ES—— THAT IS, NO!—I THINK I'LL TRY A HAIR-CUT."

A Punch cartoon
about the spy-
mania that swept
the country at the
start of the war.

PERCY T. REYNOLDS-

"RUN AVAY, YOU LEEDLE POYS; DON'T GOME HERE SHPYING ABOUT!"

SEASIDE MINSTREL, SUSPECTED OF BEING AN ALIEN, IS MADE TO REMOVE THE BLACK FROM HIS FACE FOR PURPOSES OF IDENTIFICATION.

Any suspicious person was immediately suspected of being an alien.

suspected spies but this did not stop German residents, mostly tradesmen, from becoming targets for attack. German grocers were said to be lacing their foodstuffs with poison and barbers were liable to cut their customers' throats. Stories were told of Governesses who kept bombs in their trunks. Railway signalmen were being overpowered in the their signal boxes by roving bands of Germans – in response to the threat of sabotage on the railways the army kept hundreds of men guarding long stretches of track. Then there was the case of the 'nurse' in a railway carriage, who, when she removed her gloves, had hands like a butcher. Anti-German messages were carried in *The Daily Mail* telling people to refuse to be served by a German or Austrian waiter and if they said they were Swiss, the paper suggested that customers ask to see his passport.

Innocent people were harried because of misplaced patriotism, revenge and spite. Florence Mower from remembered that anyone was fair game for a spy:

If you saw somebody in the street that was a bit strange, somebody perhaps with a black beard, kids would run after them shouting, 'You're a German spy.' Someone you hadn't seen near your terrace before, who just happened to be looking around, was automatically a German spy.

It was not just children that were accusatorial:

Grown-ups as well as children were just the same with the Irish. Irish people

20

were just spies for the Germans. We had some near us down St Paul Street, Patsie Kelly and his housekeeper. Patsie used to wear one of these Catholic round hats, and they used to follow him and shout after him, 'Irish German spy'.

A Swiss waiter was taken to Scotland Yard in the belief that he had been drawing military installations when in reality he had been sketching, on a menu card, a plan of the tables in the dining room.

Anti-German feeling did not just stop at words. Alfred Dee recalled that:

There was a pork butcher's shop on Spring Bank, Kress and Wagner's. They were from Germany. There was [sic] a lot of German pork butcher's [sic] in England at the time, and quite a number in Hull. Rumours went round that Kress and Wagner were spies and, in fact I was one of the lads that went and stoned the shop: a big gang of us under the trees that lined Spring Bank, chucking big stones through the windows.

A QUICK CHANGE OF FRONT.

Having a German name became very unfashionable and many families adopted an Anglicised version of their name to avoid persecution.

German surnames were very distinctive and many established naturalised families chose to anglicise them just to be on the safe side. Common changes were Steineker to Stanley, Stohwasser to Stowe, Rosenheim to Rose and Schact to Dent. Even members of the Royal family could not escape from this sort of pressure. At the end of October Prince Louis of Battenberg was force to resign as First Sea Lord and later changed his name to Mountbatten. Later in the war even the King felt it necessary to adopt an English name for his dynasty.

Hand in hand with spy phobia came strange war stories born of hysteria. Two have become famous. During the retreat from Mons, Arthur Machen had written a story in which the ghosts of the archers of Crécy helped the British troops. Shortly after its publication soldiers were seeing visions of St George, angels, and arrow wounds on German bodies. And in September, thousands of Russian soldiers were supposed to have passed through England, in closed and blacked-out railway carriages, on their way to France.

Britain prided itself upon being a democracy; DORA was to change that. On 8 August, Parliament passed the Defence of the Realm Act in just five minutes and effectively signed away the traditional freedoms of the British people putting Britain under martial law and virtually suspending civil rights for the duration. It gave the executive almost unlimited powers, including court-martialling persons breaking security regulations and allowed the police to stop and question suspects, who could be imprisoned on refusal to

TAKING NO RISKS.

Anti-German feeling even went as far as dogs!

Coastal areas were closed and anyone entering these areas had their papers and permits inspected.

OPENED BY CENSOR. ·

4671

DORA imposed on every aspect of life. The censor inspected every letter coming into the country.

answer, and arrest without a warrant. And as the war continued, DORA continued to be added to and refined so that it eventually encroached on every activity of the British citizen.

Following on from DORA came press censorship. The Press Bureau was set up in Royal United Services Institution on 10 August to perform two functions. Firstly, it was the official dispenser of war news for the War Office and Admiralty and secondly, it was authorised to censor any war news that the papers had obtained independently and sent to them for censoring. Although not obliged to send in news stories for censoring, newspapers that published anything that was false or gave out restricted information were liable to be prosecuted under DORA.

Special constables made their first appearance during this period, guarding tunnels, bridges and railway stations alongside troops and Boy Scouts. There were fewer cars and taxis in the street as the army had commandeered many of them, there were also fewer buses as these were in use in France as troop carriers. In September street lamps were dimmed along with shop lights. To further the gloom, County cricket was no more, golf courses were mostly deserted and women's fashions grew more sober. Casualty lists grew and the West End plays reflected the times with such plays as *Tommy Atkins*; people quickly grew used to the sight of ambulances carrying the wounded.

Although it was wartime, there was no change to the Lord Mayor of London's banquet in November. As usual large quantities of champagne were used to wash down the traditional turtle soup and 'barons of beef', served by smart white-coated stewards.

In 1914 each area of the country had specified licensing hours, differing across the country in a complicated way. The serving hours that existed meant generally easy access to alcohol that the government

A Special Constable in the Ilford area. Note the three-striped armband that signified his position of authority.

After brief military training, a number of army battalions were used to patrol sensitive areas of the country. These King's Own Lancashire troops guarded the railway line from London through to Swindon and beyond. This photo shows a section responsible for guarding the track near Reading.

Very quickly the wounded became an everyday sight. These are recovering on the seafront at Brighton.

I.

II.

III.
"-MORNING, MATE. BIT BREEZY FOR
GETTING A LIGHT, AIN'T IT?"

Army guards and Special Constables longed to catch a saboteur.

quickly restricted under the DORA regulations, giving military authorities the power to specify the opening hours of public houses in or around defended harbours. This was quickly superseded by the Intoxicating Liquor (Temporary Restriction) Act on 31 August that gave local Chiefs of Police the power to restrict licensing hours as appropriate to the maintenance of order and the suppression of drunkenness. The act was to be valid till a month after the end of the war. By the end of the year half of the licensing authorities in England and Wales had restricted their hours with a consequent massive decrease in intoxication and disorder.

While the men marched, most of the women stayed at home, but according to *The Times* they were not idle.

From the first the women of title or position, led by the queen, gave time, money and ability to organising or helping on some movement for the care and comfort of the broken soldier and the bereaved among their sister-women. First and foremost, there were hospitals which needed women's aid. The superb response of the women of England to the call for nurses, the work of the Red Cross and the Voluntary Aid Detachments... Then there were

DORA even restricted that haven of Britishness – the pub. Hours were controlled and the government determined the quantity of alcohol sold, as well as its strength.

"WOT'S THE USE OF THIS 'ERE EARLIER CLOSING?"
"WY, IN CASE OF A ZEPPELIN RAID. IF THE 'UN SMELLS
BEER 'E'LL 'AVE IT!"

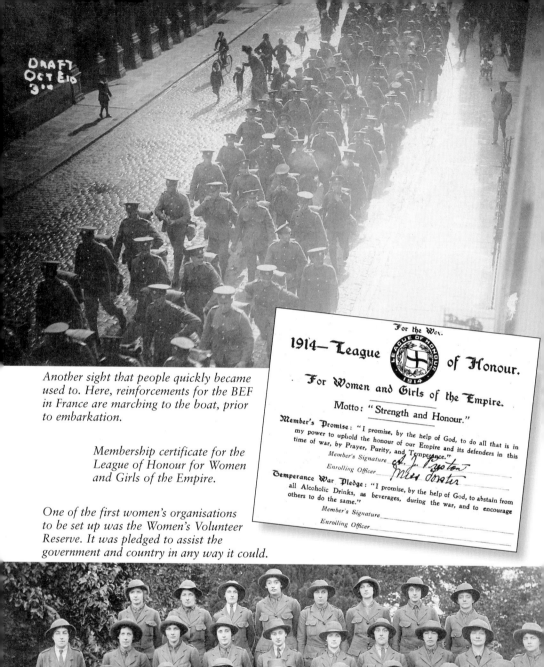

DRAFT
OCT £10
3/0

Another sight that people quickly became used to. Here, reinforcements for the BEF in France are marching to the boat, prior to embarkation.

Membership certificate for the League of Honour for Women and Girls of the Empire.

One of the first women's organisations to be set up was the Women's Volunteer Reserve. It was pledged to assist the government and country in any way it could.

For the War.

1914— League of Honour.

LEAGUE OF HONOUR
1914

For Women and Girls of the Empire.

Motto: "Strength and Honour."

Member's Promise: "I promise, by the help of God, to do all that is in my power to uphold the honour of our Empire and its defenders in this time of war, by Prayer, Purity, and Temperance."

Member's Signature _A. I. Payston_

Enrolling Officer _Miss Forster_

Temperance War Pledge: "I promise, by the help of God, to abstain from all Alcoholic Drinks, as beverages, during the war, and to encourage others to do the same."

Member's Signature _____

Enrolling Officer _____

matinee performances to be arranged in support of this or that object, concerts to be promoted, bazaars to be organized. The 'flag' day, an ingenious but rather over-worked plan for collecting the spare money of the multitude by selling them small button-hole emblems which secured them immunity from appeals for the rest of the day, provided another form of war service for women of the leisured classes. They created and carried on free buffets for soldiers and sailors at railway stations, largely in response to a letter published in The Times *from a soldier who signed himself 'On leave and Tired.' They showed taste and tireless energy in the decoration and staffing of Y.M.C.A. huts in the military camps and near the railway termini... Tea parties were given in private houses, motor cars were provided.*

And in any other way they could help, they did so.

Britain was slowly moving in industrial terms, towards mass production in armaments and other war necessities; it was on a war footing but the country itself was not yet a war zone. It was to be a further month before it became a true 'Home Front' in a military sense.

After a disastrous holiday season, Christmas promised to be a bright spot in a miserable year for Scarborough. For the inhabitants, soldiers and barbed wire barricades soon became familiar sights as Norman Hodgson, whose family lived behind Foreshore Road, recalled:

Active service was not an option for women in 1914, so many joined the voluntary services and helped look after the wounded. Pictured is a St John VAD nurse.

All the steps leading from the seafront to the cliff and to the main streets were barricaded with barbed wire, only one narrow stairway being left for our use. When we emerged from our stairway, the first thing we saw was a sandbagged barricade across Eastborough, six feet high and six feet thick. There was a staggered passage through it, so that there was no gap through which a bullet could pass.

Members of the Royal Field Artillery guarding the East Coast, Christmas 1914.

The damage done to Whitby Abbey.

There were some trained soldiers stationed in the town but most were Territorial Force recruits of the 2/5th Yorkshire Regiment. At sea, naval patrols kept a watch for intruders. Scarborough looked like it was at war but it felt at peace. That would change on the morning of 16 December.

Ironically, defeat in the Falkland Islands had given the German navy a temporary strategic superiority that Admiral Von Ingenohl was prepared to use. On 2 November a German battle cruiser squadron shelled Yarmouth. The raid was designed to test the Royal Navy's response rather than inflict any real damage (the shells fell short and there were no casualties). To the British the raid was a failure but to the Germans it showed that a fast moving squadron could both attack a coastal town and evade the Royal Navy. The plan that was conceived was to lure out a British squadron from the Grand Fleet using an advanced force and lead the British ships to the waiting guns of the German fleet. The advanced force would then crown the victorious sea battle with a raid on the English coast, providing a great victory and a considerable amount of national and international publicity.

By 14 December, British Intelligence was aware that an attack was being prepared but the reports did not indicate where. As the whole of the waters off the northeast coast were a German-laid minefield, Admiral Jellicoe positioned his fleet 25 miles southeast of Dogger Bank and waited. The wait was in vain for the main German fleet was ordered home when it came across British destroyers

Scarborough Castle was not fortified in any way. German shells damaged the wall and destroyed the coastguard building.

Another sight that was becoming more common – trainloads of troops being moved around the country; in this case a Territorial Battalion of the Royal Scots Fusiliers.

that it thought were part of a screen covering the entire British fleet. The raiding force, under Admiral Von Hipper, was left off the English coast without support.

The foul weather, that had been encountered by the main German fleet and caused them to return to Germany, worked to the advantage of the raiding force. Under cover of the dark and mist, it steamed through a gap in the minefield off Whitby and, nearing the coast, split into a north and south attack force. Shortly after 8 am the raiding group fired on the castle and then on the

October 1914 – captured German sailors being escorted to an internment camp.

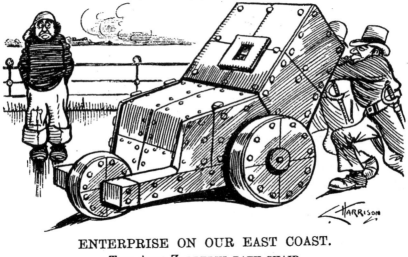

ENTERPRISE ON OUR EAST COAST.
THE ANTI-ZEPPELIN BATH-CHAIR.

Long promised, the Zeppelin threat had not yet materialised.

town. Whitby lay on their return journey and an hour after they had shelled Scarborough they were shelling Whitby. Further to the north, the German raiders were also shelling Hartlepool, the only legitimate military target. The two raiding parties regrouped and slipped through the minefield and returned to their base, leaving behind a civilian war zone of death and destruction with over 130 killed and nearly 600 injured.

The German air attacks on Britain started at 1 pm on 21 December when an enemy seaplane appeared over the Admiralty pier at Dover, dropped two bombs into the sea and made off. Just three days later an aeroplane again flew over Dover, dropped a bomb that exploded in a cabbage patch near the castle, and flew off. On Christmas Day a German seaplane flew over the Thames estuary, passing above Sheerness at 12.35 pm, pushing on as far as Erith. Here it was engaged by three British aeroplanes and turned back, making good its escape.

At Christmas there were few signs of wartime austerity, food was plentiful,

Princess Mary sent a Christmas card and brass tobacco case to every British soldier.

With Best Wishes · for a · Happy Christmas · and a · Victorious New Year.

From The Princess Mary and Friends at · Home · · · · ·

M · 1914 ·

Friends all.

The war would be over by Christmas. A 1914 Christmas card from F C Bowring. The message inside reads: 'At this time of National Trial may you be of good heart, spend a Pleasant Christmas and look forward with confidence to a Happy and Prosperous New Year.'

especially luxuries, which had actually fallen in price due to the decline in entertaining; shops were packed with goods and war toys were very popular. By now the war should have been over but it was clearly not. At the front men celebrated with a truce, while at home the bells rang – until silenced by DORA regulations. Many homes were in mourning, with thousands more to follow:

What do you clear bells ring to me
In this glad hour of jubilee?
Not joy, not joy. I hear instead:
So many dead! So many dead!

Four years later the war would indeed be over for Christmas!

1

1915 – Towards Total War

Prices had risen during the preceding months. In February the General Federation of Trade Unions issued a pamphlet which argued that wages were being eroded by the increasing cost of food. Primary necessities such as wheat and meat, according to government statistics, comprised about twenty per cent of an average working class family's expenditure. Compared with 1914, wheat prices had risen 72 per cent, barley by 40 per cent and oats by 34 per cent. There had been no failure of supply for meat but prices had rushed up,

The crews of many drifters and smaller boats were in the service of the Royal Navy causing prices to rise due to a scarcity of fish and seafood.

Customer. "BUT THAT'S A FEARFUL PRICE FOR SHRIMP-PASTE."
Grocer. "AH, BUT THESE ARE NORTH SEA SHRIMPS, MADAM."

A postcard sold to raise funds to support the Belgians in Britain and Belgium.

particularly in respect of the poorer quality cuts. Neck of mutton had previously cost between $2^1/_2$d to 3d a pound but by 1915 the lowest grade of this cut – scrag of mutton – was fetching from $4^1/_2$d to 6d per pound while brisket had risen from around 5d a pound to 9d. However, by the middle of the year the Board of Trade was able to announce that the government had been able to check the advance in meat prices. Fish had also become so expensive that the Archbishop of Westminster allowed his parishioners to eat flesh on Fridays instead of the traditional fish.

The recruitment of large numbers of mineworkers (by December 1914 around 14 per cent of miners had joined up), coupled with transportation difficulties caused by the military use of the railways, resulted in shortages and an increase in coal prices. At the start of February 1915 the cost of best quality Derbyshire coal had risen about 20 per cent. By the middle of the year the government had 'persuaded' coal-merchants to curb their profits and taken powers to limit the price being charged by the collieries.

Measures like this only limited price rises, further increases were inevitable. Only two major increases were actually 'pegged' during the year, one as a result

Voluntary limitation of food consumption was mooted early in the war but was not a success.

WAR-TIME ECONOMIES.
"Eat two ounces less meat a day."—*Daily Press.*
Conscientious Youth. "FATHER, YOU'VE GIVEN ME AN EIGHTH OF AN OUNCE TOO MUCH."

Many railwaymen joined the colours, especially the Royal Engineers and the specially raised Railway Companies and Battalions. The shortage of men on the railways meant that travellers had to deal with their own luggage.

of nature, the other as a direct result of government action. In the first case a bumper wheat harvest reduced prices, while in the second, the government passed legislation in November that fixed the rents of working-class housing, of whatever sort, to their pre-war levels. This was in order to prevent demonstrations like that in Glasgow when 15,000 demonstrated against a 20 per cent increase and also to prevent situations like that on Tyneside where workers were paying 18s a week for a half-share in a bed that was occupied by two other tenants as soon as they had vacated it.

The effects of price rises varied from family to family. While a family on a fixed income was worse off, a similar family whose trade was buying and selling could profit considerably from the situation. A family with a number of wage earners would enjoy a higher real income compared to a family of the same size with only one wage earner and a number of young children. In the East End of London, Sylvia Pankhurst recorded the level of poverty caused by the situation. One story she recounted in her 1932 book *The Home Front* was of a woman who was supporting a bedridden husband and five children on 10s a week from the Poor Law guardians. Her rent was 7s and the Relieving Officer forbade her to take in a lodger to supplement her income. To make the situation even worse her children were forbidden free school meals because their mother was getting Poor Law relief. On the other side of the coin, there was a marked increase in the demand for children's shoes, a sign of family prosperity. The general conclusion drawn at the time was that children were better fed and clothed than ever before.

Alcohol once more became an issue when Lloyd George spoke out against the excesses of certain workmen who 'were doing more damage than the enemy'. As a result of this, the King took the pledge for the duration as did many other

35

[According to a publican who gave evidence the other day,
the earlier closing of public-houses owing to War regulations
has led to a larger jug trade.]

Workman (grappling with the difficulty). "STRAFE THE
KAISER! THERE GOES ANOTHER HALF-PINT!"

*Pinning up posters to remind
patrons that they could not buy a
drink for someone else.*

*A Punch cartoon pointing out
that the new licensing hours
might have little effect on
consumtpion.*

patriots across the country, but very few influential figures joined him. Heavy
drinking was found to be affecting war output and in an attempt to combat this,
the government passed a DORA amendment that took over licensing in certain
sensitive areas of the country, eventually fourteen areas in total. The act
restricted licensing hours, thereby reducing the time available for drinking. A
further act established a Central Control Board for Liquor that prohibited
treating, that is the purchasing of a drink for someone, even someone as close
as a wife, unless the drink was taken with a meal.

Another cause for concern was public morals. There was talk of 'war babies'
blamed upon the new freedom being enjoyed by women and the feeling that life
for a serviceman might be short. A Member of Parliament even went as far as
to suggest that such children should be adopted by the state.

There was dissatisfaction with the way in which the government was
prosecuting the war, which was exacerbated by the acrimonious differences

between Churchill and Sir John Fisher, the First Sea Lord over the Gallipoli campaign. A coalition government was mooted and was eventually formed at the end of May as a result of the political and military fallout from the shell shortage that, according to *The Times*, was the cause of the failure of the British attack at Festubert. The new government immediately created Lloyd George as Minister of Munitions, with the task of organising munitions production and eliminating piecemeal industrial methods. The nation's factories and civilian workforce were to be coordinated into a gigantic arsenal to produce sufficient war material to meet the ever-growing demands of the military. Mass production would help to win the war, and, in order for this modernisation to proceed efficiently, Lloyd George managed to get 40,000 skilled workers recalled from active service. There was still a shortage of labour that could be alleviated by the use of semi and unskilled workers; much of this new workforce would be women.

The massive need for munitions needed an equally large industrial base. This meant employing tens of thousands of workers in factories all over the country. Shown is an application form for such employment.

An employment certificate that showed the importance of the employee. A year later this would almost certainly guarantee his exemption from military duty.

March of the Church Nursing and Ambulance Brigade of Young Women and Girls past Nelson's Column.

Initially frustrated in their attempts to assist the war effort in other than minor ways, such as money-raising, helping refugees, knitting socks (of all possible shapes and in such numbers that the army cried halt) and the like, women were given their chance to assist in March when the Board of Trade issued an appeal for women to take paid employment of any kind. Any woman who was prepared to work in trade, commerce or agriculture was asked to put her name on the Register of Women for War Service at her local Labour Exchange. In an attempt to attract the patriotic, the appeal stated that,

> *...any woman who by working helps to release and equip a man for fighting does national war service.*

The response was both immediate and tremendous. Over 124,000 women signed up and many quickly found themselves working in government offices, doing remount work in military camps (looking after and caring for horses), working as gardeners, laboratory and plumbers' assistants, driving delivery vans, sorting the mail, replacing RAMC orderlies and so on. A march through London in July demanded 'the right to serve'.

A shortage of shells was not the only problem the government faced. In order to cope with its next problem the government introduced The Munitions of War Bill to deal with the

A member of the Women's Legion that was formed in July 1915 by the Marchioness of Londonderry. It became the most widespread and successful of the voluntary organisations.

settlement of labour differences and prohibit lockouts and strikes. The bill also controlled any establishment producing munitions, limited their profits, controlled the workers (and provided them with a badge that identified them as munitions workers) and provided for the voluntary enrolment of munitions workers who were prepared to work wherever they were directed. New factories, of varying size, sprang up all over the country and by the end of the war the government controlled over 2,000 separate establishments.

New munitions plants required workers. At the start of 1915 there had been women working at Woolwich Arsenal but it was not until the creation of the Ministry of Munitions that they entered such work in large numbers. Initially moving into munitions work from other factories, the early workers were usually given automatic or semi-automatic processes to look after but in some factories they were given responsibility for making a shell from start to finish and with their fine hand control they were found to excel at fuse making. The patriotic appeal of munitions work also attracted women from the upper classes. There was such a shortage of munitions workers that eventually fourteen-year-old girls were employed in an unskilled capacity.

As conditions across the country changed, women left domestic service in large numbers to work in the new factories; one estimate puts the loss of female servants during the war at 400,000. Although their labour was urgently needed there was in many cases resistance to their employment, particularly from Trade Unionists who were concerned that men's wages would be affected. Although agreements were reached about equality and parity for piecemeal work, there was little evidence of it in reality. For example, one Croydon factory which paid a man £3 for the week's work paid the woman who replaced him just 12s 6d for exactly the same work.

Like men, women munitions workers needed relaxation and exercise. One popular sport was football.

Trade Union regulations tended to limit output.

THE LAST WORD.

First Munition Worker. "LOOK HERE, MATE, YOU'RE WORKING TOO HARD. YOU'RE A ΤΑΙΤΟR TO YOUR UNION."
Second Ditto. "WELL, I'D SOONER BE THAT THAN A TRAITOR TO MY COUNTRY."

Munitions Courts, with the power to fine and/or sentence an offender to a term of imprisonment, dealt with defaulting workers. These courts could be strict in their interpretation of the rules, for example in their decision to fine workers at Cammel Laird's in Liverpool when they arrived late on Monday morning. The fine of up to £3 resulted from them working many hours of overtime over the weekend! However, the act was not without its challengers and in July, 200,000 Welsh coalminers went on strike. Only the personal intervention of Lloyd George resulted in a return to work. There was further unrest in the south Wales coalfields later in the year as well as unrest among the railwaymen in the same part of the county.

As part of this new aggressive approach to the war and in an attempt to maximise the country's manpower potential, the government passed a bill for a National Register. Everybody between the ages of fifteen and sixty-five had to carry a registration card which, along with their name, carried details of their place of residence, age and employment. Anyone not registering was liable to a fine of £20 and a sentence of three months hard labour.

By the middle of 1915 it was increasingly felt that unenlisted men were dodging their duty and leaving the sacrifice to others. Posters urged men to do their bit; many were obviously not. It was around this time that a new patriotic phenomenon occurred – the white feather. The idea caught on quickly and, soon any man not in uniform (including the medically unfit – the givers of the feather were not fussy) was liable to be given a white feather as a sign of cowardice. Widows and grieving mothers stopped young men in the street to find out why they

This is to Certify that
(a) Ernest Alfred Muskett
(b) Secretary to a Public Co
(3s
(c) of "Warwick Cott" Kings View
Chase Side Enfield

has been Registered under the NATIONAL REGISTRATION ACT, 1915.

Signature of Holder. E. A. Muskett

GOD SAVE THE KING.

NATIONAL REGISTRATION ACT, 1915.

The National Registration Act of 1915 meant that everybody between the ages of 15 and 65 had to carry an identification card.

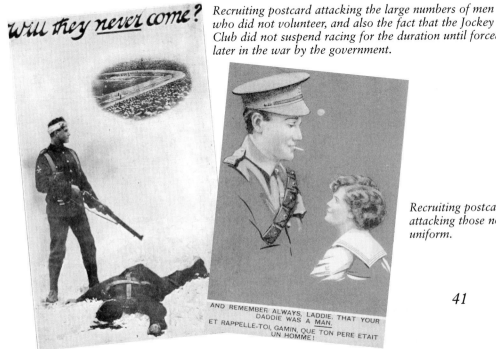

Recruiting postcard attacking the large numbers of men who did not volunteer, and also the fact that the Jockey Club did not suspend racing for the duration until forced later in the war by the government.

Will they never come?

AND REMEMBER ALWAYS, LADDIE, THAT YOUR DADDIE WAS A MAN.
ET RAPPELLE-TOI, GAMIN, QUE TON PERE ETAIT UN HOMME!

Recruiting postcard attacking those not in uniform.

were not in the army and often insulted them, while young women formed leagues pledging themselves not to marry young men who had not enlisted.

The white feather attacks were a sign that there were still many men not in uniform. After the initial rush to colours in August and September 1914, recruiting figures had fallen to the point where conscription was inevitable.

ENLISTMENTS FOR THE REGULAR ARMY
AND THE TERRITORIAL FORCE
between August 1914 and December 1915

Year	Month	Total enlistments	
1914	August	298,923	
	September	462,901	
	October	136,811	
	November	169,862	
	December	117,860	
			1,186,357
1915	January	156,290	
	February	87,896	
	March	113,907	
	April	119,087	
	May	135,263	
	June	114,679	
	July	95,413	
	August	95,980	
	September	71,617	
	October	113,285	
	November	121,793	
	December	55,152	
			1,280,362

The National Register enabled the government to find out, after deducting workers essential for the war effort – munitions workers, farm workers and the like, the potential numbers of men available for the armed forces. Before introducing conscription the government tried one more time to raise enlistment totals. This last resort was to be gentle coercion.

On 11 October Lord Derby was appointed Director General of Recruiting and on the 16th he introduced the 'Derby Scheme' by which men between the age of 18 and 41 were still allowed to enlist voluntarily; others could attest with the obligation to serve if called upon. This latter group was divided into twenty-three call-up groups according to age. As a further stimulus a *War Pensions Act* was passed that took into account all a soldier's dependants. The War Office notified that voluntary enlistment to any arm except the infantry would shortly cease.

The 'Derby Scheme' lists were closed on 15 December. Total voluntary enlistments were 215,431 while a further 2,184,479 had attested, leaving, after

As casualties mounted, the sight of a military funeral in Britain became more common as many of the badly wounded were returned to 'Blighty'. Many died after they had been officially discharged from the army. This is the funeral of Lance Corporal Thorpe.

Another sight that was becoming common were the Kitchener Battalions leaving the country for active service. This photograph shows four friends, serving in the 6th East Yorkshires, shortly before they left for Gallipoli. Of the four, two were killed in their first action and another taken prisoner, dying after his release from injuries suffered as a Prisoner of War. The survivor, Pte Charles Bilton, top left, was the author's paternal grandfather.

Volunteers who attested under the Derby Scheme wore a special brassard.

1,500 M H W V W 13090—4672

Name _Richd Barlow_   No. _138_

Address _28 New Hall Lane_   **BOLTON**

SA 26491
H 63301

Group Number _1_   8-12-1915.

Date of Attestation _____

The above-named man has been attested and transferred to the Army Reserve, until required for service, when he will be sent a Notice Paper, informing him as to the date, time and place at which he is to report himself. Fourteen days' notice will be given.

N.B.—Any change of address should be immediately notified to the Recruiting Officer.

RECRUITING OFFICE
8 DEC 1915
TOWN HALL, BOLTON

Station. _____   _B.R.L. Closs?_ Signature.

Date. _____   _major_ . Rank.

Attestation form for a Derby Scheme man.

deductions for starred (reserved) occupations and the physically unfit, a further 650,000 men who had evaded enrolment for service. As the majority of these were single men, the government carried out its threat of compulsory service and on 4 January 1916 introduced the *Military Service Act.*

From the beginning of the war British propaganda had stirred up dark emotions in the public with stories of the atrocities perpetrated on the French and Belgians by the Germans for the least little provocation. In 1915 there was a story about a crucified British soldier (discounted after the war for lack of proof but possibly proved in 2002 to have actually occurred, the only difference being that the soldier was a Canadian soldier). The sinking of the *Lusitania* on 7 May by a German submarine, with the loss of over a thousand lives, further fuelled anti-German feeling. Rioting crowds, mostly, but not all, spontaneous, attacked

WORDS—AND DEEDS.

A Punch cartoon lampooning the difference between words and deeds during the war.

The Germ-huns want the Word you bet.

But, let's hope 'this' is all they'll get."

The sinking of the Lusitania *fuelled anti-German hatred. A postcard showing the German obsession with the Iron Cross.*

Thousands of satirical Iron Crosses were sold to riase money for charity.

German shops, smashing windows and looting. In Hull, as in London, the crowds rioted, as Florence Mower recalled:

> *There was a Pork butcher's down Wincolmlee, Barmston Street... There was the shop downstairs and they had a piano upstairs. They broke all the windows and I can remember seeing the piano actually thrown through the upstairs window. Where the poor butcher and his wife and children where, I really don't know. They just raided them all. It was terrible.*

One Hull Pork butcher was in luck; one of those about to go on a planned rampage warned him about the coming attacks. On 12 May Charles Hohenrein received an anonymous letter:

> *Dear Sir,*
>
> *I belong to a secret gang but I want to be your friend. I wish to warn you that your shop's in danger and perhaps life, for God's sake take this as a warning from one who wishes you no harm (Don't treat this as an Idel (sic) joke) -*
>
> *Friendship*
>
> *I have signed friendship but I don't know you and you don't know me.*

Also enclosed were the details the butcher needed about the dates of the planned attacks.

On the same day an unstamped letter arrived, costing the butcher twopence in surcharge costs. The letter explained the reason for his concern:

ARMS & BADGES

OF

RUHLEBEN.

1915.   1916.

Concentration Camp for British Civilian Prisoners of War. Ruhleben. Germany.

A comic postcard showing anti-German feeling.

While pork butcher, Charles Hohenrein, was being accused of being German, his son was a civilian prisoner in Ruhleben concentration camp in Germany because he was British.

WE GERMANS MUST ALL HANG TOGETHER.

Dear Sir,

I hope you got my last letter and I hope you have taken notice of it as your shop is going to be broken up on ... and ... . I dare not let you know too much as I would be found and I would have to suffer. The reason I have taken such an interest in warning you is because when I was a boy your parents and those who kept your shop were very good to me many a time when I was hungry and needed bread so you see I wish you no harm in any way. Your shop is not the only shop but there are others and I am warning you and I shall have to carry out my work when I am ordered by my chief the captain. Sir, if you will put a letter in the Daily Mail I will know you have got my letter. I do not mean a bold one but one of a mild kind. The reason is to av............

LUSITANIA

Friendship ... 2nd

Throughout Hull there was an orgy of violence. The local press reported the attack on Charles Hohenrein's shop:

Ransacking a German baker's shop in Caledonian Road after an air raid on London.

A Tower Hill meeting demanding reprisals as a result of the air raids.

About midnight a crowd of youths and men were in Waterworks Street, assuming a threatening attitude in front of the premises of Mr Hohenrein, pork butcher. Later two youths threw a large stone through the window, smashing the same. The delinquents were pointed out to the police and arrested, the crowd making no attempt at rescue. A Territorial remonstrated with the offenders.

The irony was that Hohenrein's son was interned in Germany as an enemy alien.

Further damage to the German cause, and a tragedy that fuelled further anti-German feeling was the execution of Nurse Edith Cavell on 12 October at Brussels. Working with the Red Cross in German-occupied Belgium, she had nursed Belgian, British and German soldiers, but because she had assisted in helping Allied soldiers to escape, she was court-martialled and shot.

As a result of this the government took action and interned all male enemy aliens between the ages of seventeen to forty-five while the women and children were to be repatriated. Most of the internees were sent to the security of the Isle of Man but some of the London resident aliens were held at Alexandra Palace. Meanwhile the King announced that the Kaiser, the Austrian Emperor and other German royalties were to be struck off the Roll of the Knights of the Garter. Two British Dukes, who were also German Dukes resident in Germany and serving in the German Army, were deprived of their British peerages before the end of the war.

The anti-German feeling expressed during the *Lusitania* riots had been further fuelled by the Zeppelin raids that had started in January when the Kaiser had agreed to allow the bombing of military targets, exempting the residential

A German concentration camp in England. Sentries were placed in a position that allowed them to see the whole camp.

" So vast is Art, so narrow human wit."

Cubist Artist (who is being arrested for espionage by local constable). " MY DEAR
MAN, HAVE YOU NO ÆSTHETIC SENSE? CAN'T YOU SEE THAT THIS PICTURE IS
AN EMOTIONAL IMPRESSION OF THE INHERENT GLADNESS OF-SPRING ? "

Constable. " STOW IT, CLARENCE ! D'YER THINK I DON'T KNOW A BLOOMIN'
PLAN WHEN I SEES ONE ? "

Spy phobia continued throughout 1915.

districts of London and historic buildings, especially the Royal Palaces. On 19
January three airships left Germany on the first airship raid of England. At
around 8 pm two of the airships reached the Norfolk coast where they dropped
some bombs before proceeding to King's Lynn, an unguarded and non-military
town. The total casualties for the raid were two men and women killed and
sixteen injured, including one child.

The raids that followed caused few if any casualties, but they were
threatening and getting closer to London. During the raid on Southend and
district on 10 May, the Germans dropped a postcard with a prophecy, 'You
English. We have come, and will come again soon. Kill or cure. German.'

On the night of 31 May, Zeppelin LZ 38, commanded by Captain Linnarz,
took off from Brussels and headed for the London dock area. At about 10.40
pm he was cruising over the capital's northeast suburbs heading for the East
End. By 10.50 pm he was over his target area and released his bombs, thirty
explosive and over ninety incendiary, over Stoke Newington, Dalston, Hoxton,
Shoreditch, Whitechapel, Stepney, West Ham and Leytonstone. He had missed
the docks and done £18,500 worth of structural damage to the closely packed
housing. Seven civilians (three of whom were burned to death, and four of
whom were children) had been killed and a further thirty-five people injured.
The inquest on a middle-aged couple, Henry and Caroline Good, burned to
death by an incendiary bomb, was national news. When they had been found
their bodies were almost naked; the man's arm had been round his wife's waist,

Scenes at King's Lynn, Norfolk after the air raid of 19 January. Destroyed houses in Albert Street. Inset: removing furniture from the ruined houses.

Maldon, Essex, 19 January 1915 after the first air raid.

London at night.

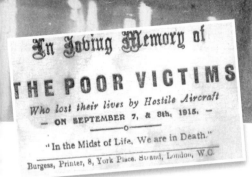

Funeral card for the victims of the air raids on the nights of 7 and 8 September. These raids were spread across the country and results in the deaths of 44 people.

Incendiary dropped at Maldon during the air raid of 16 April.

Incendiaries and a bomb dropped on the East coast on the night of 12 September.

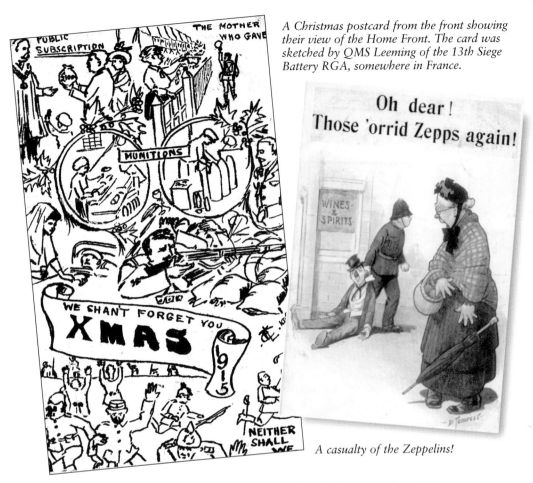

A Christmas postcard from the front showing their view of the Home Front. The card was sketched by QMS Leeming of the 13th Siege Battery RGA, somewhere in France.

A casualty of the Zeppelins!

The ruins of Edwin Davies' department store after the first air raid on Hull.

Christmas, 1915.

FROM

Mr. & Mrs. S. H. Stansfield

40 Guildford Road,
Levenshulme, Manchester

*A patriotic Christmas card
for Christmas 1915.*

**Just a token of Remembrance,
From a friend of olden time,
May God grant you every blessing,
While the Xmas joy-bells chime.**
—H. S. Hammond.

❧ ❧

With Hearty Greetings

and Best Wishes not only for Christmas,

but for all time.

and they were assumed to have died as they knelt by their bed and prayed – 'innocent victims of the baby killers.'

Six nights later it was the turn of Hull. Nearly sixty bombs were dropped and buildings were damaged in seven streets. Casualties were far heavier than those of London; twenty-four civilians killed and a further forty people injured. There was no real deterrent in Hull and the people knew it, even though the military pretended that one vital factory was guarded. Rose, Downs and Thompson was a munitions plant where women filled shells. On the top was a dummy gun made out of wood with a single soldier on guard.

There were to be a further twelve raids during the year, with two of them surpassing the total killed in Hull. The raids on 8 September, spread across the North Riding, Norfolk and London, killed twenty-six while the final raid of the year on Norfolk, Suffolk, London and the Home Counties killed seventy-one. By the end of the year the death toll from air raids amounted to 209. Small when compared with the 2,371 lives that had been lost from the sinking of British Merchant vessels and minute when compared with the losses on the Western Front; small, but disturbing. As a young officer, home on leave was heard to say, during a raid on London's theatre area, 'it's no business to happen here.'

PIER THEATRE,
EASTBOURNE.

Monday, December 13th, 1915,

Every Afternoon, 3 to 5.
Every Evening 7 to 10.
(Continuous)

Alfred West's Pictures—

"**Our Navy**"

— and —

"**Our Army**"

Doors open 2-30 and 6-30.
Seats, 1/6 to 3d. Soldiers and Sailors half-price to all parts.

Cinema advertising flyer for 'Our Navy' and 'Our Army'.

1916 – Great Endeavours

At the dawn of the New Year, probably the most singularly important aspect of the war for the government to deal with was the manpower shortage facing the army. Without men the army could not prosecute the war.

Before the war the idea of conscription had been seen as being totally against the British ideals of individual liberty but now it was no longer 'the symbol of tyranny' but a necessary evil; without it there would be insufficient recruits to replace the inevitable casualties of the coming offensives. In order provide these recruits the government passed the Military Service Act on 4 January that became law on 27 January. By this act all voluntary enlistment, even for the Territorial Army ceased, and every male British subject between 18 and 41 years of age who (a) on 15 August 1915 was ordinarily resident in Great Britain (Ireland was excluded) and (b) on 2 November 1915 was unmarried or a widower without child or relative dependant on him, was deemed to have enlisted for general service in any unit as directed by the military authorities.

Provision was made for exemption on a number of grounds: being a member of an indispensable profession or trade or being trained or educated for that work; for serious hardship, financial or domestic if called up; for ill-health or infirmity; and for conscientious objections. To deal

A married couple inspect the proclamation calling up the first eight groups of married men.

The calling up of groups 33-41. Married men from 27-35 waiting to be examined at the recruiting booth at the Horse Guards Parade, London on 29 May 1916.

with the exemptions, the government set up tribunals. If a man preferred to serve in the Royal Navy, then the Admiralty had first call on his services.

On 25 May the government extended the act to cover married men. The men about to be called up were 'Derby Scheme' volunteers and in order to differentiate them from those who would later be conscripted, they were organised into year groups (as opposed to classes, for those being involuntarily conscripted). The classes corresponded with their year of birth, class 1 being 1875 and class 23 being 1897; married men of the same ages were in Class 24 (1875) to 46 (1897).

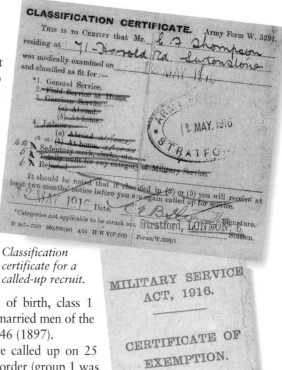

Classification certificate for a called-up recruit.

Certificate of exemption for an agricultural engineer granted by a tribunal. He was only to remain exempt while he was in that job.

Single men of groups 2 to 5 were called up on 25 January, with the others following in order (group 1 was the last) between then and 28 March. Class 1 to 13 followed this between 3 March and 28 March. Groups 24 to 46 were called up between 7 March and 13 June while classes 24 to 46 were drafted quickly between 3 June and 24 June. This mass call-up had the potential to produce tens of thousands of new recruits but instead the net increase was just 43,000. There were 748,587 exemptions granted on top of the 1,433,827 who were already in reserved occupations or wore an official war work badge. More worryingly, 93,000 men simply did not turn up when called. With the army in France 46,200 men short in April and 165,000 men below establishment at the end of the year, conscription was going to have to be applied with a less gentle hand.

Unidentified Conscientious Objectors from Hull after their release from prison.

ENLISTMENTS THROUGH 1916

Year	Month	Total Enlistments
1916	January	65,965
	February	98,629
	March	129,493
	April	106,908
	May	125,768
	June	156,386
	July	88,213
	August	111,771
	September	81,195
	October	97,684
	November	76,058
	December	52,005
Total enlistments for 1916:		1,190,075

Conscription was seen as harsh but necessary. Among war workers it caused some disquiet because its almost immediate failure to swell the ranks of the army meant that the government would soon begin the process of comb-out, taking those it thought could most easily be replaced by other labour. The comb-out could even be used as a way of enforcing industrial peace with Trade Union members who were too militant, perhaps having promoted a strike or fostered any form of industrial discontent, suddenly finding themselves being called-up – their exemption counting for nought. Throughout the remainder of the war there would be constant comb-outs in order to provide sufficient manpower for the army.

There was considerable criticism of the final exemption from military service that allowed men, whose personal principles did not allow them to support the war, to go before a local tribunal to claim exemption. Predictably, this exemption became a burning issue. These 'Conchies' or 'Cuthberts' were, according to the popular press, 'sickly idealists,' 'pasty faces,' or worse, suffered from a 'fatty degeneration of the soul' and had as much pluck as a rabbit. According to the *Daily Express*, the term 'conscientious objectors' was the new name for slackers, while the journal *John Bull* accused them of being human toadstools which needed uprooting without further delay. In order to inflame opinion there were even reports of mock tribunals being set up to teach these 'curs' all sorts of pious humbug in order to escape the drill sergeant.

Feelings were so inflamed that even the Society of Friends, a body with profoundly pacifist beliefs, was attacked. It was alleged that they had totally ignored Christ's teachings on wealth and become one of the richest communities in Britain but were escaping the responsibilities of wealth by exaggerating the doctrine of non-resistance. However, there was another strand of opposition, the Socialists, who believed in international brotherhood among working men. Meetings held to express their views were broken up by demonstrators who

A London tribunal. Hearing an applicant for postponement to a later group.

HOW I FELT BEFORE THE TRIBUNAL.

A contemporary postcard about going before the tribunal.

threw stink bombs and rushed the platform in order to close proceedings. Even the church seemed to be against them when a writer in the Anglican quarterly, *The Optimist,* suggested

> *that the objector who in the name of conscience refused to fight was really supporting an immoral German militarism and should be exiled from the community he was defying.*

Even academics gave the objectors little sympathy. In July, Bertrand Russell lost his position as lecturer in Logic and Mathematics at Trinity College, ostensibly as a consequence of his conviction under DORA for making statements calculated to prejudice recruiting. H McLeod Innes wrote to Bertrand Russell on 11 July:

> Dear Russell,
> It is my duty to inform you that the following resolution was unanimously passed by the College Council today:
> 'That, since Mr. Russell has been convicted under the defence of the Realm Act, and the conviction has been affirmed on appeal, he be removed from his lectureship in the College'.

Going before a tribunal, a conscientious objector would be questioned by a group of local tradesmen and other worthy figures (generally elderly men), including a dominant soldier who was the spokesman, and sometimes a woman. These bodies were notably inconsistent in their handling of the claimants, asking such difficult and demanding questions such as whether they took exercise, whether they washed and what they did on Sundays. A favourite question was 'What would you do if a German attacked your mother or your sister?' The *Bradford Daily Telegraph* of 16 March 1916 contained the following from a Tribunal board:

Member:	*What would you do if a German attacked your mother?*
Applicant:	*If possible I would get between the attacker and my Mother but under no circumstances would I take a life to save a life.*
Member:	*If the only way to save your mother were to kill a German, would you still let him kill her?*
Applicant:	*Yes.*
Member:	*You ought to be shot.*

There was little sympathy for such men and few exemptions on conscientious grounds were granted with most tribunals being guided by the government's promise to make the path of the conscientious objector a hard one. A further problem was that the act did not define what was meant by 'conscientious objection' so the interpretation was left to the individual members of the tribunal, and of course many of these were unsympathetic. There were also appeal tribunals, but most conscientious objectors fared little better with these. Even physically unfit objectors were drafted into the Non-Combatant Corps, despite their appeals, where they were made to do physical labour beyond their health. When their health broke down they could legitimately be refused a pension on the grounds that their disability was not caused by war service.

A majority of the objectors agreed to assist the war effort in some form of non-combatant service like the Quaker ambulance units that had served on the Western Front since the start of the war (winning many medals for bravery), but those who turned down such service were deemed to have enlisted. There were also those men who were termed 'absolutists' who refused to help in any way, who were also deemed to have enlisted. They could then be taken to a military camp where they were under military law. If they refused to obey a legal order they could be punished. In a similar way, if after being refused, they did not report for service, they could be arrested as deserters, handed over by the police to the military and tried by court-martial in the same way as their fellow objectors who had refused to obey an order.

In total around 6,000 men were imprisoned and seventy died during their captivity. Mrs Pankhurst

A few months after this photograph was taken, newspaper adverts like this were banned by law to save paper.

58

"I'M NOT ASKING TO BE LET OFF—I'M ASKING FOR MORE TIME. I'VE GOT A LOT OF CONTRACTS TO FINISH."
"HOW LONG WILL THEY TAKE?"
"OH, ABOUT THREE YEARS—OR THE DURATION OF THE WAR."

Not all applicants at a Tribunal were sincere.

recorded that those who refused to wear khaki and accept military training were bullied – one man was made to stand in a waterlogged pit for days – and terrorised and kept in handcuffs. Others were kept in dark punishment cells and given bread and water; if they went on hunger strike they were forcibly fed. Some were shipped to France where they would be classed as being on active service – disobeying an order on active service resulted in a death sentence rather than a prison sentence as in Britain. Shortly after their arrival they were sentenced to death. The pacifist Professor Murray found out and questioned Lord Derby who confirmed the sentences. Murray then contacted the Prime Minister who notified Field Marshal Haig that no executions must be carried out without the Cabinet's knowledge. Such excesses were classed as 'British Prussianism' by the No Conscription Fellowship and condemned by the *Daily News* which asked 'Where are we drifting?'

With this sort of behaviour directed against them, the objectors won some sympathy. As if to confirm this, an Army Order of May decreed that henceforth such prisoners would be kept in civil prisons. However, this was not an end to their suffering. Six months later a statement in the House of Commons confirmed that such prisoners who were suffering conditions like heart problems were being kept with venereal disease patients at Woolwich Hospital, where the sanitation was defective and there was no protection from infection. The life they experienced in prison was not easy. After being court-martialled one conscientious objector was given a sentence of hard labour which meant that 'you had to spend the first month in solitary confinement with the exception of forty minutes exercise, also you had to sleep on a bare wooden board without mattress.' Another, who had asked to join The Quaker War Victims Relief Work in France, was given 112 days' imprisonment at Wormwood Scrubs, including

Married men signing-on for munitions training. Married men, beginning with group 36 were given free instruction in munitions making, in order that they might be substituted for single men.

a number of weeks in solitary. After doing alternative civil service he was allowed to go to France to join the Friends Relief Service.

However, the tribunals were not just for conscientious objectors: they were designed to see who was essential to the war effort at home and who was not; in essence they gave panels of ordinary citizens the power of life and death over their fellow citizens. From the start they could do no right. 'If they spared the widow's son they were reviled by Lord Northcliffe. If they gave short shrift to scrimshankers they were guilty of dumping unassimilable dross into the Army. They were accused of robbing industry and of allowing industry to hoodwink them. They were attacked for browbeating conscientious objectors and for allowing themselves to be browbeaten by them.' The left-wing view of their activities was that 'nervous wreck, semi-idiots and consumptives were forced by red-faced presidents of tribunals to get into khaki, and dragged out to France to die, cursing the country which had enslaved them in a military despotism and in whose service they had been forced to swear loyalty.' In reality the leniency of tribunals varied but there are many stories of strange applications and different decisions in different areas. While a tripe-dresser was sent into the army, a man who could kill, pluck and have a fowl ready for market in two minutes was indispensable to the war effort; while twenty-one single men working for Lord Northcliffe's *Comic Cuts*, *Home Chat* and *Forget-Me-Not* were granted exemption by the Southwark tribunal, in Croydon a woman had to plead to keep her final son (the other ten were serving) at home as her sole support; and in Hull, an elderly infirm widow sought exemption for her son (an ex-regular

An advert in Piccadilly asking the public not to use motorcars.

Lowestoft shelled from the sea by German ships. The photograph shows the damage in Cleveland Street.

Bombardment damage on The Esplanade at Lowestoft.

An unexploded German naval shell that was fired at Lowestoft.

The incendiary device dropped on Dover during the night of 22 January.

Bombardment damage at Lowestoft.

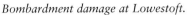

who was time-expired and had served in France) as her only means of support because two of her sons had died so far in the war, and her third son was crippled with a spinal injury. All over the country, last sons were being exempted but only sons were not. There was also some evidence of class bias when 'at Huntingdon, a nurseryman stepped down from the bench to argue the case for his own exemption, which he was conditionally granted, and then ascended the bench again.' In other places the panel were undoubtedly too soft; one Welsh tribunal exempted all but six out of 2,000 men. On the whole though the general impression was that they were careful, sympathetic and thorough.

Following the pattern of 1915, the air raids started in January and continued through until the end of November, six weeks' further nocturnal activity. The 1916 season began with a small raid on the night of 22 January that resulted in one fatality, a raid the next night resulted in no casualties. A week later the air raids would begin in earnest. On the night of 31 January nine airships took off to bomb the Midlands; weather conditions made navigation impossible and bombs were dropped on Stoke-on-Trent, Burton-on-Trent, Derby, Birmingham, Loughborough and a field near Holt. In all 379 bombs were dropped, killing 71 and injuring 113.

One of the airships, L19, suffered engine trouble and dropped into the North Sea after being hit by Dutch gunfire over Ameland. On 3 February:

> The trawler King Stephen *came into Grimsby stating that at 7 am on the 2nd she had found L.19 floating, but in a sinking condition, 120 miles east of the Spurn Light. The Captain of the ship had implored the* King Stephen *to take the crew off, but the skipper had declined, fearing that his own small crew might be overpowered by the more numerous Germans (Captain Loewe and fifteen crew), and his steamer taken off to Germany.*

The Captain of the trawler maintained that he searched for a British Naval vessel to aid the men but could not find one. As a result all the Zeppelin crew died. Weeks and months later bottles containing messages from the airship were found in Swedish waters. The last message was dated 7 February and gave a different and accusatory version of the incident that provided the Germans with a propaganda opportunity they were quick to exploit. A second propaganda opportunity was provided by the Bishop of London who praised the skipper's behaviour and then went on to denounce the air crew as baby killers.

In 1916 there were to be a further thirty-five air raids spread out over most of England, resulting in considerable damage and a total of 272 civilians and 39 servicemen being killed. The Official History reached the conclusion that, fortunately for Britain and the British people, 'the enemy authorities, having once committed themselves to Zeppelin warfare, failed to exploit it to the full'. Nevertheless the psychological effect of the raids was considerable. The airship menace was now assuming serious proportions and a massive re-organisation of the air defences was necessary.

By 16 February, the anti-aircraft role had been transferred from the Admiralty to the War Office and an air defence branch created, with the country split into eight air-defence areas. With speed of communication being essential, telephonic equipment was used and every railway station and railway signal box given facilities for instant communication.

Blackout was another problem that needed to be controlled more closely. In 1914, the lights had been merely screened against the sky but this method resulted in throwing pools of light on the roads. As time went by the level of blackout had improved, but places like London could never be disguised because of the reflection of the River Thames and Lea Valley reservoir (the lake in St James's Park had been drained early in the war to avoid this problem for central London). Some towns insisted on a complete blackout while others thought that the only protection lay in searchlights and artillery. Norwich had strict lighting regulations, so strict that men were fined for striking matches in the street to light their cigarettes or pipes.

Other aspects of lighting also caused problems. Throughout the war there were stories about car headlamps being used by enemy agents to direct the raiding airships over England. Both police and military authorities spent considerable amounts of time and manpower investigating each sighting; only one case was brought to the point of prosecution but this was eventually dropped. As a result of this, drastic orders for the reduction of motorcar lamps were enforced. Speeding trains gave off light from the their funnels and from the railway carriages; as a result trains slowed down and in some cases services ceased. While these were useful for defensive purposes, they also aided the enemy because they disrupted the flow of munitions. Even 'arc-ing' (intermittent flashes of light caused by faulty contact between pick-up arm and conductor-rail or wires) from trams caused a problem at night, reducing night services. And on air raid nights many electric train and tram drivers refused to work 'so that measures had to be instituted to keep compulsory "slow-motion" services going, in order to evacuate the crowds attempting to leave any seemingly threatened area.'

During the first two years of the war it had been thought unnecessary to warn of impending air raids. However, as the number of munitions plants grew and had to be open twenty four hours a day, it became necessary to have a warning in order to prevent workers from abandoning their factories. This need resulted in an air raid warning system with warning maroons and all-clear bugles. With the advance warnings came the better protection brought by artillery and searchlights and also the formation of Home Defence Squadrons of the Royal Flying Corps, capable of night operations.

With such massively improved defences the War Office, in the shape of the Royal Flying Corps, equipped with suitable planes and a new type of explosive ammunition, was now in the position to expose the vulnerability of the Zeppelin. The chance came on the night of 2 September when the largest airship raid of all was launched against London. Sixteen German Army and Navy Zeppelins carrying 460 bombs attempted to bomb the City of London but were met with bad weather and gunfire; little material damage was achieved and casualties were low (four dead and eight injured). The loss of an airship over England was further proof of lack of success. This new airship, SL11,

commanded by London-born Hauptmann Schramm, was caught over north London in the beams of two searchlights that he was unable to shake off. The gunfire was more intense than ever before and, although inaccurate, the airship scattered its bombs on the Enfield, Ponders End, Tottenham, Edmonton and Finsbury Park districts. Thousands watched from the sky as three pilots from 39 Squadron attacked, with Lieutenant Leefe Robinson in the forefront. After firing three drums of New Brock and Pomeroy ammunition into the airship the rear part of the craft started to burn. In a few seconds the whole airship was on fire and falling out of the sky. To the crowd below it was an unbelievable spectacle, regardless of whether people were burning to death inside. Before their eyes a tremendous fireball was plunging to earth. A nine-year old remembering this experience sixty-four years later recalled that the:

Lt William Leefe-Robinson was awarded the Victoria Cross for shooting down a Zeppelin. He was to die later in the war.

> *Spontaneous barrage of cheering and shouting made the roar of a hundred thousand people at a pre-war Cup Final sound like an undertone. People danced, kissed, hugged and sang.*

For this attack, Leefe Robinson was awarded the Victoria Cross. The Zeppelin menace to London had effectively been mastered. However, in November a cheaper and more dangerous menace made its appearance – the bomber.

While the war over the sea was not going as well as planned, there were problems

A supposedly genuine photograph of the Zeppelin falling to earth on 3 September and the remains of the Zeppelin the next day.

A machine-gun section in action in central Dublin.

Ruins to the north of Sackville Street, Dublin. A view from Nelson's Pillar.

A crowd of Clyde strikers on Glasgow Green.

A Royal Flying Corps funeral cortège in Aldershot, July 1916.

The increasing demand for labour meant employment for all.

WORK FOR ALL

APPLY

THE MISFORTUNE OF WAR.

Tired Tim. "'Ere, I don't arf like the look o' this, Bill."
Work-shy Willy. "No, more don't I, mate. Cuss that there Kaiser!"

In
Loving Memory

The Man who saved the Empire.

Lord Kitchener had the foresight of seeing at the beginning of the War where it was leading us. He will never be forgotten. He has died a noble death in the service of his Country.

East London Printing Co., London, E.C.

In Loving Memory of
Field Marshall Right Hon.
EARL KITCHENER
of KHARTUM, K.G., K.P., G.C.B., O.M., G.C.S.I.
G.C.M.G., G.C.I.E., Sec. of State for War.

Born June 24th, 1850,   Drowned June 5th, 1916.
He will live in history as the World's Greatest
Military Organiser.

Mourning card for Earl Kitchener who was drowned when HMS Hampshire *was sunk by a mine.*

VAD hospital, Holbrook Lane, Chislehurst on 6 April 1916.

across Britain's other channel. At Easter, the Irish problem reared its head again, this time extremely violently. The rebellion broke out in Dublin and took a week to suppress, and was the signal that the great Anglo-Irish reconciliation brought about by the German threat, had finally broken down. When the British government had introduced conscription they had excluded Ireland, making the point that this was not really Ireland's war (in reality the government was aware that it would have difficulty enforcing conscription). According to historian Trevor Wilson, the Easter Rising simply took this process of separation from Britain a step further. The German war offered the Republicans the chance to break away from Westminster completely. After many deaths and a number of executions the uprising was put down. While of great importance to Irish history, it was a relatively minor occurrence in the history of the British Home Front.

In early June the country suffered a major military loss when HMS *Hampshire* struck a German mine off the Orkney Isles while on a mission to Russia. The ship sank, with the loss of nearly everyone on board. One of those lost was Lord Kitchener, Secretary of State for War. His death caused widespread shock and there were those who could not believe it was true, preferring to believe the rumour that it was a ruse to confuse the Germans.

A further problem faced the government in the form of worker unrest. Lloyd George blamed the problem on the conditions of work, subjection to new disciplines and the loss of prized rights and privileges, the shifting of workers from their homes to often inadequate accommodation and a sense that, despite high wages, they were really only working to enrich their employer. When 15,000 Liverpool dockers, 20,000 munitions workers in Glasgow and 30,000 jute workers at Dundee walked out, the unrest had turned into strikes. Lord Sandhurst blamed the problem squarely on the shoulders of the younger workers, who he felt cared little about the war and thought of it only in terms of their own financial rewards. However, later in the year, Lloyd George was able to report to the House of Commons a massive increase in munitions output: taking two examples as illustrations, he announced that the annual

production of 18-pounder shells (1914-15) was now being made every three weeks and of heavy shells every four days. And although there had been considerable unrest affecting 284,000 workers in 581 disputes, these were the lowest figures since 1907.

The change to a war footing was felt in most industries, which, as the demand for their normal product died, switched over to war work.

> *Jewellers abandoned their craftsmanship and the fashioning of gold and silver ornaments for the production of anti-gas apparatus and other war material; old-fashioned firms noted for their art productions... turned to the manufacture of an intricate kind of hand grenade. Cycle-makers turned their activities to fuses and shells; world famous pen-makers adapted their machines to the manufacture of cartridge clips; and railway carriage companies launched out with artillery, wagons, limbers, tanks and aeroplanes; and the chemical works demoted their energies to the production of the deadly TNT.*

A lack of skilled men was already having a marked affect on dilution and female employment before conscription; with its advent many more women would be needed. By August 766,000 women were replacing men in various forms of civil employment. There were a further 340,000 employed in munitions and War Office establishments. In February the government had called for 400,000 women to assist in agriculture and in March the Home Office and the Board of Trade asked employers to organise their work so that women could replace called-up men. By the end of the year women were seen doing most of the jobs that had previously been the sole preserve of men, such as driving cars, and collecting tickets on the Underground. Women replaced men in the London Clubs and on the doors of the big hotels; there

were 'conductorettes' on the buses, and even women police.

Women workers faced many hardships and dangers as they replaced men in industry. The varnish used on aeroplane wings produced toxic fumes and it was common for them to be found lying ill or unconscious outside the workshop; the TNT used in artillery shells

A certificate presented to school children who assisted the Empire in some way.

Women took over the roles vacated by men, in this case as a conductress on the buses.

Female labour helping unload wagons on the dockside.

turned their skin yellow, gaining them the nickname 'Canaries'. During 1916, 181 'munitionettes' were diagnosed as having toxic jaundice as a result of working with TNT, of whom 52 died; in 1917 there were 189 cases, with 44 fatalities, and in 1918 there were 34 diagnosed of whom 10 died.

More dangerous still were 'the monkey machines', in which a heavy weight was dropped to compress explosive into shell cases. Death at work was not an unusual occurrence under such conditions, but it did not stop work. A story is told of one of Lloyd George's representatives arriving at a factory, where, just before his arrival, there had been an accident. An explosion had killed four women, who had been screwing shell fuses in place. He found work in progress in the bloodstained hut just as normal. Sylvia Pankhurst recorded a similar situation when a group of women asked to see round a National Factory prior to starting work:

> *The workers wore rubber gloves, mobcaps, respirators, and leggings. Their faces were coated with flour and starch, to protect them from the TNT dust. Yet in spite of these precautions their skin was yellow. They asked the manager whether the work was dangerous. He answered: 'Not so very dangerous'. They questioned the women workers, but they whispered they dare not speak of their conditions... A few days later the factory was blown up. Thirty-nine people, including the manager, were killed.*

MUNITIONS PRODUCTION DURING THE WAR

Weapons	1914	1915	1916	1917	1918
Guns	91	339	4,314	5,317	8,039
Machine guns (thousands)	0.3	6.1	33.5	79.7	120.9
Rifles (millions)	0.1	0.6	1.0	1.2	1.1
Shells (millions)	0.5	6.0	45.7	76.2	67.3
Aero-engines (thousands)	0.1	1.7	8.4	11.8	22.1
Tanks	-	-	150	1,110	1,359

Women workers producing bandages.

In 1916 Bank Holidays were stopped in order
to increase war output.

THE BIG PUSH.

Munition Worker. "WELL, I'M NOT TAKING A HOLIDAY MYSELF JUST YET, BUT
I'M SENDING THESE KIDS OF MINE FOR A LITTLE TRIP ON THE CONTINENT."

Discharge certificate for a
member of the Territorial Force

Certificate for children who sent Christmas
gifts to members of the armed forces.

A Glasgow crowd
waiting to buy whisky.

For the first time, many working class women were independent, not only because there were fewer men but also because of the higher level of wages they were earning. They spent their money on things previously only dreamt about, make-up, powder and silk stockings. Skirts were shorter and trousers were worn and many felt able to smoke in public. In contrast to this, it was now the fashion for middle-class women to dress plainly. However, for many of the wealthy the war brought little change; they attended the fashionable events dressed as they had before the war.

There were other restrictions and changes to cope with but for most Britons the war was becoming a way of life and its impact was noticeable everywhere. In February, for the hours between sunset and sunrise, the striking and chiming of public clocks (including Big Ben) was prohibited, followed by a ban on whistling for cabs between 10 pm and 7 am. Both the Whitsun and August Bank holidays were cancelled to increase munitions output; the later cancellation resulted in Hull dockers refusing to work unless they received holiday rates of pay. However, people still managed to get away for holidays as in pre-war days. There were fewer arrests for drunkenness but at the same time there was an increase in the use of cocaine; to reduce this it was necessary to prohibit its import except under licence. Newspapers became thinner due to paper shortages while the casualty lists grew longer, and the sight of wounded soldiers in their blue uniform became more and more common. Matches became difficult to buy and luxuries like restaurant cars disappeared. Top hats disappeared because they would not fit into the forms of transport left to the public. Fuel shortages reduced the number of cars and postal deliveries became less reliable due to a lack of workers. The statues in London and the tombs in Westminster Abbey were covered in sandbags to protect them against bomb damage. There was an increase in

A claim against the German government, presumably for damage to his residence.

A death on active service left the bereaved without a body to grieve for or bury. Silk markers were made to commemorate the soldier's passing. Private Banning, a railwayman with the LNER Battalion of the Northumberland Fusiliers, was the great-uncle of the author.

spiritualism among bereaved mothers and wives trying to get in touch with dead sons and husbands. Tramps, according to a police report, had disappeared from the scene, being either employed or in the army, and even 'Guy Fawkes' night was banned, courtesy of DORA.

One change that is still with us was the invention of William Willet, a master-builder in London. Originally rejected as the idea of a crank, his idea of advancing the clock by one hour in the summer was accepted in 1916, becoming British Summer Time. While the farmers objected, to the civilians working on their allotments and to the war workers, the idea had much to commend it, both giving an extra hour of daylight and reducing the need for artificial light.

As well as a housing shortage there were the inevitable price rises. A poor potato harvest caused the price to double over the period from April to the end of the year. A 4lb loaf had risen from around 6d at the start of the war to 10d at the end of the year, while butter and milk increased by 100 per cent during the year. Sugar, which was becoming ever more difficult to get hold of, also showed a 100 per cent price rise. The average increase in the retail price of the principal articles of food between July 1914 and September 1916 was 65 per cent.

PERCENTAGE FOOD INCREASES
from July 1914 to September 1916

Food stuff	Percentage increase
Sugar	166
Fish	over 100
Eggs	over 100
Flour	66
Bread	58
Potatoes	53
Butter	54.5
Cheese	52
Bacon	49
Tea	50
Milk	39
Margarine	19

However, there was no shortage of the luxuries and for the better-off there were still large joints of meat available, along with geese and turkeys at Christmas. While some were spending their newly found prosperity on furs and cheap jewellery, in general the consensus was that there was little to celebrate and that almost everyone looked sad and depressed, while at church services across the land many of the congregation were dressed in mourning. The government's only concession to Christmas was to waive a recent restriction in order to allow people to have a bigger meal for Christmas lunch. One diarist recorded that 'to wish each other "Merry Christmas" is a mockery.' The weather in London summed it all up – dank and foggy. No one would mourn the end of 1916.

1917 – So Long, So Far

One casualty on the Home Front was the railway system, which even though heavily used by the military had managed to continue to provide a high level of service to the ordinary traveller. However, this would only last as long as the French government could provide sufficient locomotives for the British army's needs as well as its own. When the French government wanted more than 600 of them returned, the only place that they could be replaced from was Britain. As well as taking trains, the army needed rails and coal; added to this the Italian railways were entirely dependent on British coal. As a result of this, services vanished or were curtailed and many reduced in speed and many stations closed. When no extra trains were put on for Easter, and the operators would only sell tickets to the capacity of each train, it was a sure signal that there would be tough travel times ahead.

The 1917 Girl !

A postcard showing how the perceived role of women had changed since the start of the war.

The civilian population was further controlled by additions and extensions to DORA with many harmless actions becoming potentially serious offences.

Apart from prohibitions against 'careless talk' and so on, there were scores of 'don'ts' which themselves seemed very silly but which added up to a very necessary code of safeguards for the protection and promotion of the war-effort.

A civilian could not:

Send abroad any letter written in invisible ink; trespass on railways or loiter near railway arches, bridges or tunnels; buy binoculars without official authorisation; fly any kite that could be used for signalling; buy whisky or other spirits on Saturday or Sunday, or any other day except between noon and 12.30 p.m., pay for any intoxicating liquor for any other person, except as a host of that person, at lunch, dinner or supper; give bread to any dog, poultry, horse or any other animal. More obviously sensible than most was the rule restricting the entry of civilians into special military areas around the coasts.

In December 1916, Lloyd George had become Prime Minister, bringing in a new

The call-up of 'combed-out' men on 1 January.

What time does the balloon go up, please?

The shortage of petrol resulted in a number of delivery vans being converted to use coal gas for fuel.

Wives and sweethearts accompanying the recruits.

The Hotel Metropole in London was taken over by the Ministry of Munitions in 1916 as offices.

The Great Central Hotel was another large building commandeered by the government for office use.

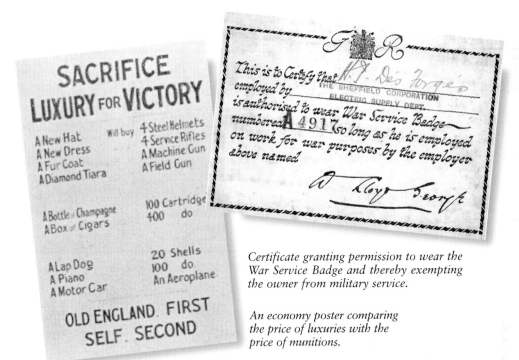

SACRIFICE LUXURY FOR VICTORY

A New Hat	Will buy	4 Steel Helmets
A New Dress		4 Service Rifles
A Fur Coat		A Machine Gun
A Diamond Tiara		A Field Gun
A Bottle of Champagne		100 Cartridges
A Box of Cigars		400 do
A Lap Dog		20 Shells
A Piano		100 do.
A Motor Car		An Aeroplane

OLD ENGLAND. FIRST
SELF. SECOND

This is to Certify that N. I. Des Forges employed by THE SHEFFIELD CORPORATION ELECTRIC SUPPLY DEPT. is authorised to wear War Service Badge numbered A 491 so long as he is employed on work for war purposes by the employer above named

D. Lloyd George

Certificate granting permission to wear the War Service Badge and thereby exempting the owner from military service.

An economy poster comparing the price of luxuries with the price of munitions.

style of government. His five-man cabinet were the decision makers and under them were 'old' Departments of State and the new ministries of Food, Food Production, Labour, National Service and Shipping. As the ministries grew in size it was necessary to provide working space for them; requisitioning many of the London Clubs, some of the hotels as well as office blocks, achieved this. There were clashes between ministries about who controlled what and they proved to be clumsy bureaucracies that were expensive to run. The new style of government was a rapid movement to state control.

In March 1917 the Ministry of National Service started its work administering the National Service Scheme that was intended to introduce a system of National Industrial Service. This industrial army of volunteers was to be created to fill vacancies in industry caused by men being drafted. Launched with much publicity, 500,000 volunteers were hoped for but by mid-April only 163,000 had registered and by August only 20,000 of these had been placed in employment. As can be seen, the scheme was not a success and was sharply criticised as a waste due to the excessive amount of administrative labour it employed to achieve so little.

At the same time the call-up was not producing sufficient men for the army and in the same month there was a comb-out of the younger miners. In order to

The SS Cooroy was sunk on 29 August 1917.

London by night – the view from Hendon.

make sure there were enough recruits, many of those previously classified as unfit for service were re-examined and given a classification that allowed them to serve at home, thereby releasing someone for the front. Later in the year all doctors of military age were called-up to increase the number serving overseas. This was because of the danger in sending men home in hospital ships. Although they were clearly marked as hospital ships, a number of them had been torpedoed.

Police powers were increased, giving them the power to arrest any suspect or enter any premises at any time. Spies remained on everyone's mind and anyone could be accused. Married to a German, D H Lawrence was exiled from Cornwall, his house ransacked and his notebooks confiscated because he and his wife had been heard singing German songs – supposedly they were signalling to German submarines.

While the Zeppelin had effectively been defeated they were to be replaced by much higher-flying airships, flying so high that in some cases they were inaudible and invisible. Replacing the airships came the Gotha aeroplanes and later in the year a handful of Riesen (giant) aircraft. Unlike the Zeppelins, the initial aeroplane raids were during the day, a time when people were up and about. How dangerous these early daylight raids could be is shown by the figures for the first Gotha raid on Britain and for the first raid on London. On 25 May, Gothas dropped a total of 139 bombs on Folkestone, killing 95 and injuring 290, resulting in mass graves. In London, although Liverpool Street Station was the main objective, fatalities occurred in other areas. One particularly tragic instance was the killing of sixteen children and the wounding of thirty others, when a bomb went through three floors of a school and exploded in the cellar where they were taking shelter. In total, 162 civilians were killed and 432 injured during this, the most deadly raid of the war.

After such initial successes, the air defences were strengthened and the Gothas later flew by moonlight. Although this lessened their accuracy, the raiders were still dangerous and the lives of many Londoners became severely disrupted, especially in the East End where the housing density was the highest

Six sergeants in the WRAF, which was founded in April 1918.

First Aid Nursing Yeomanry; by 1918 there were 116 of them driving ambulances for the Red Cross. February saw the formation of the Women's Land Army, followed the next month by the formation of the biggest women's active service force, the Women's Army Auxiliary Corps (WAAC) from the embryonic 1914 Women's Legion of cooks and drivers. Later in the year the Admiralty set up the Women's Royal Naval Service (WRNS) under Katherine Furse. The women's services provided the armed forces with drivers, clerks, cooks, storekeepers, typists and many other roles but the most important work was done by the WRNS who were involved in coding and decoding operations. There were also women serving in the Royal Flying Corps but it was not until April 1918 that they had their own service – the Women's Royal Air Force. Also in 1918 the WAAC became the Queen Mary's Army Auxiliary Corps following their gallant behaviour during the German March offensive. This level of war participation was acknowledged in the Commons at the end of March. Approval was given for women's suffrage to be included in the electoral reforms at the end of the war.

While many women flocked to join the new military units, the majority stayed in the jobs making munitions. The dangers of working with high explosives have previously been mentioned. Over the course of the war many women, producing shells for the front, died in accidents. A major disaster occurred in January at the Silvertown ammunition

A member of the Women's Land Army, which was founded in 1917.

Munitions workers and two nurses. The gun is a Hotchkiss Mark I machine-gun that was produced at Enfield.

Munitionettes wearing their 'On War Service' badges.

A VAD driver in Belfast before going overseas.

A VAD driver with her charge.

By 1917, the early war problems of separation allowances had been sorted out.

food; the calling-up of younger workers (who had thought themselves to be protected from the draft); the restriction on the mobility of labour; liquor restrictions; industrial fatigue due to weekly overtime and Sunday work; lack of adequate housing in some areas; lack of consideration for women workers by some employees; delays in granting pensions to soldiers; want of confidence in fulfilment of government pledges and the inadequacy of the compensation under the *Workmen's Compensation Act*. Over the year there were 688 disputes involving 860,000 workers.

As well as the many thousands of young women working in industry there were many tens of thousands in uniform. On the civilian side were the policewomen, described as the 'true friends of the girls', whose successes in combating disorder, theft and drunkenness led to most cities in the country setting up their own female police service. In hospitals around Britain were the VADs (Voluntary Aid Detachment), working as nurses or orderlies, many of who came from middle and upper class backgrounds. And to assist with animal forage, hay baling, sack making, driving and tarpaulin sheet mending there was a Women's Forage Corps that had been formed in 1916. There were already women serving in the army at the start of the war (Queen Alexandra's Royal Army Nursing Corps, founded in 1897 as the Army Nursing Service). Another pre-war corps also served in uniform and abroad, was the

Members of the WRNS aboard HMS Dolphin.

The WAAC was the biggest of the female military organisations.

A member of the First Aid Nursing Yeomanry.

and the homes offered less safety. The anticipation of, and the actuality of, an air raid had two effects. Firstly, many simply moved to safer areas, like Brighton, during moonlit periods and secondly, many families and their pets simply moved into the Underground stations for the night, often just in anticipation of a raid – this was eventually banned by the government. Citizens in Dover also hid from the enemy in the caves cut into the chalk cliffs. But for most of the country, there was little danger from aerial attack and the main cause for concern was the blackout regulations.

As in 1916, there was considerable industrial unrest, especially on the subject of 'dilution' of skilled labour in engineering and munitions plants during the winter of 1916-1917. Culminating in April and May, they involved nearly 200,000 men and caused the loss of 1,500,000 working days. To help alleviate the problem Lloyd George set up eight area commissions to investigate and then report on the causes of the discontent. A number of factors were highlighted: high food prices in relation to wages and the unequal distribution of

An anti-aircraft gun in action at night somewhere in the London Defence area.

Munitions workers in Bradford.

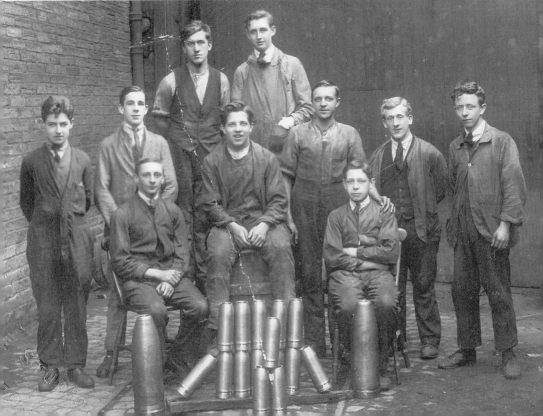

Eton boys working in a potato field. In order to grow as many vegetables as possible any spare piece of ground was cultivated.

With the shortage of food, it became essential for those that could, to cultivate their own allotment.

Girl land workers in the Lord Mayor's show.

Germans declared unrestricted warfare on all merchant ships arriving and leaving Allied ports. The Food Controller, Lord Devonport, launched a voluntary rationing scheme. Cancelling the order to limit the number of courses for lunch or dinner in a hotel or restaurant, he asked consumers to limit themselves to 4lb of bread a week, 2½ lb of meat and 4 ounces of sugar. Further impositions in hotels and restaurants were two potato-less days a week and one meatless day; also banned were afternoon teas that cost more than 6d. The voluntary imposition was 'Eat less bread and victory is secure'. In order to aid the voluntary economy campaign, the King and Queen adopted the voluntary scale of national rations in February. Bread-economy worked and by the end of May consumption was down by ten per cent.

Food shortages were to some extent ameliorated by the great patriotic allotment campaign that started during the year. By May of 1917 it was estimated that there were half a million allotments and vegetable plots under

Supplying commandeered margarine to a small dairy for distribution.

the complaints about its unpalatability, more bread was being consumed than ever before, even in pre-war days.

However, the use of other cereals meant that there was less food available for animal use, thereby reducing the availability of eggs, pork, bacon and other meat. The police were even tasked with taking an inventory of livestock, to prevent the unnecessary consumption by animals of grain, that was fit for human consumption. Food was available but it was not being distributed fairly and in many areas shops were stormed to force the shopkeeper to release the commodities. There was now an urgent need for the government to provide everybody with an equal supply of whatever foodstuffs were available.

Earlier restrictions under DORA had made reference to bread and animals. Picking up bread crusts thrown away by navvies constructing a new aerodrome, and then feeding them to his pigs, resulted in a £50 fine for a farmer. A rigid interpretation of the law meant that many people were punished for perfectly normal things like giving meat to a dog (£20 fine) or leaving a loaf on a shelf in cottage from which the worker was moving (£2 fine) or, after running out of cattle-cake, feeding the cattle with bread so they did not die (three months in jail). The year also produced regulations that attempted to stop food hoarding, under which the authorities could enter any premises thought to contain more food than was required for normal consumption. The government also prosecuted anyone selling above the maximum price; fines were high with one potato farmer being fined £5,500 plus costs. With bread being wasted at the rate of 10,000 tons a week, there was a real danger of supplies not lasting until the next harvest. The government was also strict on shopkeepers; they were not allowed to turn away non-regular customers or charge what they thought the market would bear.

A major reason for the food shortage was the U-boat campaign. During the last four months of 1916, 632,000 tons of shipping had been sunk and the President of the Board of Trade had reported that a complete breakdown in shipping would come before June 1917. On 1 February the

As well as food, paper was also in short supply.

NOTICE.

In order to meet the national need for economy in the consumption of paper, the Proprietors of *Punch* are compelled to reduce the number of its pages, but propose that the amount of matter published in *Punch* shall by condensation and compression be maintained and even, it is hoped, increased.

It is further necessary to restrict the circulation of *Punch*, and on and after March 14th its price will be Sixpence. The Proprietors believe that the public will prefer an increase of price to a reduction of matter.

Readers are urged to place an order with their Newsagent for the regular delivery of copies, as *Punch* may otherwise be unobtainable, the shortage cf paper making imperative the withdrawal from Newsagents of the "on-sale-or-return" privilege.

In consequence of the increase in the price of *Punch* the period covered by subscriptions already paid direct to the *Punch* Office will have to be proportionately shortened.

A butter queue at Tonypandy during the winter of 1917.

1917; thereafter a good harvest ensured supplies, at a price. By the end of the year, queues (a new word in the English language) had reached epidemic proportions with shortages in a whole range of everyday foodstuffs like meat and tea. One queue, reported *The Times* on 10 December, for margarine, in Walworth Road, London was estimated to consist of 3,000 people and, after two hours of sales, 1,000 went away empty handed. To make sure of supplies on Saturday mornings people started to queue at 5 am, babes-in-arms and children at their skirts. However, the queuing was not just confined to the final purchaser. By the end of the year, butchers were having to do the same to make sure they got their supplies to sell to the public.

Food was not in short supply and there was no danger of anything vaguely resembling famine, as there was in parts of central Europe. Bread was still easily obtainable, and had been lowered to the same price as a year previously. Foods, then classed as exotic dishes, such as tinned fish, were readily available, although few would eat them. With changing government directives the quality of bread had slowly diminished as various other substances had been added, like potato flour, wheat husk and other cereals. The population wanted white bread and for a while bakers had tried under these circumstances to provide this but by the end of 1917 this was no longer possible. Even with all

Renewal notice for aircraft and bombardment insurance.

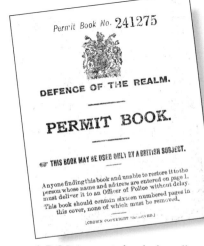

A DORA permit book that allowed the bearer to enter certain restricted areas.

A crowd waiting to purchase potatoes.

As well as a sugar shortage there was a lack of many of the raw materials needed for beer production. With production reduced by government order, 'pubs' were rationed and, when sold out, stocks could not be replaced until the next week. A decrease in sales meant a comparable decrease in profits so price rises were inevitable. When prices rose to 8d a pint in Liverpool, the dockers wrecked some pubs and boycotted others, forcing the government to increase beer production by a third. As in America, there was a strong temperance element that tried to get the government to ban alcohol during and straight after the war. The movement had the support of the Bishop of London and Harry Lauder, a popular entertainer. Fortunately for public morale the idea was not adopted.

On the other hand, some foodstuffs like potatoes, were only difficult to find at certain times of the year, before the arrival of the new crop in the summer of

A potato queue in North London.

A new word in the English language – queue. In this case waiting for the Sunday joint at Smithfield meat market. Earlier in the war, the bars in the top of the picture would have been covered with carcasses. By 1917 there was a shortage of meat.

KILLED IN ACTION AT THE BATTLE OF ARRAS,
EASTER MONDAY, 1917,
SEC.-LIEUT. PERCY BLEZARD DUCKWORTH,
WARWICK BATTERY, ROYAL HORSE ARTILLERY,
AGED 23.

Mr. and Mrs. Duckworth desire to thank you very sincerely for your kind expression of sympathy in their bereavement.

Bank House,
Barbourne,
Worcester,
April, 1917.

As casualties rose, letters like this became more common.

sportsmen from their estates and the consequent diminution of shooting parties' had the effect of largely increasing the number of pheasants and partridges which for two years had been left largely unmolested. Complaints appeared in the daily papers concerning the 'ravages of the birds in the fields and gardens in many parts of England,' and it was suggested that there should be a relaxation of the Game Laws. Writing in 1917 Reverend Reeve complained about the problem in his home area of Stondon Massey, Essex.

> We have been sufferers in this neighbourhood from the overstock of game. The Rectory Garden has been constantly visited by pheasants from the adjoining woods, and early and late they have battened upon our green-stuff. Nearly every form of green vegetable has been stripped to the stalk, and this is when we are being urged to make every yard of ground profitable!

Female agricultural workers.

worse by amount of money that the working-classes were now earning and the fact that rationing entitled them to it. As well as coal there was a paper shortage and in an attempt to save newsprint, newspaper posters were banned in March and the number of pages in a newspaper reduced. This was coupled with a price rise for many of the leading papers:

> *Waste paper became a marketable commodity. From Leeds it was reported that customers of whatever social standing were expected to bring their own bags or sheets of paper when shopping.*

The reason being that waste paper by this time was nearly as valuable as the perfect product itself.

By far the most pressing shortage was that of food; not that there was always a shortage, some of the problem had to do with price. Well-stocked butchers in London were charging prices 250 per cent higher than before the war. And by the end of the year 'bloaters' had reached 6d each. Price rises caused the most hardship on those with fixed incomes (the rentier class) but those with higher incomes sometimes had no advantage. Some commodities remained hard to obtain, like butter and sugar, and even margarine proved difficult to get in some areas and queues became the norm. Sugar supply was a major grievance and many areas were quick to introduce their own system of rationing followed at the start of 1918 by a national scheme. Eventually sugar scarcity restricted brewers, grocers and sweet manufacturers. In January, sweet and chocolate production were reduced and beer production reduced to half that of 1914. Jam making became impossible causing the wastage of large quantities of fruit and 'sugar days' attracted large queues outside grocers' shops. Substitutes for ordinary sugar included syrup made from sugar beet, honey sugar, glucose and generic products quaintly named as 'Consip' and 'Sypgar'. When the sugar bowl disappeared from the tables of Lyons' cafes (instead a bowl was carried from table to table) it was obvious there was a severe shortage. By April there was less than ten days' supply.

One food of which there was no shortage was game. 'The absence of

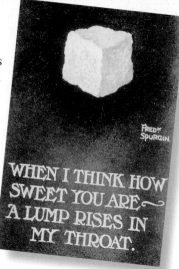

By 1917, sugar had become a very scarce commodity.

A certificate given to women who worked in agriculture.

The manpower shortage in the army was becoming critical during 1917. It would not be long before men such as these would find themselves being drafted.

more common, fuelled by:

> *...broken homes, the new freedom of women, constant mobility, the crowding of men into camps and barracks, the loosening of social restraints and the strains and general tensions of wartime life. Life was cheap, so the moment was precious and as a result by the end of the war the illegitimacy rate was thirty per cent above its pre-war baseline. The divorce rate rose rapidly but so too did the marriage rate and the Chief Commissioner of Police in London stated that over the last three years 19,000 women had been arrested on soliciting or similar charges and that they and the welfare societies were disturbed 'at the state of things in London's Parks and open spaces.*

Then there were the shortages to contend with. In April there was a shortage of coal in London, which by the onset of autumn had not been solved. Indeed it had been made

A leaflet sent to every household informing the occupants of how much coal they could buy.

*Scheduled Occupation
Certificate for R Robertson.
The original owner in 1917 was
a 23-year-old metal turner with
Ross Courtney & Co. Ltd in
the Canonbury Munitions Area.*

factory in the East End of London. A multi-coloured fireball lit up the sky followed by a violent explosion, heard fifty miles away, and an earthquake tremor that reached the City. A square mile of buildings was razed to the ground; two thousand people were made homeless, sixty-nine killed and 450 injured, many of whom were women.

Further changes occurred that changed the sportsman's year. In May the Jockey Club suspended racing at the insistence of the War Cabinet and during the year the Oxford and Cambridge boat race, the Henley and Cowes Regattas, the football league cup final and county cricket all disappeared. In their place people could now see women playing organised football.

As well as an increase in juvenile delinquency (see *The War and National Education* in section three) there was much flouting of convention. For many the only compensation for the war was pleasure in whatever form it took. A new word was coined – 'flappers' – to describe the young girls who wore 'high heels, skirts up to their knees and blouses open to the diaphragm, painted, powdered, self-conscious, ogling.' There was a relaxation of sexual taboos caused by the now ephemeral state of life. This stemmed from the here today, gone tomorrow attitude that was becoming

*Owing to the shortage of labour during the winter of
1916/17, many well-to-do people had to fetch their own coal.*

*Women even
replaced men on
heavy manual
work.*

cultivation. Tennis clubs dug up their courts while private gardens dug up their flowerbeds. Everywhere people grew vegetables and even the King and the Prime Minister took part. The Archbishop of Canterbury sanctioned Sunday labour and services were held on allotments, while tea on the allotment became a normal Sunday event. Those too lazy to garden simply stole, resulting in allotment guards and the introduction of severe penalties for thefts – £100 fine or six months in prison. In order to increase home production the Board of Agriculture introduced a further scheme. A special food production department was set up in January, with the telegraphic address 'Growmore', whose remit was to increase Britain's food-growing capacity to a maximum, creating a country free from food imports. To do this required three million extra acres under cultivation and a massive increase in the agricultural workforce. The shortfall in workers on the land was quickly addressed by the introduction of the voluntary Women's Land Army, and at harvest time there were many holidaymakers who were happy to be involved. Also assisting, were a number of prisoners of war. One particular group in Essex were left unguarded to do their work and as a result had access to the main roads of the area. On the Ongar road they regularly intimidated the baker out on his rounds, jostling around trying to buy bread. The purchases were not, however, to do with hunger; there was an ulterior motive. They were collecting the bread with a view to escaping.

The Food Controller introduced a 'Voluntary Scale of Rationing'. This scheme was not a great success and it was eventually replaced with rationing. Families that adopted the voluntary scale were asked to display this notice in a prominent place.

German Prisoners of War such as these were used to help on the land; initially in small numbers.

A school party digging for victory – in this case potatoes.

By 1918 the amount of land under cultivation had risen from 5.2 million (nearly 13 million acres) to 6.4 million hectares (nearly 16 million acres). The target for cultivation had been met.

Even though vegetables were never rationed, and many tens of thousands of people were now growing their own, it was still necessary to supplement the diet with extras provided by nature like dandelion leaves instead of lettuce – and then there were nettles. 'One thing we used to eat – and it was surprising how nice they were – were boiled nettles. They were nice as a vegetable.' The government also recommended them in a food economy pamphlet:

Stewed Nettles
  Wash the nettles, and put them into boiling salted water, and boil until they are nearly done. Strain off the water, put in two teaspoonfuls of milk and a heaped teaspoonful of butter or margarine, and stir briskly till boiling point is reached.
  Another way of serving nettles is to cook them in fast-boiling water until tender, drain them carefully, and press into a pie-dish. Sprinkle over a few crumbs, seasoning to taste, and a little grated cheese, with a few tiny pieces of butter. Place in a brisk oven for a few minutes.

During harvest time local servicemen were used to help in whatever way they could.

In order to combat the shortage of agricultural workers, the Food Production Department opened a school for soldiers of low medical classification, many of whom had seen service at the front.

Other foods were also collected from the hedgerows. Reverend Reeve recorded in his diary for 27 September

> *...school children are everywhere employed gathering the blackberries in School Hours under the control of their Teachers. The fruit is packed in baskets provided of regulation size, and sent by rail to the Army jam factories, while cheques are sent to the Teachers and payment authorized to the children of threepence per pound.*

In March, towards what became known as the 'turnip winter', the general food prospects were so unsure that arrangements were made to set up communal kitchens and, soon after, the first one was opened on Westminster Bridge Road by the Queen. Even though there was a decrease in shipping losses, some kitchens were continued in order to provide cheap well-balanced meals for factory workers. However, a lot of food had been lost to the U-boat campaign; between January and June 1917, 47,000 tonnes of meat and 87,000 tonnes of sugar were lost. The introduction of the convoy system in May eventually cut ship losses and improved the food situation so that there was no longer a chance of the country being defeated by starvation. In June Lord Rhondda was appointed as Food Controller and rapidly imposed stricter controls: no throwing rice at weddings, feeding pigeons in London or stray dogs anywhere became illegal, potato flour was put in bread to reduce wheat consumption. And along with match seller and the bootlace vendor, the muffin man also disappeared.

BRITISH MERCHANT VESSELS LOST BY ENEMY ACTION

Year	Ships Lost	Lives Lost	Gross tonnage
1914	64	69	241,201
1915	278	2,371	855,721
1916	396	1,217	1,237,634
1917	1,197	6,408	3,729,785

Year	Ships Lost	Lives Lost	Gross tonnage
January	49	276	153,666
February	105	402	313,486
March	127	699	353,478
April	169	1,125	545,282
May (convoys)	122	591	352,289
June	122	416	417,925
July	99	468	364,858
August	91	462	329,810
September	78	356	196,212
October	86	608	276,132
November	64	420	173,560
December	85	585	253,087
Total	**1,197**	**6,408**	**3,729,785**

There were still inequalities in supply; while meat prices rose and queues grew longer it was still possible to get a lavish six-course meal at the Ritz, with illegal quantities of bread. The Lord Mayor's Banquet went ahead despite opposition; there was little concession made to the food shortages being felt across the country by the menu that consisted of clear soup, fillets of sole, casserole of partridge, roast beef and sweets, washed down with punch, champagne and port. In ordinary homes the food was considerably blander than this as shortages of sugar, tea, butter and bacon made themselves felt. A December day's menu in a typical suburban home was very uninspiring and would include porridge (without milk or sugar), tea with milk and sugar, potatoes fried in fat for breakfast, while dinner would consist of meat (salt brisket) and two vegetables (generally carrots and potatoes), milk pudding and cheese. Tea would consist of bread and jam, while supper was maize semolina.

Even with all the problems being experienced on the Home Front and the general war-weariness, the prevalent attitude of the people was that the struggle must go on. This was backed by the attitude of the church and the government's rejection of German peace moves. The population had no time for pacifists, or British peace moves as made by Lord Lansdowne in November or International Socialism, as demonstrated by the Seamen's

Getting enough sugar for a wedding cake now needed a licence.

TO THE WEDDING CAKE LICENSE OFFICE

THE FOOD CONTROLLER ADDS A NEW TERROR TO MATRIMONY.

CITY
BIRMINGHAM
LIVERPOOL
MANCHESTER   762349
SHEFFIELD   466000
LEEDS   438254

National War Bond tank on Trafalgar Square during late 1917. The cities previously visited by the tank are displayed on the wall behind the tank, together with the amount of money raised.

Union when it refused to man the ship taking Ramsay MacDonald to the International Socialist conference in Stockholm. In fact resolution was stiffened by the arrival of American troops in the middle of August.

In an attempt to make Christmas a little better than the previous one, the Ministry of Food planned a set Christmas dinner of French rice soup, filleted haddock, roast fowl and vegetables, plum pudding and caramel custard at 10s for four people. But even this could not stop Christmas 1917 being the gloomiest of the war.

Many churches and villages sent their men a personalised (but mass produced) Christmas postcard.

YOUR KING AND COUNTRY THANK YOU.
Glynde Church will remember every Sailor and Soldier this Christmastide.

1

1918 – The Year of Victory

As 1917 turned into 1918, the problems remained the same and would do so for some time. There were shortages of food and men for the army, prices were rising, and there were industrial unrest and air raids to contend with. Apart from final victory there was to be one other high point of the coming year, the granting of the vote to many women.

By 1918 there were one-and-a-half million women replacing men in just about every sort of employment. As a reward for their contribution to the war effort, parliament had agreed in 1917 to women's suffrage. There was a need to reward the soldiers, sailors and airmen during the reconstruction of a better post-war world. The *Representation of the People Act* gave the vote to men over the age of twenty-one and women over the age of thirty provided they were householders or wives of householders or fulfilled certain other property qualifications. Although revolutionary, the act passed quietly into law during June 1918 giving 8.5 million women the vote and in November women over the age of twenty-one could stand as Members of Parliament (with one woman serving in 1918). What the act gave to many it also took away from a few; conscientious objectors were disenfranchised for five years after the war as a punishment for not fighting.

Bus conductors, 1918 style.

CHANGES IN WOMENS EMPLOYMENT DURING THE WAR

Type of Employment	Number of Women 1914	Employed 1918	Percentage of of 1914 total
Munitions	212,000	947,000	446
Textiles	863,000	818,000	95
Clothing	612,000	556,000	91
Other industries	452,000	451,000	99
Transport	18,000	117,000	640
Agriculture	190,000	228,000	120
Commerce	505,000	934,000	184
Self-employed	430,000	470,000	109
Hotels, Theatres	181,000	220,000	121.5
Professional	542,000	652,000	120
Domestic service	1,658,000	1,250,000	75
Local and national govmnt. (incl. teaching)	262,000	460,000	175
Totals	5,925,000	7,103,000	19.88%

As had been the case in 1917, food was a continuing problem although food supplies were now better – the 1917 harvest had been a record one. There were still lengthy queues and much resentment about the ways in which the wealthy always got their share. Worryingly there were signs of malnutrition among the poorest members of society. The government had no choice but to introduce rationing, initially in London and the Home Counties, slowly extending it to the rest of the country. The first commodity to be rationed was sugar – January – followed in April by meat and bacon (recorded on the meat card) and butter, lard and margarine (on the food card); over 40 million of each of these types of card were issued. After registering with a butcher and a grocer, each individual's ration of 16 oz of meat, 5 oz of bacon and 4 oz of margarine or butter every

Purchaser's Shopping Card for sugar.

Food was a major concern by 1918, resulting in postcards like this.

I CANNOT SEND YOU BANKNOTES,
I CANNOT SEND YOU GOLD,
BUT THIS SUGAR AND POTATO
ARE MORE THAN WEALTH UNTOLD.

MINISTRY OF FOOD.
R1.—(September) Sugar.

Purchaser's Shopping Card (Sugar).

Demonstration of Manchester workers in favour of compulsory rationing, 28 January 1918.

Indexing applications for sugar cards at the Imperial Institute.

The Food Controller's Registration Headquarters at the Imperial Institute.

Women postal workers.

week was guaranteed (children under six received half the meat ration of an adult, while adolescents and heavy workers received extra allowances). With fair distribution of these basic commodities, queues disappeared. In July, ration books replaced the ration cards. The food was there, the only problem was that the price was not affected by rationing. Compared to the Central Powers, Britain was comparatively well off. Throughout the war most things were still available and were never nationally rationed, while in Germany and Austria every foodstuff was rationed, with some becoming unobtainable.

COMPARISON OF FOOD RATIONING

Foodstuff	Britain*	Germany	Austria
Bread	Not rationed#	3 lbs 13¼ oz	2 lbs 2oz
Meat	16 oz	7 oz	4.6 oz
Fish	Not rationed	0.87 oz	Not obtainable
Milk	Not rationed	1½ pints	0.58 pints
Eggs	Not rationed	0.25 of an egg	Not obtainable
Butter	4 oz	1.05 oz	1 oz
Sugar	8 oz	8 oz	3½ oz
Cereals	Not rationed	2.19 oz	1.4 oz
Cheese	Not rationed	1.09 oz	¾ oz
Jam	Not rationed	3½ oz	2.4 oz
Syrup	Not rationed	0.87 oz	0.58 oz
Fruit	Not rationed	Not obtainable	11.7 oz
Tea	Not rationed	Ersatz – 1.75 oz	Ersatz – 1.1 oz
Coffee	Not rationed	Ersatz – 2.19 oz	Ersatz – 1.4 oz
Cocoa	Not rationed	Not obtainable	Not obtainable
Potatoes	Not rationed	6 lbs	7 lbs
Vegetables	Not rationed	5-10 lbs	2 lbs 12 oz

* Not rationed but some, like milk, were restricted or locally rationed.
# By the end of the war a working man received 1lb per day and a working woman 4lb a week.

Food hoarding was a crime and a man was fined £500 and sentenced to one month's imprisonment for his private stock of food: 144lbs of sugar, 14 hams, 37 tins of sardines plus other things. While food shortages were forcing some people to hoard, it was encouraging others to try different foods, like horseflesh at 1s a pound.

Local authorities also assisted the population in receiving adequate food provided by the national kitchens. They quickly spread from their point of origin in the poorer parts of London and by August there were 623 of them spread across the country (not always in the poorer areas). They were not restaurants (although some did have dining facilities) and most of the meals purchased were taken from the premises to eat at home. Their cheapness came from their ability to buy in bulk and, using large scale preparation they could produce meals that were far more appetising than a wage-earner's household could easily manage. Such meals were purchased in exchange for the ration coupons issued to each member of a family. A typical range of food offered by a National Kitchen included oxtail soup, Irish stew, potatoes, beans, bread, jam roll and rice pudding.

WEEKLY PER HEAD CONSUMPTION
of essential foodstuffs in an average working class family

Foodstuff	Lbs in 1914	Lbs in 1918	% change
Bread and flour	7.33	7.55	+3
Meat	1.49	0.96	-36
Bacon	0.26	0.56	+115
Lard	0.22	0.17	-23
Butter	0.37	0.17	-54
Margarine	0.09	0.20	+122
Potatoes	3.41	4.38	+28
Cheese	0.18	0.09	-50
Sugar	1.29	0.62	52

The success of the German March offensive started a new wave of anti-German feeling. A two-mile long petition, carrying over a million signatures, demanded the internment of all enemy aliens. Abuse was directed at both German people and German street names, many of which were changed as a result. Even the Royal Society expelled enemy aliens from its membership, and as late as the end of September the crowds were demanding the removal of Sir Eyre Crowe from the Foreign Office because his mother was German and he had been educated in Europe (conveniently they ignored the fact that since 1885 he had followed a very unfriendly line towards Germany). Conscientious Objectors once again

Soldiers and sailors, home on leave, applying for emergency ration cards in Camberwell.

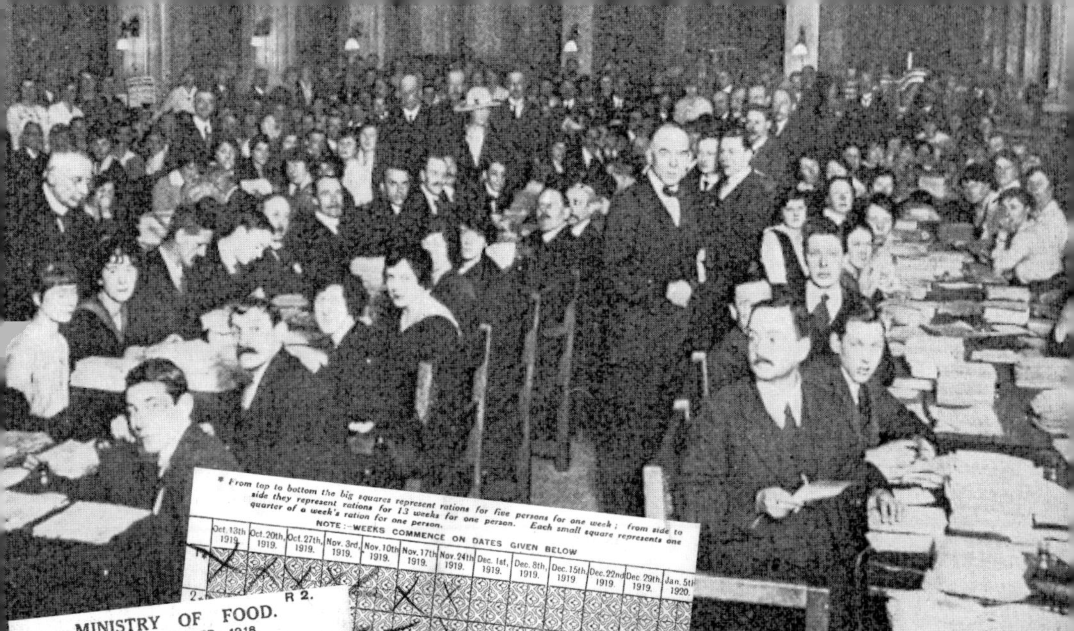

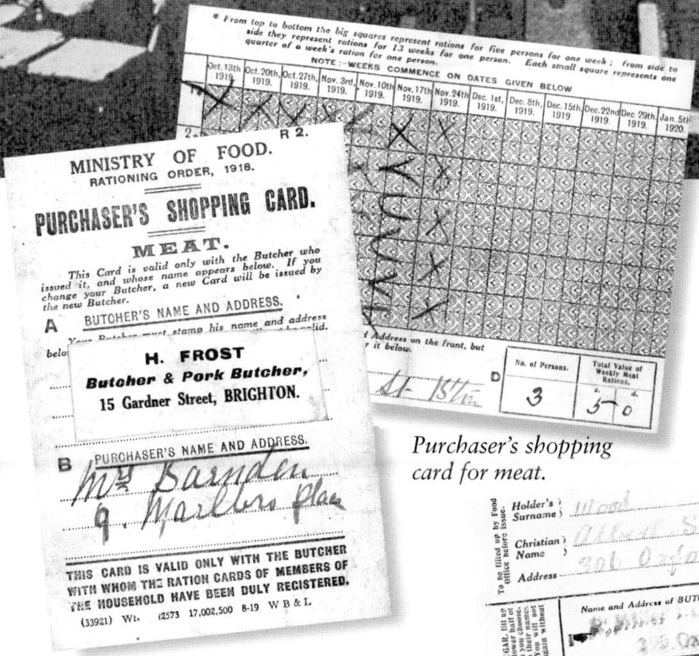

Preparing Birmingham's 900,000 meat cards in the Council House.

Rationing card to allow the owner to register for meat, butter and sugar.

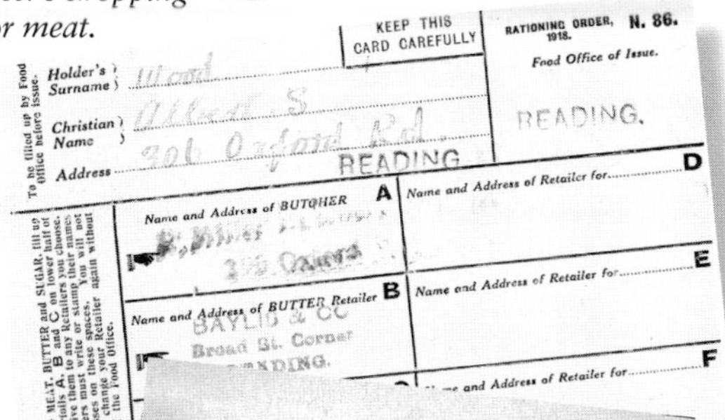

MINISTRY OF FOOD.

RATIONING ORDER, 1918.

PURCHASER'S SHOPPING CARD.

MEAT.

This Card is valid only with the Butcher who issued it, and whose name appears below. If you change your Butcher, a new Card will be issued by the new Butcher.

A   BUTCHER'S NAME AND ADDRESS.

Your Butcher must stamp his name and address below...

H. FROST
Butcher & Pork Butcher,
15 Gardner Street, BRIGHTON.

B   PURCHASER'S NAME AND ADDRESS.

Mrs Barnden
9. Marlbro Place

THIS CARD IS VALID ONLY WITH THE BUTCHER WITH WHOM THE RATION CARDS OF MEMBERS OF THE HOUSEHOLD HAVE BEEN DULY REGISTERED.

(33921) Wt.   (2573 17,002,500 8-19 W B & L

Purchaser's shopping card for meat.

Commandeered food hoard. In this particular case nearly a ton of food was removed, and a fine of £90, with £28 7s costs, was given.

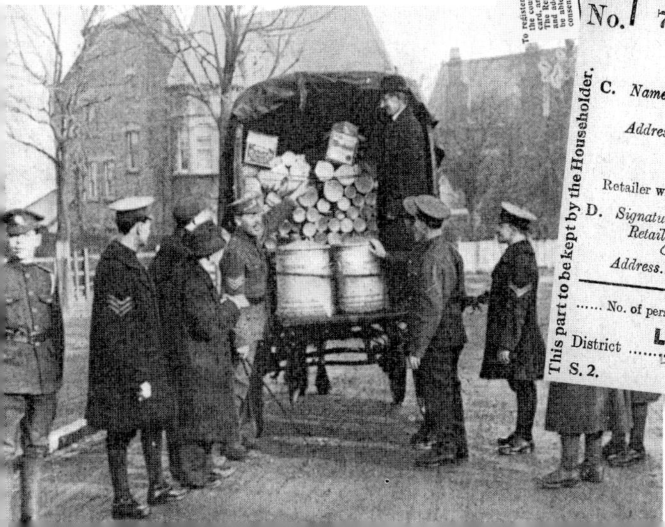

KEEP THIS
CARD CAREFULLY

RATIONING ORDER,
1918.

N. 86.

Food Office of Issue.

READING.

Holder's Surname } Wood

Christian Name } Alfred S

Address 206 Oxford Rd

READING

A   Name and Address of BUTCHER

B   Name and Address of BUTTER Retailer

D   Name and Address of Retailer for

E   Name and Address of Retailer for

F   Name and Address of Retailer for

BAYLIS & Co
Broad St. Corner
READING

MINISTRY OF FOOD.

No. 1 722078

BUTTER
SUGAR
REGISTRATION CARD.

C. Name William Alfred Parkes

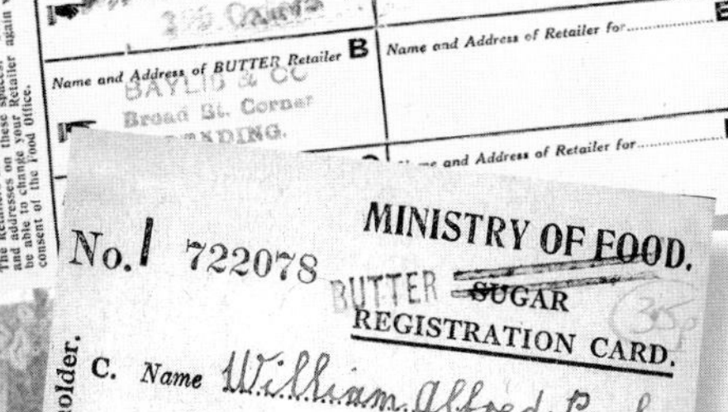

Address 50 Stoughton Rd Highfield

LEICESTER

Retailer with whom the Householder has registered:—

D. Signature of Retailer Leicester Cooperative

Address Upper Conduit Str

No. of persons three   Initials. R.R.

District Leicester Co-op Society Ltd   **LEICESTER**

S. 2.   UPPER CONDUIT ST. BRANCH

This part to be kept by the Householder

A butter registration card.

A soldier's ration book.

A classification certificate, issued after a medical inspection, prior to being drafted into the army.

S_10 817

Mr. *William A. Banks*

was medically examined at RADSTOCK 18 MAY 1918, and classified as :—

A I. (One) NATIONAL SERVICE MEDICAL BOARD

TAUNTON
For Medical Board Stamp.

B II. (Two)
C III. (Three)
R

W^d Banks
DEPUTY COMMISSIONER OF MEDICAL SERVICES,
TAUNTON AREA.

Signature of Man
N.B.—Categories not applicable will be struck out in RED INK. The category in which the man is placed will be described as follows :—B iii (Three), etc.

This Certificate will be handed in when the holder reports for Service.

Chairman
President
Medical Board.
(P.T.O.)

Ongar Rural District Council.

ARNOLD RICHARDSON, SOLICITOR,
CLERK TO THE COUNCIL. R.S.

The Council House,
Chipping Ongar,
Essex.

13th March 1918.

Dear Sir,

ONGAR LOCAL FOOD CONTROL COMMITTEE.

The ladies of Chipping Ongar are desirous of setting up a Centre for the preparation of supplies of Soup &c to the School Children and poor of Chipping Ongar and they wish to know whether they might have the use of your Premises in the Bull Yard, for establishing this Centre and if so whether you would grant this use at a nominal figure having regard to the objects for which it is required. If you will you be good enough to let me have the key of the Premises in order that the ladies may inspect them and decide whether they are suitable for the purpose.

Yours faithfully,
Arnold Richardson

J.E. Fisher Esqr.,
Auctioneer,
Broadway Offices,
TOOTING.
S.W.

Half the rent The Educational Authority pard

Request by Ongar Council for the use of Bull Yard as a Soup Kitchen for local schoolchildren.

became the target of much public venom.

The March offensive was a severe setback and one that placed further demands on the nation's men. In April a new Manpower Bill was rushed through Parliament, which, regardless of its effect on production, removed the youngest age groups from munitions and coalmines; above this the comb-out was more selective. This resulted in over 100,000 munitions workers and 50,000 pit workers being released for the army. Instead of negotiation with certain groups of workers, the army now took, for example teachers. The age of conscription was raised to cover men aged 41 to 50, while for those in specialised occupations like doctors, it went even higher. This extension of conscription had a detrimental effect on many families, resulting in many exemptions; it also hit key people in science, industry and business. In May,

Lady Rhondda opening a government information bureau in a large retail store. These were also present in other places like railway stations. Their aim was to provide leaflets and books explaining the food regulations.

CERTIFIED COPY of an ENTRY OF MARRIAGE. Pursuant to the Marriage Acts, 1836 to 1898.

Printed by authority of the Register General.

M..Cert. Church.

Registration District

Insert in this Margin any Notes which appear in the original entry.

1918. Marriage Solemnized at *the Parish Church* in the Parish of *Angmering* in the County of *Sussex*

No.	When Married.	Name and Surname.	Age.	Condition.	Rank or Profession	Residence at the time of Marriage	Father's Name and Surname.	Rank or Profession of Father.
492	March 23rd 1918	Reginald Arthur Hammond	22	Bachelor	Soldier	Watt Lane Angmering	Arthur Hammond	Bricklayer
		Lilian Mary Penn	22	Spinster	—	Seldon Patching	Frederick Penn	Stockman

Married in the *Parish Church* according to the Rites and Ceremonies of the *Church of England* by — or after *Banns* by me,

This Marriage was solemnized between us. { Reginald Arthur Hammond / Lilian Mary Penn } in the Presence of us. { Fredk: Pelham / Frederick Penn } E.L. Bull (Priest in charge)

I, *E.L. Bull Priest in charge* of Parish of *Angmering*, in the County of *Sussex*, do hereby certify that this is a true copy of the Entry No. 492 in the Register Book of Marriages of the said Church, and that such Register Book is now legally in my custody.

WITNESS MY HAND this 23rd day of *March* 1918.

E.L. Bull (Priest in charge)

The Act 2 & 4 Geo. V., cap. 27, section 3, enacts that "FORGERY of the following documents, if committed with intent to defraud or deceive, shall be FELONY and punishable with Penal Servitude for any term not exceeding fourteen years:—Any register or record of Births, Baptisms,..... Marriages, Deaths, Burials,........which now is, or hereafter may be, by law authorised or required to be kept in the United Kingdom, relating to any Birth, Baptism Marriage, Death, Burial........or any part of any such Register, or any Certified Copy of any such Register, or at any part thereof."

There might have been a war on, but it didn't stop people getting married. Private Hammond was lucky enough to get married on the day the German offensive started.

all males born in 1899 and 1898, regardless of their employment were called-up, and a month later this was extended to include all those born between 1895 and 1897, except workers in ship building and at oil shale works. In order to counter any invasion it was even proposed to form a militia of every male up to the age of 60. A further proposal to conscript both the Irish and the clergy was reversed before it went through Parliament.

The Bishop of Kensington opening the 'Feed the Guns' campaign in Trafalgar Square, 7 October 1918.

By 1918, men were being called-up as soon as they reached the age of eighteen. By nineteen, they were fully trained and ready for the front. This is a group of new recruits in the 52nd (Graduated) Battalion of the West Yorkshire Regiment. The author's grandfather (Private H. Cook, later a regular soldier with the 2nd East Yorkshire Regiment) is circled.

MEN IN RESERVED OCCUPATIONS
at 31 October 1918 (from National Service registers)

Age period	Railway & Transport	Coalminers	Agricultural	Munitions, shipbuilding & ship repairs	Other certified occupat.	Total
1900	18,824	36,498	22,849	29,850	15,157	123,178
1895-1899	42,929	67,885	36,554	91,044	6,943	245,355
1890-1894	55,610	79,261	42,148	173,079	19,232	369,330
1885-1889	78,096	96,588	63,289	225,900	44,284	508,157
1876-1884	168,462	179,836	137,733	444,379	147,391	1,077,801
1874-1875	37,720	42,641	37,933	67,929	64,816	251,039
Grand total	401,641	502,709	340,506	1,032,181	297,823	2,574,860

There was, throughout the war, a constant need for money. The government had initially relied upon the vast wealth created during the Victorian era to pay for the war. However, consecutive war budgets had increased income tax, increased taxes on all sorts of goods and imposed a super tax on the wealthy. There were also War Bonds and War Savings Certificates that gave the purchaser a good rate of interest on their capital. As well individual purchases, it was possible for a town or city to pay the total cost of an aeroplane or tank or any other piece of equipment. To assist in the collection of money from the public there were

FEED THE GUNS

Postcard for the 'Feed the Guns' campaign showing the ruins of a French village.

Voting rights were extended in 1918 to include any male over the age of 21. This is a registration card for voting issued by the army.

Tank Banks that were sent from town to town and from city to city in competition with each other to see which could raise the most money for the war effort. The sums raised by such methods were large and, when the tanks appeal started to fade, the government created a ruined French village on Trafalgar Square to raise more money. In total about £600,000 million was collected by voluntary subscriptions to pay for the war.

To many there came a feeling that the war would go on forever. Lloyd George recalled the bewilderment and hardships of the time, war tiredness, the ghastly losses, the receding horizon of victory. With non-essential work like painting having been stopped earlier in the war, most towns and cities were now drab,

An aerial view of the ruined village created on Trafalgar Square to help sell War Bonds.

Giant poster at the base of Nelson's Column.

shabby and colourless places. Even the people were shabby and the colour of their clothes matched the drabness of their lives and the towns they lived in. It was not just food that had been rationed; coal had been rationed and gas and electricity supplies had reduced, making homes colder and darker. These shortages meant a lack of hot water and made cooking difficult. Ready-made meals from restaurants proved popular, as did meetings, provided the venue was heated. In order to save both heat and light many people spent long periods in bed. These restrictions also hit restaurants under what was dubbed the Curfew Order, whereby meals could not be cooked after 9.30 pm and lighting had to be extinguished thirty minutes later. The same order also meant that all places of entertainment had to end performances at 10.30 pm. The shortage of coal did not only affect householders, for by September the furnaces on Teeside were also being affected.

CHANGES IN FUEL USE 1914 – 1918

Year	Coal (million tons used)	Oil (million galls. used)	Electricity (m Kwh)
1914	196	600	2,100
1918	207	1,350	4,000
Increase	**3.5%**	**125%**	**90%**

Whereas in previous years people had taken holidays, in 1918 they were now classed as unpatriotic. There was no sport to occupy people's minds and there had been no return of the Bank Holidays taken away in the previous year. In general travel from home to work was proving difficult so anything as exotic as a holiday would probably have been impossible anyway. The train services continued to decline while fares rose by fifty per cent. In some areas there was no longer a service because the track was now serving its country in France. Petrol shortages worsened and the London rush hour became a nightmare. The new ministries had vastly increased the number of people who needed transport across London, but at the same time the shortage of fuel meant less transport and overcrowding.

The scramble to get into some of the longer distance trains and omnibuses constituted a bear fight, out of which those of both sexes who were worsted or driven off the over-laden vehicles. retreated to the pavement with hats bashed in, umbrellas broken, shins and ankles kicked and bruised, in a shaken condition.

The general lack of petrol throughout the war meant that cycling, which had

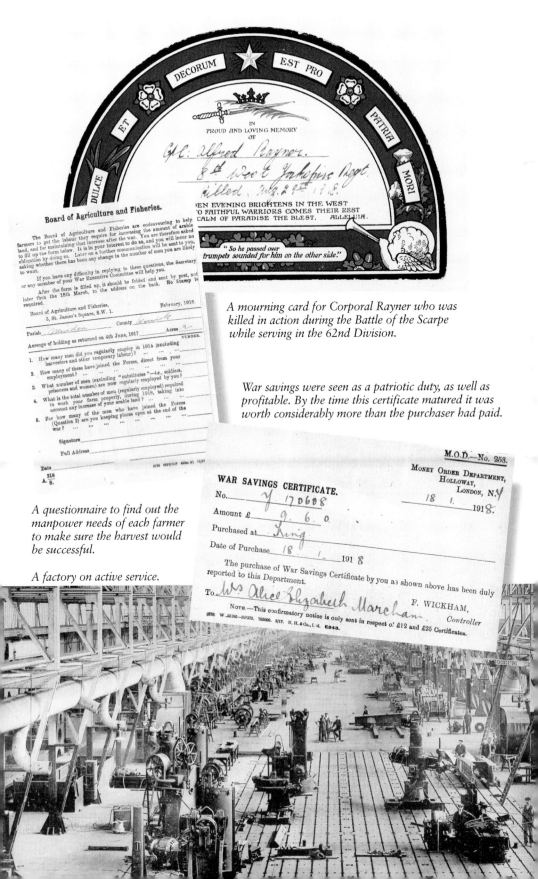

DULCE ET DECORUM EST PRO PATRIA MORI

IN
PROUD AND LOVING MEMORY
OF

C.P.C. Alfred Rayner.
8th West Yorkshire Regt.
Killed. Aug. 29th 1918.

...EN EVENING BRIGHTENS IN THE WEST
...O FAITHFUL WARRIORS COMES THEIR REST
...CALM OF PARADISE THE BLEST.   ALLELUIA.

" So he passed over ...
...trumpets sounded for him on the other side."

Board of Agriculture and Fisheries.

The Board of Agriculture and Fisheries are endeavouring to help
farmers to get the labour they require for increasing the amount of arable
land, and for maintaining that increase after the war. You are therefore asked
to fill up the form below. It is in your interest to do so, and you will incur no
obligation by doing so. Later on a further communication will be sent to you,
asking whether there has been any change in the number of men you are likely
to want.

If you have any difficulty in replying to these questions, the Secretary
or any member of your War Executive Committee will help you.

After the form is filled up, it should be folded and sent by post, not
later than the 15th March, to the address on the back.   No Stamp is
required.

Board of Agriculture and Fisheries,   February, 1918.
    3, St. James's Square, S.W. 1.

Parish _____   County _____

Acreage of holding as returned on 4th June, 1917_____ Acres ___
                                                              NUMBER.

1. How many men did you regularly employ in 1914 (excluding
   harvesters and other temporary labour)? ...   .

2. How many of these have joined the Forces, direct from your
   employment? ...   .

3. What number of men (excluding "substitutes"—i.e., soldiers,
   prisoners and women) are now regularly employed by you?

4. What is the total number of men (regularly employed) required
   to work your farm properly, during 1918, taking into
   account any increase of your arable land ? ...   ...

5. For how many of the men who have joined the Forces
   (Question 2) are you keeping places open at the end of the
   war ? ...   .

Signature _____

Full Address _____

Date _____

*A mourning card for Corporal Rayner who was
killed in action during the Battle of the Scarpe
while serving in the 62nd Division.*

*War savings were seen as a patriotic duty, as well as
profitable. By the time this certificate matured it was
worth considerably more than the purchaser had paid.*

M.O.D.—No. 253.

MONEY ORDER DEPARTMENT,
HOLLOWAY,
LONDON, N.Y

WAR SAVINGS CERTIFICATE.

No. ___ Y 170608 ___   18 . 1 . 1918.

Amount £ ___ 9. 6. 0 ___

Purchased at ___ King ___

Date of Purchase ___ 18 . 1 . 1918 ___

The purchase of War Savings Certificate by you as shown above has been duly
reported to this Department.

To ___ Mrs Alice Elizabeth Marcham ___

                                    F. WICKHAM,
                                        Controller
NOTE.—This confirmatory notice is only sent in respect of £12 and £25 Certificates.

*A questionnaire to find out the
manpower needs of each farmer
to make sure the harvest would
be successful.*

A factory on active service.

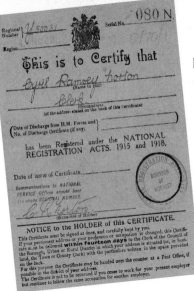

The 1918 version of the National Registration card.

been losing ground before the war, owing to the dust and danger of cars, regained its popularity.

It was not just the towns that were affected; the whole country was to feel the effects of the war in many different ways. Across the country forests were being felled and the landscape transformed. On the coast, each new tide washed up wreckage and bodies. The great country houses were experiencing financial problems with many of them having to sell the house contents to meet their tax requirements and death duties. The Reverend Reeve recorded in his journal that a large number of estates continue to be put on the market in all parts of the country '...Stondon Manor and farms will come under the hammer, I understand, early in July.'

There was the usual problem of lost output through industrial unrest, although this had been much reduced during the German offensive in March. By July the workers' patriotic support for the war effort was gone and in that month a strike in an engineering plant in the Midlands was only ended when the government threatened the strikers with conscription. In August, Yorkshire miners, London bus and tram workers, Birmingham and Coventry munitions workers, although they had specifically been asked not to by the government because of the urgent need for ammunition to keep the offensive in France going, went on strike. Even 14,000 London police joined in (albeit for only a short time) demanding higher pay and the recognition of their union (fortunately during their absence from the streets there was no sudden outbreak of crime or unrest). Munitions production kept up with demand. A previous table has shown the quantity produced but it is interesting to look at just one company's output to see where workers might feel aggrieved about the money the bosses were earning. During the years 1914-1918 the Vickers Company made for the British government:

Type of weapon/craft	Number produced
Battleship	4
Armed Cruiser	3
Submarines	53
Light ships	62
Auxiliary cruisers	3
Heavy guns up to 45cm calibre	2,328
Machine-guns	100,000
Other guns	unknown
Armour plate	unknown
Aeroplanes	5,500

An artist's view of the sky at night over London.

At peacetime prices this amounted to several hundred million pounds with stated net profits of £34,000,000 and of that 67 per cent went to one man, Basil Zaharoff.

Just to add to the nation's problems there came the great influenza pandemic that killed more people across the world in the space of a year than the war did in its entirety. It spread quickly and the death toll rose with it, from the thirty people who died from an unidentified illness in Yorkshire and Lancashire in June to over 4,000 a week at the end of October. The population faced three waves of the disease and by May 1919 somewhere between 150,000 and 230,000 people were dead (mostly from the pneumonia that followed), a large number of them being previously young and healthy; the older population were not as badly affected because they were immune from previous exposure to a

A naval officer and two soldiers home on leave pose for their photograph in front of their local street shrine.

Clearing the damage to the Odhams Press building that was caused by the air raid on London on 28 January 1918.

similar virus when they were young. The onset of the disease was very rapid and people often collapsed in the street. Ernest Cooper recorded:

> *By the latter part of Oct and early Novr [sic] it (the flu) was raging and several deaths occurred. One woman was quite well at noon and dead next morning, whole families were in bed at once and it spread in the most wholesale manner... my neighbour Docura of the Red Lion kept about with it too long then went to bed and was dead in no time, a fine strong man.*

The illness badly affected daily life, with many places being closed, such as schools due to a lack of staff and/or pupils. The entry for one school reads:

> *21 November – the attendance has become worse owing to influenza, 22 November – School dismissed for indefinite period.*

So many people were dying that undertakers were unable to deal with the situation and once again the army had to be called in to help; taking Sunderland as a typical example, the death toll was so great that the Mayor held several conferences a day with funeral directors to hear reports of the situation, and at churches and cemeteries around the city the funeral corteges were kept in queues. In total around three-quarters of the population were affected by this new disease.

While the Zeppelin threat had receded, it did not go away. There were a further four Zeppelin raids to come before the end of the war, over Norfolk, the Midlands and the north east resulting in sixteen deaths and seventy-eight people injured. The greater menace came from the Gothas and Giants that targeted London and the Home Counties and the first raid of the year was to be the worst.

On 28 January thirteen Gothas and one Giant took off in thick mist that did not dissipate as they approached England. Six turned back over the North Sea and of the remainder only three Gothas and the Giant were able to penetrate the London defences; the other four Gothas bombed Ramsgate, Sheerness and Folkestone where there were no casualties. The aircraft that bombed London caused heavy casualties, sixty-seven killed and 166 injured. Of the fatalities and

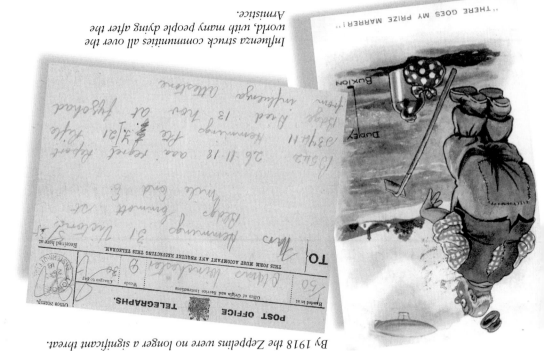

By 1918 the Zeppelins were no longer a significant threat.

Influenza struck communities all over the world, with many people dying after the Armistice.

injuries, the majority were the result of three incidents.

Londoners were still not accustomed to the sound of warning maroons and when they were fired on the evening of 28 January many people mistook them for bombs. There had already been an air raid alert and crowds were waiting for the Bishopsgate railway goods depot to open; it was an officially designated air-raid shelter. When one of the gates was partly opened there was a frantic rush for the shelter. One person is believed to have tripped and other people fell over the prostrate body. Suddenly there was a heap of struggling, fighting men, women and children. Some were suffocated, others were pushed inescapably against the wall. The entrance was blocked. And by a tragic coincidence there was a similar collective panic at Mile End Underground station in the East End. The casualties were unbelievably small – the total for both places was only fourteen dead and fourteen injured. But the greatest tragedy of the night took place at Long Acre, north of the Strand. The

Number 7 Vicars Hill after the air raid of 17 February 1918.

Gothas had gone, but at midnight there was another alarm as the lone Giant flew towards the capital. It was the biggest of them all, R39, and it dropped a 660-lb bomb outside Odhams Printing Works. The missile exploded under the pavement and the three-storey building shuddered under the impact. Fire took hold of newsprint reels in the basement. A wall collapsed and overturned printing presses. There were more than 500 people sheltering in the basement that only had one open exit. Amid the flames and smoke of burning newsreels and the danger of being drowned by the water from the fire hoses, people fought and clawed their way towards the one exit. An entrance was made for doctors to give anaesthetics, do some amputations and relieve the worst of the injuries caused by the panic. At the end of it all thirty-eight people were dead and eighty-five injured.

Only one other raid came close to causing this much damage during the year. On the penultimate raid of the year of the war, twenty-three Gothas and three Giants dropped 159 bombs on London, Southend, Ramsgate, Dover and Rochester. Forty-nine people were killed and 177 injured. The damage was estimated at £170,000.

The army had already made war preparations for 1919 and even though the public had been following the slow and steady collapse of the Central Powers, the end of the war came as a surprise. At 11am, the maroons were fired in London (the air raid signal) and church bells sounded out spontaneously after their enforced silence. Ignoring the restrictions, newspaper bills re-appeared to announce that fighting had ceased on all fronts. Crowds streamed out into the streets, screaming and shouting with pure joy. A ticker-tape style welcome to the

Cadet officers and Australian soldiers celebrating the end of the war.

The number of severly wounded meant a boom time for medical appliance sales.

In late 1918 ration cards were replaced by ration books.

peace was provided by thousands of official forms being thrown into the streets. Everybody gave up work for the day to celebrate. Boy Scouts ran through the streets sounding the 'All Clear' on their bugles as they had done throughout the war. The sound of cheering, hand bells ringing, police whistles blowing was cacophonous. People danced in Trafalgar Square and a bonfire, playfully lit by Dominion troops, permanently scarred the plinth of Nelson's column.

Shortly after the news of the Armistice became known, thousands gathered in front of Buckingham Palace to cheer and see the King and Queen. Several times during the day they appeared on the palace balcony to acknowledge the enthusiastic greeting of the assembled throng. *The Times* reported that after the King had first been out on the balcony the people turned to go, but, as they walked away, fresh throngs, flushed with enthusiasm, met them. Through Green Park came a procession of munitions girls in their overalls, carrying a very large Union Jack. Men with flags tied to sticks and umbrellas, women who had wreathed their hats with the national colours, Dominion soldiers, officers, and men of British regiments, troops from the United States, men of the Royal Air Force, Wrens, WAAC's, girls from Government offices, and children poured into the wide open space before the palace railings. Motor-lorries brought along cheering loads of passengers, some in uniform and some civilians. Motor-cars carried three and four times their normal number of people. Every taxi-cab had half a dozen men and girls on the roof, and soldiers tried to keep precarious places on the steps. Everybody seemed to have a flag, and some of these bore the words "Welcome Home". Australian soldiers climbed up the marble carving of the Victoria memorial, and secured observation posts in this way high above the heads of the crowd. Admirals and generals joined the throng, which by noon had become a wonderful surging multitude, stretching far up the Mall.

Patriotic songs were sung, and at short intervals soldiers led the calls of "We want King George". When palace servants hung festoons of crimson velvet over the balcony it was obvious that the King was going to appear. During the long wait, a band of junior army officers, carrying flags and blowing police whistles, pushed into the massed people, cleared a circle, and romped hand-in-hand round a teddy bear on wheels decorated with a flag, while an American officer, from the top of taxi, entertained the crowd with a demonstration of college yells.

The crowd had gathered to see the King, and the cries of 'We want King George' became more insistent and louder. Just before 1pm the massed band of the Brigade of Guards came in sight playing a triumphal march. As they wheeled into position in the forecourt, the King stepped out on to the balcony. Also present were the Queen, Princess Mary, Princess Patricia and the Duke of Connaught. According to The Times History of the War, a roar of cheering went up such as London had not heard during the period of the war, and above the upturned faces handkerchiefs fluttered, hats waved, and thousands of flags, the flags of all the allies, flapped and shook. The strains of the National Anthem, played by the Guards, at first were scarcely heard against the cheering, but gradually the people caught the music and with the third line of the hymn voices took up the words. Came once more 'Rule Britannia', and then another tremendous note of cheering, led by the King, while the Queen waved a flag above her head. Next the band led the crowd in singing 'Auld Lang Syne', and after this 'Tipperary', 'Keep the home fires burning', and the more stately, but beautiful, 'Land of Hope and Glory', 'Tipperary' was accompanied with nervous laughter and tears. People remembered the early days of the war, and emotion gripped and almost overwhelmed many of them. The crowd showed no wish to dissolve, and men began to call for a speech. The band quietened them with 'The Old Hundredth', and the crowd reverently took up the hymn. Enthusiasm quickly had its fling again. American and Belgian national airs provoked great cheers, and everybody sang the 'Marseillaise.' Then the King spoke. Few could hear him, but his message was well chosen. 'With you I rejoice, and thank God for the victories which the Allied Armies have won, bringing hostilities to an end and peace within sight.' 'Now thank we all our God' was played by the band after the King's words, and an historic scene ended with a final round of cheering, in which the musicians of the band and the King joined. When the crowd eventually dispersed it was to continue the celebrations elsewhere. It was drizzling as dusk fell, but this did not stop the bonfires and torch-lit processions. Searchlights swept the sky, giving the city the first night light for a long time, but while the celebrations went on, for many there was

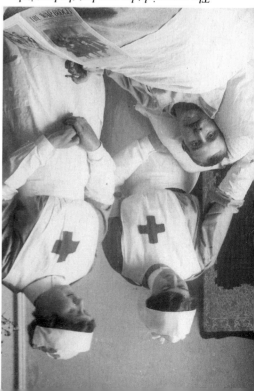

The war might be over but the hospitals were full of seriously wounded soldiers like this one.

only sorrow; throughout the country thousands queued outside churches to attend thanksgiving services and to pray for the Unreturning Army. As one man remembered,

There was a hell of a show all over the country. People went mad.

All night street parties, with beer and drinks and singing. The King also celebrated. The Royal cellars were unlocked and a bottle of brandy was opened that had been laid down by George IV to celebrate the Battle of Waterloo; unfortunately it tasted very musty.

The same sentiments and reactions occurred all over Britain to a greater or lesser extent. In Southwold, Ernest Cooper received a phone call from the County Adjutant to tell him that the Armistice had been signed and that guns were firing and bells ringing in Ipswich. At first he could not take it in, even though the papers had intimated for a couple of days that it could happen very soon. When he arrived at the Mayor's office he found that the Mayor already knew.

D.S.1.

MINISTRY OF LABOUR,
EMPLOYMENT DEPARTMENT,
NELSON...
..................................EMPLOYMENT EXCHANGE.
..........................17 SEP. 1918

Dear Sir,

We understand that you have been recently discharged from His Majesty's Forces. Quite possibly you are returning to your old employer or to your previous employment. Perhaps you are not yet fit even for work of a light kind. If, on the other hand, you wish to get work now or at a later date, may we say that we shall be very glad to see you at this Exchange at any time during the usual hours? These hours are:—

Daily, 10 to 4 o'clock.
Fridays, 10 to 7 o'clock.
Saturdays, 10 to 12 o'clock.

May we point out to you that we have set aside a special part of this Exchange for interviewing every discharged man on his first visit, and also those who are so disabled that they are likely to experience special difficulty in obtaining suitable employment? In addition to this, a Committee, consisting of local employers and workpeople, is ready to advise, and, if possible, to assist any discharged man who applies to this Exchange and finds it difficult to obtain suitable work.

(19913) 12216/578. 60M. 7/18. M. & S.

[P.T.O.

A Ministry of labour leaflet concerning employment for medically discharged soldiers.

A few minutes later a car came in from the local air station full of mad officers, cheering, waving flags and blowing trumpets. Flags soon came out, and bells began to ring and a few of us adjourned to the Mayors house and cracked some bottles of Fizz. An impromptu meeting was called and the Mayor read the official telegram from the Swan balcony, some soldiers came up on a wagon with the Kaiser in effigy, which they tied to the Town Pump and burnt amidst cheers.

Not every village knew of the Armistice by 11 am; some did not find out until much later in the day. The vicar of Stondon Massey in Essex recorded that, while some heard the distant bells at Brentwood, it was not until the afternoon

The King and Queen in the Old Kent Road during their post-Armistice week of visits.

A Hull scene, thought to be at the end of the war.

that definite tidings reached the villagers and then it filtered through chiefly in the form of private messages. As soon as he had official confirmation he allowed the bells to be chimed.

While it was a release, the end of the war would for some would be anti-climactic, a return to the problems and monotony of before the war or a time of great sadness. Then a young girl, Gladys Johnson later recalled her experience of the end of the war. Her father had been sent home after being gassed and wounded in the hand. His experiences gave him terrible nightmares and made him violent.

> *He would wake up screaming even before he was taken ill. He was always fighting. Anything that moved, curtains, anything, he'd be getting up to fight. Yet when he wasn't having nightmares, there couldn't be a nicer man... He would go absolutely mad. I can remember it so well towards the end. He was laid in bed for a fortnight and he went raving mad. It was in my mother's bedroom... All she had in there was a full size bed and a gramophone with a big green horn at the window. We never knew why we took it upstairs. But if we had not, my father would have jumped through the window that night. He got out of bed and tried to strangle my mother and me. It ended with the horn going through the window. My neck went black with the marks where he tried to choke me. He died the next day. The day after Armistice Day. We had no Armistice celebrations inside or outside the house.*

And to add insult to injury, while his own doctor had been treating him for the effects of poison gas, the locum doctor added to his death certificate a sentence that would lose the widow's pension – 'Not aggravated by war service.' For Ernest Read, the last day of the war was also dampened by sadness:

> *The only sad event was poor Docura's funeral which took place with Military Honours in the afternoon...doubly sad that a man of 37 and a keen volunteer from the start should be buried amidst the Armistice rejoicings.*

However, for the majority, it was the war to end all wars and a return to the peace that they had bought at any price.

Home Front Time-Line

1914

August

1   British ships detained in German ports.

2   The Government assures France that the British Fleet will stop the German Fleet if they attack French shipping in the Channel.
German troops invade Luxembourg.

3   The King of the Belgians appeals to King George V for diplomatic intervention to safeguard Belgian integrity.
Germany declares war on France.

4   Germany declares war on Belgium.
Sir Edward Grey wires to Sir E Goschen (British Ambassador in Germany) telling him that, unless satisfactory German assurances regarding Belgian neutrality are forthcoming, he will ask the German Government for his passport so that he can leave Germany.
British mobilisation orders issued.
Admiral Sir John Jellicoe takes control of the British Fleet.
British ultimatum to Germany ends with a state of war at 11 pm.

5   Britain mobilises for war.
Lord Kitchener becomes Secretary of State for War.

6   Appeal for 100,000 men to join the army.
Parliament votes £100 million for the war.
Prime Minister Asquith speaks in the Commons on the war.

7   BEF begins to land in France.
The Prince of Wales inaugurates the National Relief Fund.

8   *Defence of the Realm Act* (DORA) passed.

10   Aliens Restriction (No. 2) Order stopped enemy aliens engaging in any banking business without written permission from the Home Secretary.

11   Press Bureau constituted.

12   Great Britain declares war on Austria-Hungary.

17   Enrolment of Special Constables begins.

20   Queen's Work for Women Fund launched.

28   Appeal for a further 100,000 men for the army.

September

4   The Prime Minister in a speech at the Guildhall justifies Britain's entry into the war.

5   Agreement of London – Great Britain, France and Russia pledge not to make a separate peace.

6   Formation of a Royal Naval Division announced by the Admiralty.

8	Speech by Lloyd George on the need for economy.
11	Blackout in London.
18	*Trading with Enemy Act* passed imposing severe penalties by way of fine and imprisonment upon any person trading with the enemy.
19	Lloyd George makes a speech to Welsh men about German barbarities. Home Secretary grants licences to allow certain German and Austrian banks to continue operating in the United Kingdom.
25	The Prime Minister in a speech in Dublin appeals to volunteers.
28	Prince Louis of Battenburg resigns as First Sea Lord.
29	Lord Fisher appointed as First Sea Lord.

October

8	Proclamation allowing licences for trading with the enemy.
14	Certain German and Austrian banks granted licences to receive dividends on certain shares.
16	First Canadian troops arrive in England.
24	Importation of sugar prohibited.
29	Turkey enters the war on the German side. National Union of Women Workers' Police Patrols officially set up by the Home Office.

November

5	Great Britain declares war on Turkey and annexes Cyprus. The Kaiser is removed from the Navy List of Officers.
6	Carl Hans Lody is the first German spy to be shot; executed by firing squad in the Tower of London.
9	Prime Minister gives a speech at the London Guildhall setting out the war aims of the Allies; 'We shall never sheathe the sword'.
11	Parliament opens.
13	Field Marshal Roberts dies in France.
16	Asquith moves war credit of £225 million.
17	£350 million war loan issue. Lloyd George's first war budget.
27	*Trading with the Enemy Act* amended to create custodians of enemy property in Great Britain.
30	King leaves England on a visit to the army in France. The Home Secretary grants licences for certain Turkish banks to continue trading.

December

2	Seditious paper seized in Dublin.
6	Pope tries to bring about a Christmas truce.
8	Trial of Ahlers for high treason starts.
9	Ahlers convicted.

16	Scarborough, Whitby and Hartlepool bombarded by the German navy – 137 killed and 592 injured.
18	Conviction of Ahlers quashed.
21	Seaplane air raid on Dover – no casualties.
24	Aeroplane raid on Dover – no casualties.
25	Seaplane raid on Dover – no casualties.

1915

January

4	The Stock Exchange suspends traders and clerks who are not fully de-naturalised, if of enemy origin.
6	Kitchener reviews military situation in the House of Lords.
8	Licences granted to certain Turkish banks to continue transactions in France, Cyprus, Egypt and conquered parts of the Ottoman Empire.
19	Zeppelin air raids on Yarmouth and King's Lynn – 4 killed and 16 injured.
	The Court of appeal in the case of Porter v Freundenburg determines that the test of a person being an enemy, for purposes of business, is his place of business or residence and not his nationality.
27	Britain loans Romania £5 million.

February

4	Germany declares waters round the United Kingdom a war region as from 18 February.
7	Foreign Office issues statement justifying the use of the neutral flag for the purpose of evading capture at sea.
11	*SS Wilhelmina* seized and placed in Prize Court.
	Aeroplane raid on Colchester and Essex – no casualties.

March

5	Issue of 3 per cent. Exchequer bonds announced.
8	Bill introduced to give government power over munitions works.
9	Thirty-four Trade Unions agree to expedite munitions output.
16	*Customs (War Powers) Act* allows Customs and Excise officers to confiscate and condemn any goods suspected of being of enemy origin.
31	Home Secretary appoints a committee of enquiry into the recruiting of men from the retail trades.

April

| 1 | Scheme for a 'Dockers' Battalion' at Liverpool published. |
| 5 | King George prohibits use of alcoholic drinks in any of the royal households. |

John Redmond addresses the National Volunteer Convention at Dublin.

6   Government appoints committee on munitions.

7   Appeal by the churches for restraint in the use of alcohol.

13   Munitions Committee meets under the chairmanship of Lloyd George.

14   Zeppelin raid on Tyneside – 2 injured.

15   Zeppelin raid on Essex and Suffolk – no casualties.

16   Aeroplane raid on Faversham, Sittingbourne and area – no casualties.

20   Prime Minister at Newcastle denies that British operations are hampered a lack of munitions.

22   Passenger traffic between England and Holland suspended.

29   Zeppelin raid on Suffolk – no casualties.

     Lloyd George announces the government scheme with regard to alcoholic drinks – a drink tax.

May

4   Budget estimated expenditure £1,6632,654,000 introduced; estimated revenue £270,332,000.

     Drink tax abandoned.

7   Zeppelin raid on Southend – 1 killed and 2 injured.

     Lusitania torpedoed off south west coast of Ireland. 1,198 men, women and children drowned including 124 US citizens.

10   Anti-German demonstrations in London and Liverpool as a result of the sinking of the *Lusitania*.

12   Anti-German riots.

14   Internment of enemy aliens begins.

16   Zeppelin raid on Ramsgate – 2 killed and 1 injured.

19   Age limit for recruits fixed at 40.

25   Coalition Ministry formed.

     Nationalists approve the refusal of Mr John Redmond to take office.

26   Zeppelin raid on Southend – 3 killed and 3 wounded.

30   First air raid on London when Zeppelins raid East London – 7 killed and 35 wounded.

June

3   Bill to create Ministry of Munitions introduced.

     Zeppelin raid on Kent, Essex and the East Riding – 8 injured.

6   Zeppelin raid on Hull, Grimsby and the East Riding – 24 killed and 40 injured. One Zeppelin destroyed by Lieutenant R Warneford, RN.

15   Zeppelin raid on Northumberland and Durham – 18 killed and 72 injured.

     Vote of credit for £250 million.

     Daily cost of the war now £2,666,000.

16   Lloyd George takes the oath as Minister of Munitions.

19	Tribich Lincoln, ex-MP for Darlington, committed for trial on charges of spying.
23	Carl Frederick Muller, a German spy, is shot at the Tower of London. Prime Minister announces forthcoming bill on the registration and organisation of national resources.
24	Coalition government formed under Prime Minister H H Asquith.
29	National Registration Bill introduced by Mr Walter Long. This required the registration of all people between the ages of 15 and 65 resident in England, Wales, Scotland, Scilly Isles and (with reservations) in Ireland.
30	Welsh miners' dispute settled.

July

2	Ministry of Munitions formed.
4	Aeroplane raid on East Suffolk – no casualties.
12	South Wales miners' conference rejects government proposals.
13	£570 million (besides £15 million through the Post Office) subscribed to War Loan. Strikes made an offence.
14	National Registration Bill passes the House of Lords.
15	Welsh miners' strike begins. *National Registration Act* becomes law.
17	Women's right-to-serve procession starts at the Victoria Embankment, London, organised by Christabel and Emmeline Pankhurst and the Women's Social and Political Union.
19	Lady Moir and Lady Cowan establish scheme for training ladies to undertake weekend work to relieve women workers at the Vickers armaments factory, Erith, Kent.
20	Welsh miners' strike settled.
28	Debate on compulsory service.
30	Haicke Janssen and Willem Roos, two German spies, are shot at the Tower of London.

August

4	Anniversary service at St Paul's.
6	345 establishments declared 'controlled' under *Munitions of War Act*.
7	National Relief Fund stands at £5,431,671 in one year.
9	Zeppelin raid on Goole, East Riding, Suffolk and Dover – 17 killed, 21 injured. One raider destroyed at Dunkirk when returning to base.
12	Zeppelin raid on Essex and East Sussex – 6 killed and 24 injured.
15	National Registration of all males and females aged between 15 and 25 years.
16	Cumberland coast bombarded from sea – no casualties.
17	Zeppelin raid on Kent, Essex and London – 10 killed and 48 injured.

18	Offices of the *Labour Leader* newspaper raided by the government.
21	Government declares cotton absolute contraband.
27	South Wales Miners' Federation refuse Mr Runciman's award. In return government refuses to meet them in further conferences.
31	South Wales coalfield dispute finally ended after considerable government concessions.

September

7	Zeppelin raid on East Suffolk and London – 18 killed and 38 injured.
	Unrest among railway workers in South Wales.
8	Zeppelin raid on London, Norfolk and the North Riding – 26 killed and 94 injured.
9	Ernst Melin, a German spy, is shot in the Tower of London.
	Lloyd George stirs up Labour at TUC Congress 'With you victory is assured, without you our cause is lost... This country is not doing its best'.
11	Zeppelin raid on Essex – no casualties.
12	Zeppelin raid on Essex and East Suffolk – no casualties.
13	Aeroplane raid on Margate – 2 killed and 6 wounded.
	Zeppelin raid on East Suffolk – no casualties.
15	Vote of credit brings total so far this year to £900 million and £1,262,000,000 since the start of the war.
16	Taff Vale railway dispute ended.
17	Augusto Roggen shot as a German spy in the Tower of London.
	Debate in House of Commons on National Service.
19	Fernando Buschman, a German spy, shot in the Tower of London.
21	Budget introduces new taxes; 50 per cent on excess profits and on certain imports on grounds of foreign exchange and luxuries.
	Raised taxes – by 40 per cent on income tax; postal charges; imports of certain comestibles, tobacco, motor-spirit, patent medicines. Exemption from income tax limited to £130; scale of abatements on larger incomes reduced.
24	Liquor control regulations applied to the areas of Greater London.
30	Labour meeting resolves that the voluntary system with special recruiting campaign is sufficient and that there is no need for conscription.

October

7	Labour leaders appeal for volunteers for the army.
11	Lord Derby produces recruiting scheme; forty-six call-up groups with married men being the last to be called-up.
	Treating prohibited.
12	Edith Cavell executed at Brussels.

13	Zeppelin raid on Norfolk, Suffolk, the Home Counties and London – 71 killed and 128 injured.
15	State of war between Britain and Bulgaria from 10 pm.
23	King George appeals for more men.
26	George Breeckow shot as a German spy in the Tower of London.
27	Irving Reis shot as a German spy in the Tower of London.
28	King George thrown by his horse while inspecting troops in France. 'L2' circular setting out women's wages for munitions workers.

November

1	King George returns to England after his accident.
6	Suspension of *The Globe* for publishing misleading statements about Lord Kitchener.
8	Drastic criticism in the House of Lords of the government's measures, especially the press censorship.
11	Lord Derby warns unmarried men of compulsion if they fail to enlist voluntarily before 30 November.
26	Mr Stanton, Independent Labour candidate, stands as a protest against pacifist and anti-recruiting policy of late Keir Hardie, and wins the seat by 4,206 votes.

December

2	Albert Meyer shot as a German spy in the Tower of London.
8	2,026 state munitions works declared 'controlled' between 12 July and 6 December 1915.
11	Rush of recruits to volunteer during the last two days under the age group system.
12	Lord Derby's recruiting campaign closed.
16	New 5 per cent Exchequer Bonds issued at par.
20	Derby groups of single men called up.
25	The King sends Christmas message to his troops.
28	Cabinet decides for compulsion – single men before married men.

1916

January

4	Lord Derby's report on recruiting published; of the five million men of military age only half had offered themselves for enlistment.
5	Military Service Bill introduced which prioritised the order of those who would be called up.
12	Second reading of Military Service Bill.
22	Aeroplane raid on Dover – I killed and 6 wounded.
23	Air raid on Kent – no damage.

24	Military Service Bill passed by Commons.
25	Statement on contraband in parcel mails to neutral countries published by Press Bureau.
26	Commons debate on the blockade.
27	Order in council on control of shipping and a restriction of imports. Board of Trade given the power to wind-up enemy businesses.
28	Protest against closing of London Museums. Labour conference decides to allow its members to remain in the cabinet.
31	Six Zeppelins raid West Suffolk and Midland Counties – 70 killed and 113 injured. War Savings Committee inaugurated.

February

9	Air raid on Margate and Broadstairs – 3 injured. *Military Service Act* comes into operation. Extension of restrictions on lighting and on sale of sugar.
14	Remaining classes of single men called up.
15	Speeches on the war by Mr Asquith and Lord Kitchener.
16	Air debate in the Commons.
20	Aeroplane raid on Kent and East Suffolk – 1 killed and 1 injured.
21	Parliament Votes of further credit – a supplementary £120 million, bringing year's war votes to £1,420,000,000.
22	The House of Lords attacks the blockade policy.
23	Lord Robert Cecil appointed Minister of Blockade. Peace debate in Commons.
29	Government recognises The National Volunteer Force for Home Defence. Proclamation creates a blacklist of forbidden companies and individuals: trade with these is expressly forbidden.

March

1	Aeroplane raid on Broadstairs and Margate – 1 killed.
2	*Order in Council on Government of Ireland Act* (1914). Lord Derby speaks in the Lords on recruiting – system of exemptions criticised, especially in the case of agriculturalists; women must take the place of men.
5	Zeppelin raid on Hull, East Riding, Lincolnshire, Leicestershire, Kent and Rutland – 18 killed and 52 injured.
6	Women's National Land Service Corps inaugurated.
7	Prime Minister of Australia (Mr Hughes) arrives in England.
8	Special commission on commerce appointed.
9	Air debate in the Lords, with Lord Montagu urging the setting up of an Air Board and advocating the production of more powerful

machines and the construction of better anti-aircraft guns.

14   Army estimates in Parliament allow for pensions for those discharged owing to illness contracted on service with 4/5ths full pension if aggravated by service.

15   Lord Derby's pledge to married men with regard to military service.

16   South Wales coal dispute decided; miners must join recognised unions in order to maintain output.

17   Food prices risen 48%.

18   Royal Defence Corps formed.

19   Four seaplanes raid Dover, Ramsgate, Margate and Deal. Little material damage but 14 civilians killed and 26 wounded. One raider brought down at sea by Flight Commander Bone, RNAS.

20   Recruiting conference at War Office.

21   Disturbances at Tullamore, King's County. Loyalist crowds demonstrated against Sinn Fein premises, with police stopping the disturbance. Three police wounded by shots fired from Sinn Fein HQ. Four Irish volunteers arrested.

22   Central Tribunal for Great Britain set up.

23   General Cadorna received by King George.

24   Gaelic press offices in Dublin raided.

31   Army Council takes over hay and straw.
     Zeppelin raid on Lincolnshire, Essex and Suffolk – 48 killed and 64 injured. One intruder destroyed.

April

1   Zeppelin raid on Durham County and North Yorkshire – killed 22 and injured 130. Zeppelin L15 captured.
     King George presents £100,000 for war purposes.

2   Powder explosion in Kent causes 172 casualties.
     Resumption of work advised by Clyde strike committee.
     Zeppelin raid on East Suffolk, Northumberland, London and Scotland – 13 killed and 24 injured.

3   Zeppelin raid on Norfolk – no casualties.

4   Budget introduced with new taxes on amusements, matches and mineral waters. Income tax varying up to 5s in the pound. 50-60% increase in taxes on sugar, cocoa, coffee, motorcars and excess profits. Zeppelin raid on East coast – 1 killed and 9 injured.

5   List of certified trades under *Military Service Act* revised.
     Zeppelin raid on Yorkshire and County Durham – 1 killed and 9 injured.

6   First married groups called up.

10   Mr Asquith defines Allied position in a speech to French deputies visiting London.
     Lords Derby and Montagu resign from Air Committee.

11	Ludovico Zender, a German spy, shot in The Tower of London.
12	Clyde strikers tried for sedition.
14	Cabinet Council on the *Military Service Act.*
17	Committee appointed to investigate recruiting. Committee held that there was no case for extension of *Military Service Act* to all men of military age, but suggested extension of the act to include those reaching the age of 18; the retention of time-expired regulars; further combing-out of single men and perseverance with existing methods of recruiting.
18	Lord Milner advocates universal military service in the House of Lords.
19	Cabinet crisis on manpower question reported.
20	New Volunteer regulations issued. Manpower proposals to be submitted to secret session of both Houses.
	Sir Roger Casement lands in Ireland and is arrested.
	Disguised German warship *Aud* sunk while trying to land arms on the Irish coast.
22	Easter manoeuvres of Sinn Fein volunteers cancelled.
24	Outbreak of the Irish Rebellion.
25	Zeppelin raid on Lincolnshire, Cambridgeshire, Norfolk and Suffolk – 1 killed and 1 injured.
	Aeroplane raid on Dover – no casualties.
	Rebellion in Ireland – Sinn Feiners seize Dublin Post Office; serious fighting in the streets of Dublin.
	Yarmouth and Lowestoft bombarded from sea by German cruiser squadron – 4 killed and 19 injured.
26	Martial law in Dublin.
	German Battle cruiser squadron raids Lowestoft – engaged and dispersed by local naval forces.
	Great Yarmouth bombarded – 4 killed and 19 wounded.
	Zeppelin raid on East Suffolk, Kent, Essex and London – 1 person injured.
27	Zeppelin raid on Kent – no damage caused.
28	Martial law across Ireland.
	General Sir J Maxwell takes command in Ireland.
	New Military Service Bill abandoned.
30	Dublin Post Office burned by Irish nationalists.
	30 Dublin rebels surrender.

May

1	Zeppelin raid on East coast of England and Scotland.
	End of Irish uprising – leaders surrender. Total casualties for the uprising: military and police, killed 124; wounded and missing 397; civilians killed 180 and 614 wounded.

124

2	Zeppelin raid on Yorkshire, Northumberland and Scotland with 9 killed and 30 injured. A Zeppelin L20 sank off Norway.
3	Aeroplane raid on Deal – 4 injured.
	Three Irish leaders shot.
	Mr Birrell resigns Irish secretaryship.
	Military Service Bill extending compulsion to married men is introduced.
5	Four Irish rebels shot.
8	A further four Irish rebels shot.
9	Appeal of Irish nationalists to support the constitutional movement.
	Duma (Russian parliament) members received by King George.
10	Commission appointed to enquire into the causes of the Irish rebellion.
11	Debate in Parliament on Irish administration. Mr Asquith announced the execution of twelve Irish rebels and that he would visit Ireland in the near future. In total 73 sentenced to penal servitude and 6 to imprisonment for life.
12	Mr Asquith visits Dublin.
15	Statement of war aims by Sir E Grey.
	Sir Roger Casement charged with high treason.
16	Military Service Bill extending compulsion to married men passes the Commons.
17	Daylight Saving Bill passed.
	Air Board formed with Lord Curzon as President.
18	Royal Commission on Irish rebellion opens.
19	Air raid on Kent and Dover – 1 killed and 2 injured. One raider destroyed over the Belgian coast.
21	Daylight Saving Bill comes into operation.
22	Daily cost of the war recorded as £4,820,000.
23	Vote of credit for £300 million.
	Munitions workers' patriotic procession.
25	*Military Service Act* becomes law.
	Lloyd George undertakes settlement of the Irish question.
	According to the King's message to his people 5,031,000 have voluntarily enrolled since the start of the war.

June

5	HMS *Hampshire* mined off Scottish coast when proceeding to Russia: Lord Kitchener and his staff drowned – 75 bodies washed ashore, 12 survivors recovered.
8	Compulsion replaces voluntary enlistment in Great Britain.
15	*Daylight Savings Act* comes into operation.
25	Trial of Sir Roger Casement begins.
29	Sir Roger Casement found guilty of high treason and sentenced to death.

July

3   Report of the Royal Commission on the causes of the Irish Rebellion issued.

4   Ignatius Tribich Lincoln, ex-MP, sentenced to three years in prison for forgery.

6   Lloyd George becomes Secretary of State for War, with Lord Derby as Under Secretary.

7   King George sends a message of congratulations to the troops in France.

8   Order in Council rescinds Declaration of London of 25 February 1909 regarding maritime blockade, contraband and prizes.

9   E S Montagu appointed as Minister of Munitions.
Two German aeroplane raids on southeast coast (Dover and North Foreland) with no damage.

11   German submarine shells Seaham Harbour – 1 woman killed.
Three armed trawlers sunk off Scottish coasts in action with German submarine.

13   Bank Holiday suspended.
Allied conference on Munitions output held in London.
Bank rate 6 per cent.
German submarine sinks two trawlers and two fishing boats off Whitby.

17   Trade Unions recommend postponement of all holidays in connection with munitions production.
Daily cost of war now £6 million a day.

22   Silver badge granted for those disabled while serving in the armed forces.
General Maxwell's despatches on Irish rebellion published in *The Times*.

24   Vote of Credit for £450 million moved in Commons.

27   Captain Charles Fryatt of the Great Eastern Liner Brussels is court-martialled and shot by German authorities in Belgium, for attempting to ram a German submarine.

28   Zeppelin raid on Lincolnshire and Norfolk – no casualties.

31   Prime Minister in House of Commons denounces murder of Captain Fryatt. Government contemplates immediate action.
H E Drake becomes Chief Secretary for Ireland.
Zeppelin raid on Norfolk, Suffolk, Cambridgeshire, Lincolnshire, Nottinghamshire and Kent – no casualties.

August

3   Prime Minister receives deputation from Miners, Railwaymen and Transport Workers for discussions about demobilisation problems after the war.

Zeppelin raid on Norfolk, East Suffolk and Kent – no damage.
Sir Roger Casement hanged.

7   Admiralty deny allegation in German press that British Hospital ships are being used as transport ships.

9   Zeppelin raid on Northern Counties and Norfolk – 10 killed and 16 injured.

10   Mr McKenna submitted a balance sheet to the Commons, based on the war continuing until 31 March 1917 – the country would be indebted by £3,440,000,000 with a national income of up to £2,640,000,000. Premiere of the film *The Battle of the Somme* at the Scala Theatre, London.

12   Seaplane raid on Dover – 7 injured.

21   The film *The Battle of the Somme* went on general release.

22   Lloyd George gives survey of military situation and announces 35 Zeppelins destroyed by the Allies.

23   Zeppelin raid on East Suffolk – no casualties.

24   Zeppelin raid on East Suffolk, Essex, Kent and London – 9 killed and 40 injured.

25   Zeppelin raid on East and Southeast coast and London.

September

3   Thirteen airships raided the Midland and North Home Counties, Kent and London – 4 killed and 13 injured. Lieutenant William Leefe-Robinson was awarded the VC for shooting down one of the intruders over Cuffley, near Enfield.

5   Mr Balfour talked to local Glasgow trade unions about shipyard labour.

6   At Birmingham the TUC insists on the restoration of trade union customs and practices after the war.

9   In Cardiff, South Wales railwaymen resolve to strike, demanding an increase of 10s weekly on wages.

22   Aeroplane raid on Kent and Dover – no damage.

23   Big raid by German airships (probably 12) on London, Lincolnshire, Nottinghamshire, Norfolk and Kent. Two airships were brought down, one in flames. The second Zeppelin was set on fire by the crew before they surrendered; casualties due to the raid were 40 killed and 130 injured.

25   Seven airships raid Lancashire, Yorkshire and Lincolnshire – 43 killed and 31 injured.

October

1   L31 brought down at Potter's Bar after raid on the Midland and North Home Counties, Hertfordshire and London – 1 killed and 1 injured.

11   Mr Asquith delivers speech on 'No patched-up peace'.

16   Board of Trade issues average increase in retail prices of principal food articles between July 1914 and September 1916; overall increase 65%.
22   Aeroplane raid on Sheerness – 2 injured.
23   Aeroplane raid on Margate – no injuries.
31   Increased wages demanded by Cardiff miners.

November

14   Pensions Bill introduced.
15   Appointment of Food Controller and control of bread foreshadowed.
17   Food regulations issued; Board of Trade invested with wide powers to prevent waste, regulate manufacture and production, direct sale and distribution, control markets, regulate price and commandeer any article.
20   Milk and flour regulations issued by Board of Trade.
23   German destroyers raid in the Channel at the north end of the Downs – little damage.
26   German naval raid near Lowestoft – armed trawler *Narval* sunk.
27   Zeppelin raid on Durham, Yorkshire, Staffordshire and Cheshire – two raiders brought down. Four people killed and 37 injured.
28   One aeroplane raids London at mid-day injuring 10 people. The aeroplane was subsequently shot down in France.
        Brixham fishing fleet attacked by German submarine.
29   The Board of Trade takes over the South Wales coalfield from 1 December.
30   Lord Derby speaks on conditions for the New Volunteer Army - no man to lose civil employment and no compulsion to sign agreement, not to leave home save for defence of country.

December

1   Lloyd George states he is unable to remain in government because of his dissatisfaction with the leisurely conduct of the war.
3   Mr Asquith decides on reconstruction of government.
        Wage dispute in South Wales settled in favour of miners.
5   Lloyd George and Mr Asquith resign.
6   Cabinet crisis – Lloyd George asked to form administration.
        The Board of Agriculture is given powers to acquire land.
7   Lloyd George becomes Prime Minister.
9   New War Cabinet formed.
        Ministries of Food, Labour and Shipping formed.
11   Ministry of Labour comes into being.
14   House of Commons asked for fifth Vote of Credit in the financial year – a further £400 million; total cost £1,950,000,000
16   Government decides to take over Irish railways, to satisfaction of Irish people.

17	German Peace note received by the Foreign Office which lays the blame for the continuation of the war upon the Allied governments.
19	Lloyd George's first speech as Premier calls for the control of shipping, mining and food.
22	Ministries of Food, Pensions and Shipping set up.
	King George's speech to Parliament urges the vigorous prosecution of the war until the security of Europe is firmly established.
31	Total air raid casualties for the year 311 killed and 752 injured.

1917

January

11	Terms of new war loan announced – 5% interest, issue price 95 and principal repayable in 1947 or 4% interest, free of income tax, issue price 100 with principal repayable in 1942.
	Important food orders issued by Lord Devonport; millers had to increase the amount of flour extracted by additional milling (5 per cent) or to add other cereals (up to 10 per cent); the use of wheat except for seed and flour was forbidden. The same orders fixed the price for chocolates and other sweetmeats.
16	General Lawson's report recommends official employment of women with the army in France.
19	Explosion at Silvertown Arsenal, East London. Over 60,000 properties damaged, 73 killed and over 400 injured.
23	Labour Party approves acceptance of office by Labour Members.
25	Southwold on the Suffolk coast shelled at night by enemy vessel – no casualties.
26	Compulsory loan or sale to Treasury of certain foreign securities.
31	Germany declares unrestricted naval warfare on all neutral states, that is, within the war zone, German submarines will sink both combatant and neutral shipping at sight from 1 February.

February

1	Unrestricted submarine war declared by Germany.
2	Lord Devonport appeals to the nation for food economy.
	Kaiser Willhelm proposed for the Nobel peace prize by Stambul Universtiy.
3	President Wilson severs diplomatic relations between USA and Germany.
6	New Air Board formed under Lord Cowdray.
	Mr Chamberlain announces his scheme for National Service.
15	British Government takes over all coal mines in the UK for the period of the war.

17	New War Loan estimated to reach over £700 million.
	Government to revise exemption certificates for men under 31.
21	New British blockade orders – vessels sailing to and from neutral countries, which have access to the enemy, must put into a British port for examination, or be liable to capture.
22	Seven Dutch ships sailing from Falmouth are attacked by submarine U3 – 4 sunk.
25	New War Loan subscriptions amount to £1,000,312,950.
	Broadstairs and Margate bombarded for 10 minutes by Germans causing slight damage. Three people killed and 1 wounded.
26	British government requisitions Dutch ships in British ports.

March

1	Air raid on Kent – 6 injured.
3	15,000 women volunteer for National Service in three days.
5	Potato shortage suggested. Meat consumption in London falls from 31,600 tons in January to 23,450 tons in February.
7	Recruiting for WAAC (Women's Auxiliary Army Corps) temporarily completed with 114,803 enrolling for National Service.
8	A speech by Sir Edward Carson spells out the dangers of food shortages if the German naval threat is not stopped. There would be further restrictions as 500,000 tons of food had been sunk in February.
9	Lord Devonport sanctions maximum food prices.
12	Russian Revolution begins – Provisional Government formed.
15	Vote of credit in House of Commons.
	Tsar Nicholas abdicates.
16	Acute potato famine in England.
	Zeppelin raid on Kent and Sussex – no casualties.
	German aeroplanes over Westgate – no casualties.
	Albert Hall meeting in favour of National Service for women.
17	Aeroplane raid on Kent – no casualties.
18	Ramsgate and Broadstairs shelled by the German destroyers – no casualties.
19	Eight hour day legalised.
	Mr Bonar Law announced that the cost of the war was now £6 million a day for the financial year to 31 March 1917. However, over the last six weeks it had cost £7million a day. The National debt now stands at £3,900,000,000.
20	Ministry of National Service formed.
	Shortage of petrol and coal.
26	Mr Bonar Law appeals to engineers on strike at Barrow to resume work.
	Cost of bread rises to 1s for a 4 lb loaf and a new standard of flour is applied to bakers.

28	Mr Asquith announces his conversion to women's suffrage. Women's Army Auxiliary Corps formed.
29	Speech by Mr Bonar Law says 100,000 more men are needed. Military Service (review of exemptions) Bill is passed.
31	Order limiting output of beer in United Kingdom issued.

April

1	British government decides to intervene in the Barrow engineers strike.
2	Government give Barrow strikers 24 hours to resume work.
3	Barrow strike over.
4	Hotels, boarding houses, clubs and restaurants subject to food orders – a weekly meatless day; 5 potato-less days; $5^{1}/_{2}$ lbs of meat; $3^{1}/_{2}$ lbs of bread; 14 oz of flour and $^{1}/_{2}$ lb of sugar per person. Flour order increases the amount of non-wheat flour in bread.
5	Aeroplane raid on Ramsgate and Kent – no casualties.
6	Food hoarding order – prohibits anyone from buying more than the household actually needs and dealers from selling food where there is reason to believe that the amount of food allowed will be exceeded; houses can be searched if owners thought to be hoarding food.
13	Board of Trade asks farmers to limit use of human food-stuffs in fattening cattle and feeding horses not doing productive work.
16	Food orders – prices of wheat (78s for 120 lbs), barley (65s for 100 lbs) and oats (55s for 78lbs). Barley to be requisitioned by the Food Controller (other than home grown and not kiln dried).
18	Food order restricting pastry and cake making.
19	Speech by Herbert Fisher, Minister of Education on educational reform and the desire by the government for people to be good citizens. This was to cost around £40 million.
20	Germans shell Dover and neighbourhood – no casualties.
25	Corn Production Bill intended to increase the amount of arable land and guarantee minimum prices to farmers and minimum wages to labourers.
26	German Naval raid on Ramsgate, Broadstairs and neighbourhood on the night of 26/27th – 2 killed and 3 injured.
30	Jockey Club decides to stop racing after 4 May.

May

1	New schedule of Protected Occupations; agriculture protected. Under new scheme very few men, and those only in very special circumstances, who are classified A and B1 will be able to escape military service.
2	Further Food Orders extend the powers of the Food controller. Budget announced – no new taxes. Estimated expenditure

£2,290,000,000 with a revenue of £639 million.

3 British Trade Corporation founded with capital of £10 million.

5 Flat racing discontinued as the public were strongly opposed to racing in the present climate of events. Also the severe restrictions on oats made further sport impossible.

7 Daylight aeroplane raid on NE London, 1 killed and 2 wounded.

8 Combing-out of munitions workers begins.

9 Daily expenditure on the war now £5,600,000.
Vote of credit for £500 million demanded in Parliament.

12 Two new groups of attestation 41 to 45 and 45 to 50.

14 King George tours industrial centres in the North.
Labour unrest – London buses and engineers go on strike; weavers in the north threaten strike.

16 Lloyd George proposes Home Rule in Ireland at once.

18 Unit of USA Medical Corps reaches England.

19 Settlement with Amalgamated Society of Engineers agreed upon.

23 Four Zeppelins raid Essex, Norfolk and Suffolk – 3 killed and 16 injured.

25 Aeroplane raid on Kent and Folkestone – 95 killed and 192 injured; three raiders brought down.

29 Mr A Henderson goes to Russia on special mission.

31 Meat sale order published.

June

1 Lord Devonport resigns as Food Controller.
Labour party appoints deputation to Stockholm and Petrograd.

3 Socialist conference at Leeds.

5 Daylight aeroplane raid on Thames estuary and Medway – 13 killed and 34 injured; four machines destroyed while returning.

11 Sailors and Firemen's Union refuse to let Ramsay Macdonald and other delegates sail for Russia.

13 Serious explosion in munitions factory at Ashton-under-Lyne.
Daylight aeroplane raid on London, Margate and Essex – 162 killed, 432 injured.

15 Release of Irish rebels announced.
Lord Rhondda appointed as Food Controller.

17 Two Zeppelins raid Kent and Suffolk – 3 killed and 16 injured; 1 raider downed.

19 Peerages conferred on the Battenberg and Teck families.

21 Warrant instituting *Order of the British Empire* published.

25 First American troops arrive in England.

July

2 The King and Queen attend service at Westminster Abbey for jubilee of Canadian Federation.

4	Aeroplane raid on Harwich and Suffolk – 17 killed and 30 injured.
7	Big aeroplane raid on London and Margate- 57 killed and 193 injured; 11 enemy aeroplanes accounted for.
9	Secret session of House of Commons on London air raids.
11	Sinn Fein candidate defeats Nationalist in East Clare election.
13	Deputation on London Air Defences received by the Prime Minister.
17	Royal proclamation changing name of Royal House and family to Windsor.
	Changes to the government announced, including Winston Churchill becoming Minister of Munitions.
22	Aeroplane raid on Essex and Suffolk – 13 killed and 26 injured.
23	Amendment to Corn Production Bill defeated; minimum agricultural wage to be raised to 30s a week instead of the 25s proposed in the original bill.
24	Vote of credit for £650 million moved.
	Recruiting system to be transferred from War Office control to the Local Government board.
25	Irish Convention opens with Sir H Plunket in the Chair.
26	Lord Rhonnda appointed Food Controller.
27	Ramsay Macdonald's motion to approve the Reichstag Peace Resolution of 19 July defeated by 148 to 19 votes.

August

4	The King and Queen attend special service at Westminster Abbey for third anniversary of the war.
10	Labour Party Conference decides by large majority to send delegates to Socialist conference in Stockholm.
12	Aeroplane raid on Essex and Margate – 32 killed and 46 injured; 2 raiders downed.
13	Bonar Law announces that no passports will be issued for travel to the Stockholm conference.
14	American troops pass through London on their way to the front; Stars and Stripes and Union Jack flown side by side from the House of Commons.
17	Government proclamation forbids threatened strike of Associated Society of Engineers and Firemen.
21	Labour Party reaffirms their decision to send delegates to Stockholm. Parliament adjourns.
	Zeppelin raid on East Yorkshire – 1 injured. One Zeppelin brought down off Jutland.
	Ministry of Reconstruction formed.
22	Aeroplane raid on Dover, Ramsgate and Margate – 12 killed and 25 injured; three raiders brought down.

September

2	Aeroplane raid on Dover – 1 killed and 6 injured.
	Trades Union Congress at Blackpool partly settles Stockholm Programme but with much opposition.
3	Six German aeroplanes bomb Sheerness area – 132 killed and 96 injured, mostly naval ratings.
4	German submarine fires 30 shells at Scarborough – 3 killed and 6 injured.
	Aeroplane raid on London and the South East counties – 19 killed and 71 injured.
	TUC declares against Stockholm Conference by overwhelming majority.
	Edmund Dene Morel sent to prison by Winston Churchill for distributing anti-war literature in Ireland. In 1924 he defeated Churchill for a seat in Parliament. Nominated for the Nobel Peace Prize in the 1930s.
8	Price of milk fixed for three months after October at 8d per quart.
11	First party of repatriated British Prisoners of War arrives from Switzerland.
17	Ninepenny Loaf Order in force.
	Summer time ends at 2 am.
18	Sir A Yapp becomes Food Controller.
24	Aeroplane raid on London, Kent and Essex – 21 killed and 70 injured. Only two of the twenty-four planes penetrate the London defences.
25	Southeast London raided by German aeroplanes – 9 killed and 23 injured.
	Zeppelin raid on Yorkshire and Lincolnshire coasts – 3 injured.
27	National War Bonds (5 per cent and 4 per cent, latter free of income tax) started.
28	Aeroplane raid on the Home Counties; raiders headed off from London with no damage.
29	Aeroplane raid on London. Three machines penetrate the defences – 14 killed and 87 injured.
30	Aeroplane raid on London. Four machines penetrate the defences – 14 killed and 38 injured.

October

1	Aeroplane raid on Essex, Kent and London – 11 killed and 41 injured.
2	War Loan issued.
11	Government stops commercial cable communication with Holland.
12	Count Luxburg is interned in Argentina.
14	Growing shortages of foodstuffs, petrol and coal.
15	Bonar Law announces future Air Ministry Bill.

19	Thirteen Zeppelins raid the Midlands, Eastern Counties and London – 36 killed and 55 injured. Five machines brought down.
24	Franco-British convention for military service allows French nationals in the UK and British nationals in France to be drafted for military service.
	Sinn Fein convention in Dublin.
29	Attempted air raid on Essex driven off.
	Parliament's thanks voted to Navy and Army.
31	Aeroplane raid on Kent and Dover – no damage.
	Further raid on Kent, Essex and London – 10 killed and 22 injured.

November

1	Recruiting taken over by the Ministry of National Service.
8	Arrival in London of USA Mission under Colonel House.
9	Lord Mayor's banquet.
10	*Air Force Act* sets up new government department – the Air Council with a Secretary of State at its head, and a status similar to the Admiralty and Army Council.
12	New scale of voluntary rations introduced; meat was limited to 2lb, butter and fats to 10oz, sugar to 8oz and bread 3½ lb to 8lb per head per week, according to sex and occupation.
18	Rumours that Russia will shortly withdraw from the war.
21	Disenfranchisement of Conscientious Objectors passed in the House of Commons.
27	Dr Elsie Inglis dies on her return with the Scottish Women's Hospitals from Russia.
29	Germany accepts Lenin's offer of an armistice.
	Women's Royal Naval Service set up under Katherine Furse.
30	Coventry aircraft works on strike with 50,000 men and women idle.

December

6	Raid by 25 aeroplanes (Gothas and Giants) on Essex, Kent and London – 8 killed and 28 injured. Two of the raiders are brought down.
11	Balfour announces receipt in September of German peace proposals.
	Non-Ferrous Metals Bill passed.
18	Aeroplane raid on London, Essex and Kent – 14 killed and 85 injured.
22	Lord Rhonda's scheme for rationing by localities comes into force; main cause of queues removed.
31	Lord Rhondda issues model rationing scheme.
	Total air raid casualties for the year – 697 killed and 1644 injured.

1918

January

2   Air Council established.

3   Manpower conference between the government and Trades Union addressed by Sir A Geddes.

5   Lloyd George addresses Manpower Conference on war aims.
    Lloyd George forms new cabinet.

10 House of Lords adopts Women's Suffrage Clause.

14 The House of Commons reassembles.
    Sir A Geddes introduces Manpower Bill.
    Yarmouth bombarded by enemy destroyers – 6 killed and 6 injured.

15 Draft of Compulsory rationing scheme issued to Control Committees.

16 Committee of enquiry into expenditure of government departments announced.

21 Sir E Carson resigns.
    Manpower Bill passes committee stage.

23 Public Meals Order.
    Average daily cost of the war is now £7.5 million.
    Labour Party Conference meets in Nottingham and suggests an International Labour Peace Conference to be held in Switzerland.

24 Lord Rhondda outlines comprehensive scheme of national food distribution.

25 36th meeting of Irish Convention considers letter from the Prime Minister.

28 Aeroplane raid on Kent, Essex and London – 67 killed and 166 injured; one machine brought down.

29 Aeroplane raid on Kent, Essex and the outskirts of London – 10 killed and 10 injured.

February

10 Lord Beaverbrook appointed Minister in charge of Propaganda.

13 Pacifist group in House of Commons defeated.

15 Submarine shells Dover – 1 killed and 7 injured.
    Trawler and seven drifters sunk in the Straits of Dover.

16 Aeroplane raid on Kent, Essex and London – 12 killed and 6 injured; one machine brought down.

17 Aeroplane raid on Kent, Essex and London – 21 killed and 32 injured.

19 Aeroplane raid on Kent, Essex and London. The aircraft failed to penetrate the London Defences.

20 Inter-Allied Labour and Socialist Conference meets at Westminster.

21 Department of Information becomes the Ministry of Information.

25	Rationing of meat, butter and margarine comes into force in London and the Home Counties.
26	Lawlessness in Ireland; additional troops sent to aid the police.

March

7	Aeroplane raid on Kent, Essex, Hertfordshire, Bedfordshire and London – 23 killed and 39 injured; one Gotha downed. Vote of credit for £600 million.
9	War Bond week produces £138,870,240.
11	National Expenditure Committee report on extravagance in munitions.
12	Zeppelin raid on East Riding, Hull bombed – 1 killed.
13	Zeppelin raid on Durham, Hartlepool bombed – 8 killed and 39 injured.
19	The House of Lords debates a resolution approving principle of League of Nations.
28	Women's Auxiliary Army Corps formed by Army Council Instruction; headed by Mrs Chalmers Watson.

April

1	Royal Air Force formed from the RNAS and the RFC. Women's Royal Air Force set up.
7	Meat rationing extended to the whole of Britain.
9	Lloyd George introduces Manpower Bill which provides for comb-out of munitions workers, call-up of more miners, transport workers and civil servants. Military age raised to 50.
10	Manpower Bill passed with a majority of 223; to have effect from 24 April.
11	Military service for Ireland agreed to by a majority of 165.
14	Zeppelin raid on Lincoln, Lancashire and Warwick – 7 killed and 20 injured.
15	Final reading of the Manpower Service Bill passed by a majority of 198.
18	Dublin Mansion House conference, after consultation with Bishops, denies right of British government to enforce conscription.
20	First National Emergency Proclamation, withdrawing exemptions up to 23¼ years. Nationalist MPs unanimously decide to oppose conscription; Irish Bishops support them.
22	Budget proposals – Income tax to be raised to 6s and super-tax up to 4s 6d. Farmers' tax doubled. Twopenny cheque stamp. Beer and spirit duty doubled. Tobacco, match and sugar duty raised. Luxury tax introduced. Letter rate raised. Expenditure, £972,197,000, Revenue £842,050,000, showing a deficit of £2,130,147,000.
25	Red Cross sale produces £151,000.

May

11   The King reviews American troops in London.

16   Arrest of about 150 Sinn Fein leaders in Ireland for plotting with Germany. Denaturalization of Dangerous Aliens Bill issued.

19   Aeroplane raid on Kent, Essex and London caused considerable damage – 49 killed and 177 injured; five raiders brought down.

24   Government issues statement exposing Sinn Fein intrigues with Germany and the revolutionary movement in Ireland.

28   Government opens discussions with Germany for direct exchange of prisoners on lines of Franco-German convention.

29   Report of Food Production Department shows that four million acres have been added for tillage and that 4/5ths of the country's food for the year will be home-grown.

June

3   Lord French wants to rewards Irish volunteer soldiers with land.

15   Committee of Ministers for Home Affairs formed under the chairmanship of Sir G Cave.

17   Aeroplane raid on Kent – no casualties.

18   Vote of credit for £500 million.

22   Lord Curzon announces abandonment of Home Rule and conscription in Ireland for the present.

26   Aircraft workers' strike.

July

1   Serious explosion at shell factory in Midlands – 100 killed and 150 injured.

3   Proclamation of Sinn Fein as dangerous organisation.

6   King George's Silver Wedding Anniversary.

9   Appointment of J R Clynes, MP as Food Controller.

11   Government announces stricter treatment of enemy aliens.

12   Denaturalization Bill passes first and second readings in the House of Commons.

18   Aeroplane raid on Kent – no casualties.

19   Denaturalization passes third reading.

20   Aeroplane raid on Kent – no casualties.
      Threatening meeting of munitions workers in Birmingham.

21   Ministry of Munitions appeals to workers not to strike during critical battle.

22   Lord Lee resigns as Director of Food Production.

23   Munitions workers' strike at Coventry.
      King visits the Grand Fleet.

24   Birmingham munitions workers go on strike.

25   Conference of National Engineering and Allied Trades' Council decide to strike if there is no settlement before 30 July.

26	Government issues an ultimatum to munitions workers – after 29 July, return to work or be conscripted.
29	Munitions workers' strike ends.
31	Sir Charles Fielding appointed as Director General of Food Production.

August

1	Mr Balfour makes a speech about the League of Nations.
5	Five Zeppelins caught off the Wash; one brought down 40 miles from land.
	Lloyd George tells the British Empire to 'Hold fast'.
8	*Education Act* receives Royal Assent.
9	Executive of Miners' Federation appeals to miners to increase output of coal by avoiding unnecessary absenteeism.
30	London police strike. The strikers' demands were for increased war bonus, reinstatement of a dismissed constable and official recognition of the Police Union.
31	London police strike settled and the men return to work.

September

5	Arrest in London of M Litvinov and other Bolsheviks as guarantees for the safety of British subjects in Russia.
13	Railway strike begins in South Wales.
24	Railway strike, which had begun in South Wales, spreads to other lines, affecting the GWR, Midland and the London and South Western.
26	Railway strike in England ended.
30	The Chancellor of the Exchequer opens a 'Feed the Guns' campaign to raise a second war loan of £1,000,000,000.

October

1	Wages (men and women) committee begins.
	Milk to be controlled.
9	Milk controlled and jam to be rationed.
14	The King presents £10,000 to the Red Cross.
17	London subscribes £31 million in National War Bonds in nine days.
18	The Prince of Wales gives £3,000 to the Red Cross.
30	Serious influenza epidemic in London; 2,200 deaths in the last week.

November

2	Mass-meeting of Trade Unionists in London to consider Labour's part in the peace.
7	Appointment of Civil Department of Demobilisation and Resettlement.
	Health Ministry Bill introduced into the Commons.
11	Armistice.

3 Aspects of the Conflict

The Work of the YMCA

Before the Great War, the YMCA had been involved during the Boer War in South Africa, and had there provided marquees that had been used by the troops as reading, writing and recreational centres, as well as meeting places for religious services. Similar services had also been provided to Territorial soldiers during their annual two-week training camps when soldiers were provided with somewhere to write their letters and purchase tea, coffee and other light refreshments.

With the advent of the 'New Armies,' the YMCA wanted to provide similar services for the thousands of Kitchener volunteers. Money was urgently needed and a special War Work committee launched an immediate appeal for money; the £25,000 it raised was soon found to be totally inadequate for the demands being placed on them and a further £25,000 was raised. This in its turn was found to be inadequate. Owing to the urgent character of the work being undertaken, work was often started before the money was available.

YMCA flag day pin to help war work.

In the first two years of the war, subscriptions amounted to £830,000. Included in this total were donations from the king and queen, Queen Alexandra, and other members of the Royal Family, as well as gifts from rich and poor alike. As the war advanced, many gifts were made in order to perpetuate the memory of sons and brothers, and in France, at home, and elsewhere there were so many memorial huts. Children in elementary schools across the country raised over £16,000, while in 1915, Harrow School gave a complete building. Livery companies and railway, banking and commercial undertakings added their share to the funds. On a more humble scale, thousands of ordinary members of the public also contributed.

Neither barracks nor temporary buildings were sufficient at first to house the hundreds of thousands of recruits who joined the new armies.

YMCA worker J Osborne from Bexhill-on-Sea.

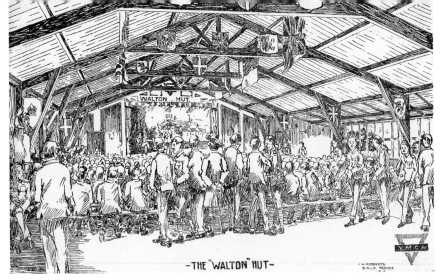

The 'Walton' YMCA hut.

Away on lonely commons, under canvas, in barns, halls and schools, billeted in private houses, or in many cases occupying empty ones – often without beds, blankets, chairs, forms or tables – their accommodation taxed all resources to the breaking point. Moreover, coming straight from middle-class families, the men found the social amenities in camp less than those usually enjoyed by the soldier in barracks.

Right from the start the YMCA came to their assistance by setting up marquees in every camp, where permission was granted by the commanding officer, to provide tea, coffee, and refreshments during the soldier's off-duty hours. This enabled the soldier to obtain an early cup of tea before going on duty at six o'clock and hot refreshments before turning in for the night. Cigarettes, matches, bootlaces, buttons and other sundries could also be obtained at the YMCA counter.

Although the work of the YMCA was under-pinned by strong Protestant beliefs, these were never pushed at the men. In order to allow the soldiers to worship in their own way, each Sunday morning the marquees and huts would be used by Church of England, Roman Catholic and Free Church chaplains for their particular form of worship; in the evening a non-denominational service would be held.

At the start of the war the organisation was relatively small and the manpower needs of the ever-growing YMCA were quickly outstripped. Fortunately the start of the war coincided with the summer holidays, and many teachers and undergraduates

Standard postcard supplied free to members of the armed forces when using the YMCA.

141

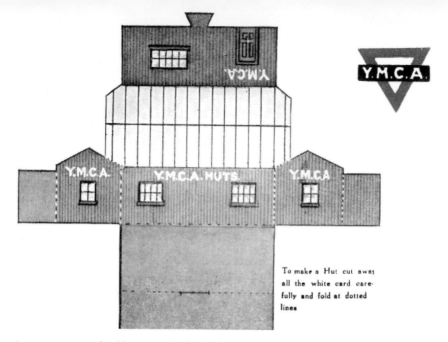

Y.M.C.A.

To make a Hut cut away all the white card carefully and fold at dotted lines

A cut-out postcard sold to raise funds for the YMCA.

offered their services. Enthusiasm carried the helpers along, and it was not unusual for them to keep at their duties in the marquees for sixteen to eighteen hours every day of the week.

The army immediately realised the importance of the work being undertaken by the YMCA and gave it every assistance that it could, smoothing away any difficulties, providing facilities for transport, and detailing orderlies for pitching the marquees and other heavy work. Marquees were usually placed within a camp's boundaries, and quickly became a part of the life of the camp.

A brilliant autumn was followed by an exceptionally wet winter in 1914; this change in the weather had a far-reaching effect upon the future functioning of the YMCA. The weather was so wet that even high and exposed country like Salisbury Plain resembled a morass, while the roads in the area were covered by four or five inches of water. Autumnal gales blew down many marquees, damaging them beyond repair. As result, it became necessary to replace these relatively cheap and portable structures with huts at a cost of around £600 to £700. Some of the first huts to be erected provided accommodation for newly arrived Canadian troops. Many improvements were subsequently made in the interior arrangements of the huts. An auditorium was provided at Crowborough to seat 2,000 men, with adequate cooking facilities to provide hot refreshments. In large camps, a double hut was built which contained a room for concerts, lectures and services and a common room for games, correspondence and refreshments from a counter.

It was also necessary, in centres occupied by thousands of troops, to hire public halls, mission rooms and other suitable buildings. One such building was Bostock's menagerie in the White City at Shepherd's Bush that was used by the 10,000 Territorial troops in training there during the winter of 1914. All the usual facilities were provided with the addition of a lending library and the provision of lectures on the course of the war.

One very important aspect of the YMCA hut and marquee was the atmosphere of being in a club, with the provision of tables and chairs being standard. The Bishop of London spent a month under canvas at Crowborough and recorded that

An early war YMCA free postcard for troop use.

the provision for writing home was always greatly appreciated by the men and was one of the reasons why the YMCA was so popular. As an added bonus, writing paper and envelopes were provided free; over the course of the war this amounted to many millions of sheets of paper and envelopes.

The soldier's love of music was recognised in the provision for the Territorial camps. Every marquee had its piano; a penny edition of 'Camp Songs' sold in hundreds of thousands. This little book contained a selection

Entertaining the troops at home and abroad.

Princess Victoria opened the Shakespeare hut in Gower Street, London on 11 August 1916.

of humorous, sentimental and patriotic songs... that proved of considerable service in promoting the success of the 'sing-song'. After a long and tedious day the camp 'sing-song' gave that happy relief to a large body of men which cannot be found in any other way.

The evening 'sing-song' closed a few minutes before the men had to be in their quarters for the night. In many cases a hymn, a short prayer and the National Anthem would follow this.

Being based on strict Protestant beliefs, the need for the huts and marquees to be open for the whole week was initially a dilemma; the Sabbath was a day of rest and prayer and was definitely not for the continuation of trade. The situation forced a modification of views, and the centres were opened for the whole week. The majority of the centres did not close, except at night, from the time they were first opened, with some huts staying open twenty-four hours a day. Sunday trading was a further problem. This was solved for the ruling body by the choices available to the men: the YMCA or the 'Wet Canteen' and its alcoholic beverages. As a compromise the YMCA sold necessaries but limited Sunday labour as much as possible and restricted amusements.

With the movement of troops to France it became obvious that the fighting man had the same needs as those back home. However, it took some time before the YMCA were allowed into France; at first it was only on an experimental basis, even though their work was fully endorsed by Field Marshal French. In November 1914, the YMCA was permitted to start its work in some of the base and rest camps. If it were successful, then it would be able to extend its activities. Initial problems included defining the exact relationship between a voluntary civilian agency and the

The YMCA served the British Forces wherever they were stationed. This is a card sent from East Africa.

army in a war zone, how it could fit in with military discipline, which of necessity was stricter than in Great Britain, and the difficulties of transport. The initial experiment was a success, as is vouched for by Viscount French, writing in November 1915:

> The problem of dealing with conditions at such a time, and under existing circumstances, at the rest camps has always been a most difficult one; but the Young Men's Christian Association has made this far easier. The extra comfort thereby afforded to the men, and the opportunities for reading and writing, have been of incalculable service, and I wish to tender to your Association, and all those who have assisted, my most grateful thanks.

After the experimental period was over, growth was rapid and by the end of 1916, there were over 180 overseas centres. The majority of these were huts, which were built in five-foot sections for ease of movement. However, various kinds of building were requisitioned, including an old church, a convent, a cinema, a winter garden and theatre, a mayor's parlour, and farm buildings and structures of various descriptions; the sign of the red triangle on any building indicated a warm and constant welcome.

Not all of the centres were situated at depots or bases; some were situated as close as practicable to the front line. The Threapwood Hut was situated within a mile or so of the enemy and was hit fifty times by shellfire before it was totally destroyed; worker safety was assured by the provision of a dugout. Another hut in close proximity to the German lines was the Heat Harrison Hut, situated near a crossroads just under four miles from the front; from early morning until late at night there was a continuous queue passing the refreshment counter.

The first YMCA building to be erected in France was named the 'Queen Mary Hut'. This was situated on the quayside and was used, in the large part, by men who came from the port of London to unload transports; although they wore a khaki uniform, they were non-combatants and did the work of ordinary dock labourers. Hanging inside the hut was a framed copy of the Queen's letter expressing warm sympathy with the YMCA work in France. This was not the

Midnight at the Waterloo hut.

full extent of royal interest in their work. Princess Victoria of Schleswig-Holstein was President of the Ladies' Auxiliary Committee for the YMCA base camps in France, paying visits to France and inspecting the arrangements in order to effect changes. Her committee collected parcels of comforts, footballs, cricket sets, musical instruments, and other articles for use by the men, and also provided 300 women helpers in order to release men for the army.

By August 1916 there were 700 staff employed on the continent, of whom only a very few were of military age; such men were generally stationed near the line where women could not serve. Many of the workers were members of the clergy who had obtained leave of absence from their parishes. University professors and many well-known people gave their services for special duties.

The movement was not only one-way. While troops going to France found a welcome in the YMCA huts at the ports, those same huts catered for the troops returning to Britain on leave. Arriving at a railhead, fully laden with rifle and kit, men knew that the sign of the red triangle secured them a wash, food and a sleep until the leave train left. At the principal stopping places, hot refreshments and other necessaries were available.

The YMCA also provided hostels for the use of wounded soldiers' relatives. They also arranged to meet the soldier's friends or relatives at the boat's side and

take them direct to the hospital where the wounded soldier was to be found. Such was the high regard in which they were held that they were afforded the full co-operation of the French authorities.

It was quickly realised after the start of the war that the servicemen arriving at

Victoria Station in the early hours of the morning, fully laden and with nowhere to go before the connection to their destination, needed some form of assistance. In response to this problem, YMCA staff met leave trains and conducted the men to a disused brewery in Westminster where they could secure beds and refreshments at moderate prices. The King allowed the Royal Mews at Buckingham Palace to be used for entertaining the troops. On arrival the men were provided with refreshments from the Palace kitchen, and, in the morning, after a substantial breakfast, the royal carriages

Huts in London: a building in Euston Square, a rest hut in the Little Theatre, Adelphi and a dormitory at the Earl Roberts Rest Home, King's Cross.

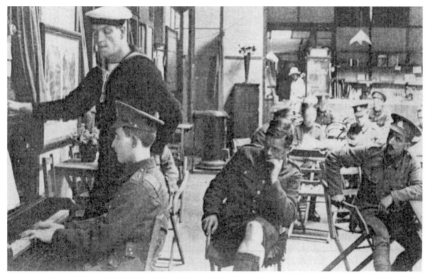

Inside the Euston hut.

conveyed the men to their respective railway stations.

As the army grew in size these developments were insufficient to meet the demand, and a hut was set up at Euston Station where a bed with clean sheets was provided for sixpence. If all the beds were taken, 2d secured blankets and a shakedown on the floor. In the morning, food was available at affordable prices and, in order for the soldier to relax, a club-like atmosphere was created by the provision of books, papers and writing materials and billiards also for a nominal charge. Instead of charging drunken soldiers, the police often escorted them to the hut where they were dealt with by the staff. Similar huts were established at King's Cross, Victoria, Waterloo and Paddington, and improvements made in the form of hot baths. Soldiers' wives often met them from the train or waved them off on their return to the front; an annexe at Waterloo Station provided accommodation for them. Overseas troops were catered for by the erection of a building abutting the Strand, at a cost of between £7,000 and £8,000.

Officers were, naturally, treated slightly differently. A hostel was erected in Grosvenor Gardens, a few yards away from Victoria Station. This was controlled by the YMCA but was erected with money provided by Mrs Charles Tufton and her friends. Designed as a comfortable club, it provided bed and breakfast and other meals. It was opened by Queen Alexandra.

Probably the best hut that the YMCA provided was at the back of the British Museum. At a cost of over £7,000 it provided a canteen, billiard room, quiet room, veranda and sleeping accommodation and baths. The YMCA was not a

The YMCA hut at Aldwych.

YMCA supplies and necessities awaiting shipment to France, Malta and Salonica.

profit-making organisation and the money for such expensive projects had to found by subscriptions. For this project the New Zealand YMCA donated £2,000, and £1,000 came from the Dean and Chapter of Westminster, the Temple Church, University College and Bedford College for Women, while the boroughs of Westminster, Kensington and Marylebone also contributed.

Not only money was donated to the YMCA. Mr Coutts provided them with the Little Theatre in John Street; it was used to house troops in transit through London.

In an average week, the London YMCA, comprising its headquarters on Tottenham Court Road, the station huts and other metropolitan centres, accommodated 7,500 men. Every building was connected by telephone so that pressure on bed space at one hostel could be relieved by another, and, to make sure that soldiers stranded at night were catered for, there were scouting parties provided with cars which picked them up.

As well as providing for soldiers on leave, the YMCA was also involved, unofficially, with enquiries about missing soldiers. With the assistance of the American YMCA in Germany, it was also able to provide relatives with information on prisoners of war.

After being discharged from the army, many disabled soldiers sought help from the YMCA

4067   *"The Times" March 5.*

"TOM"
C/o MISS MAUD FIELD,
Mortimer West, Berks., England.

Dear *Louie Wain + Caesar.*

Delighted to receive your kind subscription of —/— towards the "Dogs and Cats of Empire Fund" to provide Y.M.C.A. Soldiers' Hut at the Front.

Please tell all your dog and cat friends about it, won't you?

I am a Soldier Dog, my master is a prisoner in Germany, that is why I am working so hard for all our brave soldiers.

The Kaiser said Germany would fight to last cat and dog. Let the dogs and cats of the British Empire show what they can do!

With many wags of my tail.
From your faithful,
"TOM" (Fox Terrier).

A COLLECTING CARD FOR D.C.E.F. CAN BE SENT IF DESIRED.

to hold to dogs or cats names.

A thankyou postcard for the YMCA Soldiers' Hut fund.

in securing suitable employment. To assist, an employment bureau was set up to save the men from tramping about to find work.

The 'Snapshots League' was a method of easing the transitional separation of the soldier from his family and friends. 11,000 amateur photographers took 500,000 snapshots of family and friends at no charge. Members of the armed forces were supplied with forms upon which they stated that they desired photos of their wife, parents, or sweetheart living in the place specified. The form was returned to the Tottenham Court Road headquarters and then forwarded to the nearest voluntary helper. When the photos had been taken, they were sent, in weatherproof envelopes, to where the soldier or sailor was serving, anywhere in the world. Its cost, £10,000, was funded by private subscription.

Another voluntary activity undertaken was legal assistance. This was not directly provided by the YMCA but was facilitated by them. With the co-operation of the General Council of the Bar and the Council of the Law Society, arrangements were made to provide free legal advice in YMCA huts. This help was given by barristers and solicitors on active service and was confined to civil matters.

Naval personnel were served when they arrived at the major naval ports and also when they were in training at 'HMS Crystal Palace' for later service with the Royal Naval Division. This latter base housed up to 10,000 sailors and the YMCA was permitted to use the Egyptian, Grecian, and Roman Courts and later the Morocco and Algerian Courts as well as the North Tower Gardens. Special services provided here were a laundry and a post

Helpers preparing a meal at the Little Theatre.

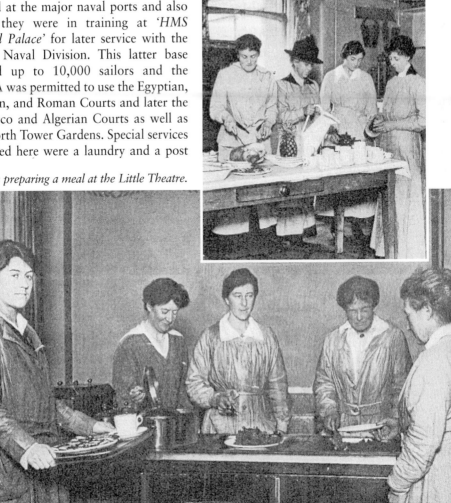

office that helped deliver mail – 1,000,000 letters and parcels between September 1914 and September 1915. During the same period over £3,000 of stamps and £9,000 of postal orders were sold and the Savings Bank had on average over 2,000 depositors. The YMCA also published a penny booklet for the sailor to record his pay and amount due. It was deliberately made to fit inside the sailor's cap. Concerts and lectures were regularly organised in the theatre and religious services were held both on Sunday and during the week.

Growing numbers of munitions workers needed both housing and feeding. To meet this new demand, The Munition Workers' Auxiliary Committee was established with Lord Derby as Chairman and Princess Victoria as President. This committee quickly organised 3,000 ladies to work, in a voluntary capacity, in district centres, across the country, which were to provide hot meals and sleeping accommodation. The major arsenal of Woolwich grew in capacity very quickly. As the work force increased in size it became more difficult for the workers to get a mid-day meal; local resources were insufficient, resulting in large queues. This affected the output of guns and shells. To alleviate this problem, the YMCA organised a kitchen that served up to 20,000 meals every day, mostly at mid-day. For a shilling the workers were provided with a three-course meal and an orchestra; a la carte meals were also provided at a reduced price. Night shift workers were also provided for.

Similarly, in London Dock centres, labourers were provided with a dinner of

Dining hall and recreation room for the shell makers at Woolwich – munitions workers going to dinner.

Lloyd George at a munitions workers' dining room at Ponder's End. Inset, his wife distributes chocolates and cigarettes to soldiers at the Temperance hut at Hampstead Heath.

hot meat and potatoes for 7d that replaced their traditional cold meat and bread. The Liverpool Dock Board adopted the idea and formed a company with capital of £10,000 to erect the huts that were then handed over to the YMCA. As a result of these cheap meals, health improved, output increased and there was less heavy drinking. Towns and cities all over the country followed suit in providing cheap meals for the work force.

Accommodation for this ever-growing work force was also a problem. In many places there were not enough lodgings to go around and in some cases landladies let out their rooms in eight-hour shifts. Looking for lodgings further afield often meant long and difficult journeys. An experimental scheme was started at Enfield to provide workers with wooden huts within easy distance of the works, affording each worker private living space. Each cubicle contained a comfortable bed, clean sheets and a box for clothes, while the use of baths and

YMCA concert room at Penkridge Bank Camp.

other necessaries was available. Close by was a common hall for meals, recreation and letter writing. For an inclusive sum, averaging around £1 per week, the munitions worker was provided with full board, lodging and washing.

Throughout the war, wherever there was a need, the YMCA did what it could to assist victory in its own way. The work it did was important and much appreciated as the following two extracts show. Lord Roberts wrote to the YMCA on the day he left for France:

> Lord Roberts hears nothing but praise for what the YMCA is doing at the various camps. The latest tribute he has received is from the Canadian contingent, who, when he inspected the men on Salisbury Plain, said that they did not know what they would have done without the facilities afforded by the YMCA.

And on behalf of the 13th Battalion, Royal Highlanders of Canada, the Captain and Adjutant wrote:

> Allow me to express our appreciation of the hospitality shown by the YMCA to us as individuals and as a regiment. Many members of the regiment have benefited by hours spent in your tents, and the accommodation granted us by you has made our weekly church parade possible.

The YMCA had achieved its aims.

3

The War and National Education

The effect of the war on National Education and the contribution of a national system of education to the effective conduct of the struggle against Germany are closely intertwined. In the first instance, the war revealed social conditions among children, adolescents and recruits that required immediate corrective legislation to improve their health. As the war developed it was found to have affected every degree of childhood, to necessitate:

> *...through economic disturbances, the increased supply of school meals, to secure subsequently by high war-wages such better conditions as practically to abolish the need for such meals.*

Educationally, children were quickly affected. A rapidly growing army needed housing and one obvious choice of premises was schools. This resulted in many schools becoming occupied by the military and unable to function as educational establishments; by May 1916 this amounted to 200 schools, mostly in the north of England. Building resources were in short supply so little school building could be done to improve the situation.

Also, many teachers rushed to join the colours (over 20,000 by 1917) leaving classes without supervision or with a substitute female teacher. This was not a

A famous teacher, John Harrison who won the Victoria Cross in 1917.

Young children being taken to an air raid shelter.

An air raid rehearsal – marching to the shelter.

problem that faced only state schools; it was mirrored across the country in both Preparatory and Public schools. Teachers were invaluable in the army: 'their high standard of education, physical training, and practising organization' makes 'them specially valuable as soldiers and officers,' and by the end of 1917 at least 1,300 teachers had been killed and three had been awarded the Victoria Cross. The shortage of male teachers particularly affected all boy classes in Elementary schools, while the general shortage of teachers resulted in much larger classes.

It was not just schools that were affected. Centres of higher learning such as universities, colleges, training colleges, medical school, technical colleges and law school soon had much reduced numbers as the young men left to join the armed forces. With reduced numbers of students, many University buildings were put at the disposal of the government for military purposes; some of the colleges of Oxford and Cambridge housing Officer Cadet Battalions, for example.

During August 1914, the Oxford Military Committee recommended over 1,100 men for commissions and by October over 1,500 men had gone. This was repeated at Cambridge where over 2,000 applicants for commissions were forwarded to the War Office. The level of service shown by such establishments is clearly indicated by the Cambridge College lists: by August 1917, 13,395 men were on service, 1,734 had been killed and 2,405 had been wounded or were missing or were prisoners. Also five had gained the Victoria Cross, twelve had been awarded the DSC, 199 the DSO and 628 the MC. The change in the numbers actually attending the university is shown by a comparison of the number of undergraduates present at Easter 1914 and 1917; this showed a decrease from 3,181 to 491. Manchester University also showed similar changes. In the summer of 1917 it recorded over 1,700 members of the university past and present serving with the colours, while over 460 students were absent on military, naval or other service, in addition to 68 members of the teaching staff.

University staff also contributed without joining the armed forces. At Manchester 'practically all the members of the Science and Medical Staff were wholly or partially engaged on war service. The ordinary research work of the scientific departments had been abandoned, and they had devoted themselves to special service, both advisory and experimental, in connexion with the war.' Each university played its own part in this research and in providing men for the front, but it was not just the men who played a part. Women university students also contributed to the war effort, with many devoting their vacations and other spare time to work on farms and in factories. The all-women Girton College, Cambridge, provided ten doctors who served in France, Serbia, Greece, Romania and Russia as well as researchers in pathology and chemistry, radiographers, bacteriologists and the inventor of an anti-gas machine. Over 100 went into educational work in schools and universities, while others were employed in munitions works as testers, chemists, inspectors, supervisors, welfare workers and heads of hostels. As with the girls' schools, many spent spare time rolling bandages, knitting sweaters, mufflers, socks and gloves. Many also helped in canteens and munitions works, VAD hospitals and government and other offices, helping, among many things, to compile the National Register.

An open-air classroom in winter.

On the other hand these stark facts reveal the impact of the educational system on the

A Guard of Honour provided by the OTC of Eton College.

conduct of the war. The schools gave to the army and navy, in the combatant and non-combatant functions, large numbers of highly-trained teachers who brought special abilities to their work. Public schools such as Eton provided the majority of the new officers, and many more were found among undergraduates. As the war progressed, more and more officers were to be commissioned from the ranks, some of whom had no more than an elementary school education though many more came from the state grammar schools.

Of course the war was unimaginably destructive, but it also gave society the chance to reconstruct on an equally wide scale, marking a way forward for the national education system and pointing out what was good in the existing system. What may seem strange or antiquated to our eyes and beliefs was not so to the writers of the period; for them, what follows was not pretentious or far-fetched; it was just the normal way to view life.

The war not only made it clear that the whole educational system needed revision, revolution, or reconstruction but at the same time showed what was of value in the old system and how it could be perpetuated in the new system.

> *The war proved that the principles of patriotism, self-sacrifice, and idealism which had permeated the schools, as the direct product of an ancient system that made Christian teaching a pervasive element in school life, must also be controlling principles in a new system which would give for the first time full training to the body, mind and personality of every child in the nation.*

The war demanded efficient womanpower, as well and manpower, and it came to be quickly realised that the reserve power of a nation lies in its children; if they were neglected physically and educated inadequately then capital had been wasted.

Serious educational reform had been hampered during the early nineteenth century by failure to understand the need for an educated proletariat. As a result of the Crimean War, which highlighted the poor physical condition of the population, a new educational effort was made which opened up education to

The war produced a realsiation that child care was of great importance for the benefit of society; Baby Week parade in West Ham.

A school class going out to tend the allotments.

more people. Between 1868 and 1878 far-reaching educational legislation affected the factory child and the university undergraduate alike; its breadth is shown by the fact that it opened up education to women. By the time of the 2nd Boer War, education had been transformed, but it had still not had the effect on the 'physical regeneration' of the nation that had been expected. According to *The Times History*:

> *It was during, and in the years immediately following, this war that the next great advance came. The war and the recruiting sergeant had revealed the physical inefficiency of a large percentage of the race. The school child was suffering, not so much from the sins as from the thoughtlessness of his forefathers and of the statesmen who had governed them.*

The

> *...far-reaching changes included the abolition of 'cul-de-sac higher elementary teaching,' the substitution of a county and borough system for innumerable small and ineffective educational authorities, the elaboration of a highly organised system of secondary schools...*

and the creation of a new central control, the Board of Education. It was hoped that this would provide measures to remove the conditions found by the recruiting sergeant, the army doctor and the new relief agencies. Further acts controlled the working hours of children, making it technically easier for them to attend school. While this had an impact on education, there was still health to improve. The Inter-departmental Committee on Physical Deterioration highlighted the paucity in improvement when it demanded 'a systematised medical inspection of school children' and that it should be imposed on every school authority as a public duty. Following this the government passed a *Provision of Meals Act* and later introduced the Schools Medical Service which quickly discovered that around a million out of the seven million school – aged children were so unfit that they could not benefit fully from the educational system. This physical neglect was quickly seen when recruitment started at the beginning of the war and a significant number of men were turned away on health grounds; with the introduction of conscription the percentage rejected was even higher.

At the start of the war, all schools and universities were closed and the early stages of harvesting were in full swing. When Lord Kitchener made his historic appeal on 7 August for 100,000 men, the appeal was soon fulfilled. While the universities emptied and boys of 18, who should have gone on to university or finished the final year in secondary school, flocked to join the colours, girls also joined in with the spirit of the times. The 'Girls' Patriotic Union of Secondary Schools', under the patronage of the King's daughter, Princess Mary, carried out administrative work, such as raising funds in schools for the Star and Garter Home for totally disabled soldiers and sailors, collecting money for Red Cross work, providing hospitality for destitute Belgian girls and so on; many also did volunteer service or made garments or cultivated the land. Large numbers of schoolgirls and university women performed voluntary aid work in hospitals, or worked for the Red Cross, driving cars, munitions – related scientific work, canteen work, munitions production, and welfare work.

Like their male counterparts, most females left school at the age of thirteen or fourteen to go to work and, like the boys, went to work in the factories, many of them producing goods for the armed forces. According to *The Times* history

> *...there was loss and great sacrifice in this work, which was soon seen to be heavier in many cases than young children and adolescents could undergo.*

As a result of this, the government became involved in child welfare work, but did not stop child labour because of the needs of the war; moreover, with an estimated 500,000 children under the age of fourteen in employment it would have been well nigh impossible.

Indeed it can be seen that the government actually encouraged the use of children. A Board of Education return on the number of children under twelve specially released from school for employment in agriculture showed that 7,934 boys and 92 girls had been employed in the spring of 1916; in the last quarter of 1915 this had been just 1,388 boys and 25 girls. By July 1916 15,750 children of school age were employed in agricultural work.

Children did not work only on farms. Earlier in the war, the Board of

War work in Bradford – a boys' class making boxes for soldiers' parcels.

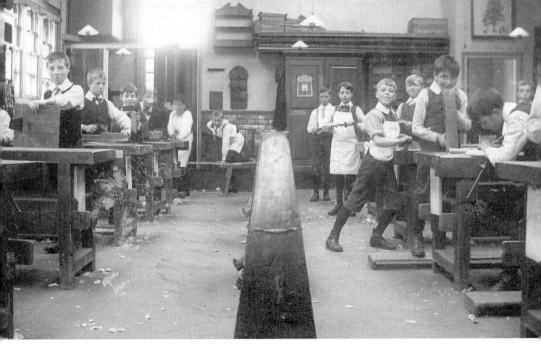

Hilda Road Boys' woodwork class, Monday afternoon, 30 June 1915

Education had given the Local Education Authorities powers to suspend attendance by-laws, thus allowing thousands of children, under the school leaving age to, in default, leave school to work in the factories. Even though the policy was officially supported by the Home Office, some cities and towns, places such as Birmingham, Hull and Bradford, kept their children at school. According to *The Times History*, the government was not strong enough to insist on the use of adult labour and many children, as a consequence, did work for which they were totally unsuited. Many children therefore lost their educational chances, but, as compensation, welfare workers were appointed, canteens provided, and the conditions and hours of labour were carefully watched.

A further reason for educational reform, a direct result of the war, was the behaviour of the children themselves. It was noted that a restlessness among children of all ages arose when the war began and that this was made worse in many cases by the loss to families of men on active service and women to war work. The result was:

> *...a good deal of rowdyism, in some cases passing into hooliganism, and a notable increase in what may be called minor crime, such as stealing fruit from orchards, and some increase in serious crime, such as robbery from the person.*

This was a general national trend but was much more prevalent in some areas than others.

It was felt that this was caused by children having no 'restraint, oversight, or mental or moral or physical training' other than what was supplied by their own homes or by voluntary clubs. Unlike middle class children, they had been cut off from any educational influences from the age of thirteen onwards and without the benefit of such bodies as Scouts and Guides or the Boys' and Girls' Brigades

159

War savings at Friern Barnet School.

they were without any system of control. Another problem was felt to be the new freedom of money. However, *The Times History*, recorded that overall, children 'behaved well throughout the war, and especially in the exciting times of air raids.' One important reason for this was that many children joined the Scouts and Brigade Corps that channelled the energy of youth into productive war activities: making sandbags, doing work for wounded soldiers, working on farms, despatch riding, air raid calls, hospital and ambulance work and so on; productive for the war effort, and work that prepared them for military service.

Not to be outdone by the boys, the Girl Guides helped with nursing duties, learned signalling and telegraphy, worked in hospitals doing the washing up, general washing and bandage work, collected money (for example £2,000 for an ambulance in France) as well as a host of other jobs. Whatever they did gained them a reputation for dedication; one Girl Guide even won an award for courage and devotion to duty while tending school children who had been killed and injured in an air raid on London.

Secondary schools also made a direct contribution to the war effort in many ways. The work of the pupils of the John Roan Foundation School serves to illustrate that contribution. 'It had its cadet corps, which supplemented the normal work of such a corps with allotment work in term time and farm work in vacation' while the Scouts group collected waste paper and assisted in the Post Office. The girls' school also made its own contribution; by February 1917 they had bought £1,318 worth of War Loan Stock and War Savings certificates. From September 1914 the girls had collected money,

> *...knitted garments, and gifts in kind for the purpose of an organised transmission of parcels to the battalions of the local regiment.*

Girls from each school form who joined together to form a Troops Committee carried out this work. And for the same regiment, 400 rifle-lock covers were sent abroad in 1915.

Kit-bags, fitted with necessaries, were made for Belgian soldiers in English hospitals returning to the front. Woollen garments were sent to prisoners of war, to Belgians at the front, and to the crews of mine-sweepers.

Other purchases included 330 books for the YMCA, and five footballs for French recruits in Cherbourg, which earned them a mention in the Orders of the Day!

Previous mention has been made of school meals provision. As with adults, food was generally a problem, especially when the government introduced voluntary rationing without due regard to the needs of children.

Schoolboys gathering horse chestnuts for use in munitions – they were a source of glycerine for explosives.

Overall this meant a reduction in the food they received. In some boarding schools the pupils were deliberately put on low war rations to make them understand the effects of war, in some it was coupled with a financial motive and in some cases caused real injury to health. In order to counter this problem, early in 1917 a special system of rations for children was instigated which laid down how much of the various food groups children needed at certain ages. A boy between thirteen and eighteen should have received 6 lb of bread, 2 lb of meat, 10 oz of fat and 8 oz of sugar per week, with girls receiving four-fifths of this allowance.

As the war continued, it became apparent that further changes were needed if the system was to provide society with well-rounded individuals and that the changes would have to start from the earliest possible age. Responding to the pioneering work of teachers like Margaret Macmillan, the government introduced nursery and open-air schools. As a result the death rate among young children reached the lowest recorded figures during 1916 and 1917.

However, this was still not enough. Further improvement was obviously still needed as was evidenced by the publication of a report in 1917 by Sir George

A London school food-control court trying a prisoner for wasting food.

A typical junion class towards the end of the war. There were very few male teachers left due to the needs of the army.

Air raid drill – schoolgirls practising carrying a wounded schoolfellow.

Newman that amplified the dangers of the nation neglecting its children: 12 per cent of all school children were physically unfit to take full advantage of schoolwork. A further restriction was placed upon improvement by the shortage of doctors.

The new Secretary of State for Education, H Fisher, produced proposals for a radical new educational system on 10 August 1917. His scheme included nursery schools, the reduction of child labour, compulsory part-time day continuation schools up to the age of eighteen, extending the school medical service and securing the physical fitness of all children and young persons. The physical problem was the basic one and Fisher wanted his bill to transform these physical conditions; conditions, it was felt, that restricted height and weight, caused spinal deformities, cardiac problems, poor dentition, and sensory deficiencies, particularly of sight. It was generally felt that

> ...the losses of the war made it not only necessary but urgent that there should be no more waste of child life, that the disease and sickness rate should be further decreased, that children should be so supervised, physically, mentally and morally, as to secure a nation clear in mind, healthy in body and wise in outlook.

His Education Bill required Local Education Authorities to provide playing fields, school baths, school games centres and equipment for physical training. Many other things were promised but before the bill could become law it was withdrawn and rewritten and eventually passed in 1918.

As can be seen, the effect of the war on national education was profound and affected large numbers of the population. For many the effect was negative, but for others it was more benevolent, and for many it raised a hope for the future: a future in which both worker and employer wanted an educated and thinking workforce. At the same time the national education system contributed massively to the conduct of the war and assisted in the final victory in many ways.

3

Prizes of War
and Trading wth the Enemy

D r Coleman Phillipson in his book on *International Law and the Great War* summarises the Prize Court as

> *...an institution of long standing. Its sources may be traced back to the later centuries of the middle ages. In order to secure protection against pirates, merchantmen associated themselves under an elected chief, called the 'Admiral', and sometimes their respective states sent out armed men to put down piracy. The piratical ships thus seized were divided among the captors according to the decision of the Admiral...*

and

> *...with the gradual development of the law of nations it became customary for the Admiralty of maritime belligerents to set up a special court to investigate the legality of captures made by their warships or privateers. In this country an Order in Council of 1589 required all prizes to be submitted to the High Court of Admiralty.*

The Prize Court had a system of litigation and jurisprudence that was peculiar to itself and it dealt with captured goods that could be considered as a prize. By the middle of the nineteenth century the court had died out but with the start of the war in 1914 it was to gain a new lease of life, one which was regretted by the very man in charge:

> *'I am sure' began Sir Samuel Evans, in his summing up on the case of the Chile, 'we all deplore the causes which render it necessary for a Prize Court to sit again within these realms after a happy lapse of about sixty years'.*

A scene in the Court of Justice, Edinburgh during a 'trading with the enemy' trial.

The SS Ophelia *was equipped as a German hospital ship, but was also provided with signalling apparatus of exceptional capacity.*

What was this court about? *The Prize Act* of 1708 sums it up:

> *...if any ship of war, privateer, merchant ship or other vessel should be taken as prize by any of HM ships of war or privateers and adjudged as lawful prize in any of HM Courts of Admiralty, the flag officer or officers, commander or commanders and other officers, seamen, and others who should be actually on board such ship of war or privateer so taking such prize should after such condemnation have the sole interest and property in such prize without further account, such ship to be sold and the proceeds distributed according to the shares of the officers and crew declared by the Royal Proclamation.*

A further act in 1864 awarded prize bounty at the rate of £5 for each person on board the enemy's ship at the beginning of the engagement. On 28 August 1914 previous schemes were cancelled and a new system of gratuities was substituted which allowed for a more general distribution to officers and men.

The purpose of these courts was to determine whether the captured vessel was an enemy vessel, or a vessel in the employ of the enemy, and if so to determine who should receive a bounty for their capture. The first case to come before the court was that of the sailing ship *Chile*, which arrived at Cardiff docks on 4 August and was detained the next day by the

The Germania, *Krupp von Bohlen's racing yacht, was condemned as a prize in October 1915.*

Collector of Customs. As the German government had not given British ships in German ports any period of grace in which to leave, the ship was condemned and became a prize. The next day, the SS *Marie Glaeser*, while sailing on the high seas, after coaling at Bristol, was captured by HMS *Gibraltar*. A prize crew was put on board and the ship taken to Glasgow.

At the start of the war many enemy vessels were captured, some of which had – legally and rapidly- been turned into British vessels in order to escape capture. Many fishing vessels could have been taken as prizes as they were working near or about the coast but these were not seized as long as they confined themselves to peaceful work.

One of the most important collective cases that came before the Prize Court was that of the *Kim*, the *Alfred Nobel*, the *Bjornstjerne Bjornson* and the *Fridland*. The owners of these ships stated that as the goods were for Denmark they were not Prize ships. When the manifests were examined, they showed that between them they were carrying, among other things, thirteen times more lard than Denmark imported in a year. As a result, the ships and their contents were given as contraband and as a prize by the court. Using neutral shipping Germany tried to maintain a stock of contraband goods throughout the war. Each capture, the legality of its ownership, and whether it was a prize, was settled by the Prize Court, a little known aspect of the war on the Home Front.

Trading with the enemy

The war presented the country and the government with a trade problem, the size of which had never before been experienced. Even though there was a war, nations could not easily be stopped from trading with Germany. There were even problems in restricting British trade with the enemy. Of the two difficulties, the former was the more simple to solve. The British fleet cleared the seas and drove German commerce in its open and obvious form out of the markets of the world while direct trade with the enemy was quickly reduced by blockade and strict application of contraband regulations.

German officers arriving at the Law Courts, London as witnesses at a Naval Prize court case.

Trading with the enemy was illegal and in some cases treasonable. However, because of the complexities of international trade, this could not easily solve the second problem. The day after the declaration of war the Crown issued a proclamation against trading with the enemy, but the wording of the document meant that the government spent over a year stopping loophole after loophole that allowed German trade to continue. In order to allow the successful continuation of British commerce during the war the proclamation had declared

> ...that any transactions to, with, or for the benefit of any person resident, carrying on business, or being in the said Empire (Germany) which are not treasonable and are not for the time being expressly prohibited by Us either by virtue of this Proclamation or otherwise, and which but for the existence of the state of war aforesaid would be lawful, are hereby permitted.

This effectively allowed German businesses in Britain to function in much the same way that they had done before the war.

The effect of this proclamation was extended to Austria-Hungary without being changed until 21 August when the Treasury expanded upon the issue. It said that there was no problem dealing with the enemy as long as it was done in Britain or a neutral country unless the business transacted was expressly forbidden – not quite business as usual but well on the way! Public feeling quickly caused a further Proclamation that revoked the previous proclamations and the explanation. The 9 September proclamation substituted a new set of rules that defined the word

The Marie Leonhardt, *a German vessel of 2,000 tons, captured in the Thames.*

A British destroyer examining a Dutch steamer.

'enemy' but essentially had the same effect as the original proclamation: it would keep German toys out of England but could not keep British gold out of Germany. Such were the technicalities of modern trade.

On 18 September the *Trading with the Enemy Act*, 1914 was passed and imposed very severe penalties by way of fine and imprisonment upon any person trading with the enemy within the meaning of the act. This new act asserted Common Law that, in simple terms, stated: trading with the enemy was illegal and could be classed as treason. From this time on it was the responsibility of the courts to decide whether or not the Common Law was ousted by the Proclamation. One early case that tested this Act was Wolf v. Carr, in which the Court of Appeal found that although the branch was in England, the cotton-waste manufacturers were resident in Germany and therefore any transaction between the two was illegal. Shortly afterwards, certain goods were claimed as 'prize' from the *Eumaeus*, even though they were the property of a Japanese branch of a Hamburg firm (Japan was an ally of Britain during the Great War). However, the parent company was found to be a German firm, thereby making the trade illegal. A further proclamation on 8 October removed further possible loopholes.

An attempt was made to make the system of control simpler. On 9 October, the Board of Trade issued a notice about future proceedings. This authorised HM Customs and Excise to require certificates of origin or declarations of ultimate destination for all goods, wares or merchandise imported into or exported from the United Kingdom in trade with any foreign port in Europe or on the Mediterranean or Black Seas, with the exception of those of Russia, Belgium, France, Spain, and Portugal.

Initially, the Home Office issued a licence by which the London agencies of the Deutsche Bank, the Dresdener Bank and the Discontogesellschaft were permitted to carry on business with certain limitations, conditions, supervision and requirements as to the deposit of money and securities. Similar permission was given to a number of Turkish banks when Turkey joined the Central Powers. In October 1914, German and Austrian Banks were even given a licence to receive dividends, while in January 1915 a licence was granted to London agencies of Turkish banks to enter into transactions at any or all of their establishments in the United Kingdom in respect of banking business with any establishments of the said banks in France, Cyprus, Egypt or any part of the Ottoman Empire occupied by the Allies. A further licence then allowed any company trading in the United Kingdom to do business with these banks. It was now possible for a previously restricted German company, registered in Britain, to deal freely in France or Egypt through an Ottoman bank. It was to be two years before the situation changed; by the end of 1916, however, the banking problem had been solved by their closure for all purposes.

The Stock Exchange was not exactly quick off the mark in restricting its business. On 12 November it laid down the rule that transactions entered

Using an X-ray to inspect cargo for contraband.

into by a member of the 'exchange' before the war on behalf of an enemy, and not completed when hostilities began, could not be completed in view of the law relating to trading with the enemy, although, like all good businesses it allowed trading with purely German firms that were registered in England and so were technically British companies. Before closing for Christmas, the Stock Exchange asked naturalised members and clerks to re-submit their papers to prove that they had been denaturalised in their country of origin. Upon their return to work only those who had proved their de-nationalisation were allowed to continue working at the Stock Exchange.

In order to stop indirect imports from enemy states, the *Customs (War Power) Act* of 16 March 1915 gave customs officers the right to seize any goods thought to be of enemy origin; the onus of proving otherwise was on the importers. This was later extended to include any goods that were thought to have been imported in contravention of the law relating to trading with the enemy.

Further legislation followed on 23 December 1915 that extended restrictions relating to trading with the enemy. During 1916, acts in February and a proclamation in April resulted in the compiling of a blacklist of people and traders. On 18 July 1916 this blacklist was greatly extended by the addition of names from all over the neutral world, including a long list – mostly with German names – from America.

On 27 January, the Board of Trade was given the power to wind up any business of enemy origin that it felt was benefiting the enemy in any way. It was also allowed to give control of enemy property to a custodian. The act made it compulsory for all enemy aliens to identify any property belonging to them or in which they had an interest; it also gave the custodian the right to have any patent granted to him. In August a further act was passed with respect to the *Copyright Act* of 1911; the copyright of works first made or published in an enemy country was deemed to have been vested in the Public Trustee as custodian under the Trading with the Enemy Acts. With acts such as these, the final legal loopholes were sealed and British money was no longer going to the enemy.

There were many cases in the courts that tested the law and its interpretation. One of the first to occur, although the case was not heard until June 1915, was that of William Jacks & Co of Glasgow, who agreed to supply the Phoenix, the Krupp and the Rheinische steel works with iron ore from Nova Scotia. Although the war had started they allowed the cargo ship carrying the ore to dock at Rotterdam where it was unloaded for Germany. In their defence they pleaded that they had tried to stop its delivery. Lord Strathclyde sentenced each of the accused to six months'

With Holland, Sweden and Norway neutral, there were many routes through which the Germans could buy the material they needed for their war effort.

A FRIEND IN NEED.

Germany. "WHO SAID 'GOD PUNISH ENGLAND!'? GOD *BLESS* ENGLAND, WHO LETS US HAVE THE SINEWS OF WAR."

imprisonment and a £2,000 fine.

The case heard at the London Guildhall on 18 January was the opposite to that of the Jacks case. Messrs. Fownes had branches in New York and Germany, the shares of the latter branch being all held in London by the parent company, and were charged with obtaining goods from Germany between 15 September and 15 December 1914. Although the goods were sent straight to New York, then a neutral state, the payment came from, and the sale proceeds went back to, London. Although the defendants pleaded that they had no intention of helping the German war effort, two of the three were given terms of imprisonment.

Court powers were also used to effect the break-up of companies deemed to be owned by the enemy even though they were registered in the United Kingdom. One such firm was the Groedel Brothers Steamship Company (Limited) that consisted of four steamships registered in Great Britain to an English company and flying the British flag. Even the steamers, intended to load timber from the forests of Transylvania, had been built in England. However, when it was discovered that of the 500 shares, 496 were owned by Hungarian businessmen living in Budapest, the ships, which had been requisitioned, were sold by auction for £288,500, twice their normal price. By October 1916, £2,312,224 of enemy funds arising from the liquidation of German interests in England was in the hands of the Public Trustee.

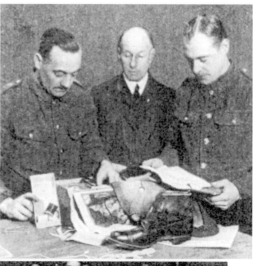

All incoming and outgoing mail was censored and searched for contraband.

3

The Royal Family and the War

On the afternoon of 4 August, the king held a council and issued proclamations calling out the Army Reserve, embodying the Territorial Force, and bidding all naval officers on the Reserves and Retired List to hold themselves in readiness for active service. The next day he and his naval equerry spent several hours at the Admiralty inspecting the elaborate plans of the probable field of naval operations. Meantime, the Prince of Wales put himself at the head of a high-powered committee and issued a national appeal for funds for the relief of distress.

A few days later, when the Expeditionary Force was ready to depart on active service, the King sent the following message to the troops:

> *Buckingham Palace*
> *You are leaving home to fight for the safety and honour of my Empire.*
> *Belgium, whose country we are pledged to defend, has been attacked, and France is about to be invaded by the same powerful foe.*
> *I have implicit confidence in you, my soldiers. Duty is your watchword, and I know your duty will be nobly done.*
> *I shall follow your every movement with deepest interest and mark with eager satisfaction your daily progress; indeed, your welfare will never be absent from my thoughts.*
> *I pray God to bless you and guard you and bring you back victorious.*
> *GEORGE R I*

A typical day in London for the King began before 9.30 am when he read the newspapers;

A Christmas card sent by King George and Queen Mary for Christmas 1914.

A portrait of George V issued at the start of the war by a French insurance company.

During the war the King inspected thousands of troops. This photograph shows the inspection of the Honourable Artillery Company Infantry Battalion on 12 September 1914.

even when he was travelling on the Royal train the papers were brought to him before the day's programme began. After reading the news he began work with one of his secretaries, dealing with correspondence. At 10.30 am the first of the interviews arranged for the day was given. It was a common thing for five or six people to be received on one morning. The range of people having an audience with the King was considerable and ranged from a journalist who had previously been imprisoned in a Bolshevik prison, to original descendants of Midshipman Young, the sole mutineer officer on the HMS *Bounty*, to an escaping Prisoner of War officer.

If engagements permitted, the king liked to take a walk in the grounds of the palace at some time in the morning, but usually his interviews lasted until lunch. At luncheon a distinguished visitor was often present, so that the king might talk to him. In the afternoon, at least four times a week, generally accompanied by the Queen and Princess Mary, the king drove out to visit hospitals to see and converse with wounded officers and men. Once or twice a week there were investitures to be added to the routine. After tea the king was involved in state work, talking with Ministers, reading government documents and further work with the secretaries. At 8.30 pm he dined.

Outside London this routine was changed. The king left the capital to visit factories, hospitals, training camps, aerodromes and other scenes of war activity across the country, and at frequent intervals to visit the Fleet in its stations off the coast and the Army at the Front.

The King was very interested in munitions production. He toured a number of such plants during the war and spent a considerable part of the summer of 1915 visiting such companies. His first visit, with Lord Kitchener, on 30 April 1915, was to the Government Small Arms works at Enfield and at Waltham Abbey. Ten days later he was at Portsmouth dockyard. On 17 May the king went to the Clyde, where he received a unanimous resolution passed by the workmen of Fairfield Shipbuilding and Engineering Company expressing their determination to put forth their best

King George invented the modern day 'walkabout' of the Royal family. Where this photograph was taken is unknown.

King George at the review of the 20th Division on 24 June 1915 on Knighton Down before it left for France on 20 July, and below – Princess Louise inspecting the Argyll and Sutherland Highlanders of 152 Brigade on 12 February 1915 when they were stationed at Bedford.

The King's visit to the Clyde, 18-21 September 1917 – watching the operation of a riveting machine.

efforts to turn out as efficiently and rapidly as possible the government work entrusted to them.

From the Clyde the king passed on to Tyneside, where he went over the Wallsend Slipway and Engineering Company's works. The tour was then carried to Barrow 'where the visit was remarkable for the long conversations between the king and the workmen'. In July the king went to Coventry and the Birmingham district, where he saw a variety of operations. His round of visits included the Birmingham Small Arms Company, the Wolseley Motor Company and Kynochs, where Mr Arthur Chamberlain showed him the making of quick-firing 18-pounder shells, the capping of cartridge cases, and the packing of cartridges. In Saltley, he visited the Metropolitan Carriage, Wagon and Finance Company where he made a short speech about increasing output.

After a short break, the king once again started touring at the end of September. This trip took him to Yorkshire. Here he visited munitions works, hospitals and Leeds University where poison gas warfare was demonstrated to him. At Sheffield he actually fired an armour-piercing shell through armour plate.

In 1917 the King once again started up his visits to areas producing ships and munitions, in England and Scotland. What was to make these trips different was the access provided to journalists who reported the visits at length. In May, the king visited Chester, some works in Flintshire, Hawarden, shipbuilding yards at Birkenhead, the Mersey, Manchester and Liverpool, Barrow a second time, and finally Carlisle and Gretna, where a great new munitions factory sprawled over land which before the war had been open country.

At an explosives factory on the Welsh borders, the king and queen saw 3,000 women and girls engaged in the production of TNT and the

174

conversion of cotton waste into guncotton. Hundreds of trousered young women surged along in the wake of the Royal visitors. At Gretna 10,000 of the operatives were women, out of a total workforce of 13,000. At Liverpool the King watched 500 women at the lathe, converting rough forgings into carefully tested shell bodies, while the Queen visited an explosives factory largely staffed by women. On the same day, the king had been to the docks, visited two armed American liners and talked to the gunners in the sterns of the vessels. From the northwest the king and queen returned to London, where, the next day, they paid an impromptu visit to a newly installed fuse factory in the suburbs.

Three weeks later their majesties left for the northeast to visit the shipbuilding yards. During this visit they made a steam tug journey along the Tees and landed at Stockton Corporation Quay. Motorcars were waiting to take them to the shipbuilding yard they were to visit, but both the king and queen chose to walk. As the Royal Party passed through the old-fashioned thoroughfares the people gave them a rousing reception. Children in bright clean pinafores waved tiny flags; on the pavements, in the doorways, and at upper windows women cheered heartily. Hundreds of people fell in behind the official party, cheering as they rushed along. During this five-day trip the king and queen visited munitions establishments along the Humber, Tees, Tyne and the Wear.

The King had to make a serious personal decision about his name. At a meeting of the Privy Council, to which Dominion Ministers as well as the Duke of Connaught, the Archbishop of Canterbury, the Lord Chancellor, the Prime Minister, Lord Curzon, Lord Rosebery and others had been summoned, the King signed a proclamation announcing that for the future the Royal House and Family should be known as 'of Windsor', and

The Royal Tour of the northeast coast – inspecting munitions girls at Stockton.

A senior Air Force officer greets King George.

relinquishing and discontinuing the use of all German titles. The text of the proclamation read:

By the King
A Proclamation

Declaring that the name of Windsor is to be borne by his Royal House and Family and relinquishing the use of all German titles and dignities.
GEORGE R I

Whereas we, having taken into consideration the name and title of our Royal House and Family shall be styled and known as the House and Family of Windsor:

And whereas we have further determined for ourselves and for and on behalf of our descendants and all other the descendants of our grandmother Queen Victoria of blessed and glorious memory to relinquish and discontinue the use of all German titles and dignities.

And whereas we have declared these our determinations in our Privy Council:

Now, therefore, we, out of our Royal Will and Authority, do hereby declare and announce that as from the date of this our Royal Proclamation our House and Family shall be styled and known as the House of Windsor, and that all the descendants in the male line of our

King George visiting munitions factories in Birmingham.

said grandmother Queen Victoria who are subjects of these realms, other than female descendants who may marry or may have married, shall bear the said name of Windsor:

And do hereby further declare and announce that we for ourselves and for and on behalf of our descendants and all other the descendants of our said grandmother Queen Victoria who are subjects of these realms, relinquish and enjoin the discontinuance of the use of the degrees, styles, dignities, titles and honours of Dukes and Duchesses of Saxony and Princes and Princesses of Saxe-Coburg and Gotha, and all other German degrees, styles, dignities, titles, honours and appellations to us or to them heretofore belonging or appertaining.

> *Given at Our Court at Buckingham*
> *Palace, this seventeenth day of July,*
> *In the year of our Lord One thousand*
> *nine hundred and seventeen, and in*
> *the eighth year of our reign.*
> *God save the King.*

In September the King and Queen toured independently; the King toured the shipbuilding areas of Western Scotland while the Queen and Princess Mary visited Coventry where they saw aeroplane and other factories. The next month the two Royal ladies visited Woolwich where they inspected equipment and stores and met the women who sorted and stored them.

The Royal visits were not always war-related and during the visit to Bristol, as well as visiting shell factories, they also found time to visit the Wills tobacco factory where they spent half an hour watching the various aspects of cigarette production. Moreover, at Bath, for the first time in two hundred years, a reigning King of England drank the waters in the Grand Pump Room.

King George greets Lloyd George at the gates of Buckingham Palace.

The King and Queen at Farnborough 1917 inspecting the newly formed WAAC.

In November the King visited the National Physical Laboratory at Teddington, where Sir Richard Glazebrook showed him such processes as the minute setting of the gauges of shells and similar operations. A little later he visited a factory that made tents and gasmasks for horses.

The Royal family took a deep interest in the food question and had practised voluntary food economy from the day that it was suggested. When compulsory rationing of meat, sugar and fats was introduced, the King and Queen both had ration cards and, according to *The Times History of the War,* lived strictly within the allowance permitted by the cards.

The first visit of 1918 was made by the King to Harwich to view a vast number of auxiliary craft and on the same day the Queen, the Prince of Wales and Princess Mary explored the London docks to see the huge stores of grain and the processes by which it

George V invested hundreds of officers and men with military awards and decorations. An officer leaving after an investiture.

was unloaded. On several other occasions they visited towns associated with the food supplies of the country. At Reading they watched the manufacture of biscuits at Huntley and Palmer's works and the packaging and distribution of vegetable seeds at Sutton's seeds. The King, like the Queen, spent hours going round the food warehouses of the London docks.

King George being piped aboard HMS Barham *on 26 July 1917.*

During a tour through Lincolnshire they went to the fish docks at Grimsby, where they saw fish being slung in baskets from trawlers to the quay, and long lines of cod, plaice, whiting and turbot exposed for auction in the sheds. As they walked through the docks the King and Queen were almost hemmed in by crowds of cheering fish workers. Next they moved to Lincoln where they visited workshops as well as the Cathedral and a military hospital, and while in Lincoln the King held a sword given to the city by Richard II. Lincolnshire was the birthplace of the 'tank' and while he was there he watched them being made and tested; breaking his schedule, he took a ride in one of them over a course, selected by him, which included all of the steepest places. The tour of this part of the country was concluded with a visit a new aerodrome where Prince Albert was serving as a Captain in the Royal Air Force.

Prince Albert in 1918. He would later become King George VI.

The next tour, which proved to be the last of its kind before the war ended, was to the West Riding of Yorkshire, where three busy days were divided among the cloth producing towns. Due to the expansion of the army, towns like Bradford, Leeds and the surrounding areas were boom towns: before the war the army had purchased less than one per cent of the wool produced in the area; after three years of war the War Office had purchased 1,600,000,000 lbs, worth more the £100 million. Most of the cloth came from this small area but Scotland, Ulster and the Midlands also provided some. The majority of this work was done by women and during the Royal visit to Yorkshire the women sang instead of cheering.

During the war, the King left the country on a number of occasions to visit the Western Front. His first visit started on 30 November 1914 and

Corporal Beesley (from Nuneaton) of the Rifle Brigade receiving his Victoria Cross from the King in France.

The King decorating Private Harry Shelly with the DCM on 12 August 1918.

lasted until his return on 5 December. While in France he visited hospitals, conversed with army, divisional and brigade commanders, visited the Commander in Chief, Sir John French, and distributed a number of decorations. He also inspected a number of troops, most especially the Indian Army units. The visit was political as well as military and on the first day he met with President Poincaré, the French Prime Minister, Monsieur Vivianni and General Joffre the French Commander in Chief. At the end of the first day he presented General Joffre with the Grand Cross of the Bath. For the remainder of the visit the procedure was very similar, inspecting units, giving out medals to generals and soldiers and meeting and talking to members of the High Command.

Nearly a year later this visit was repeated with one major difference. On 28 October, towards the end of the eleven-day visit, the King was reviewing First Army troops when the mare he was riding reared as the troops cheered. The horse rolled over, crushing the King's leg. With five distinguished surgeons in attendance, the King was quickly transported to England by ambulance, hospital train and hospital ship. On the train, the king invested Lance-Sergeant Brooks, of the Coldstream Guards, with the Victoria Cross, although he was so weak that he needed assistance to pin the award through the thick uniform cloth.

The crossing, on the hospital ship *Anglia*, with only fifty other injured men, was rough but uneventful. On arrival at Victoria Station he was put in a motor ambulance and taken to Buckingham Palace where an English and Canadian nurse attended him; the English sister had, in fact, attended King Edward when he was suffering from typhoid. Public anxiety was allayed by a cheerful bulletin. The King was confined to his rooms for six weeks of convalescence during which time he was prescribed alcohol as a stimulant. After his recovery he made a further four visits to France, the last

in August 1918 just before the Allied offensive.

The Prince of Wales joined the army at the start of the war and was gazetted ADC to Sir John French at GHQ in France. In October 1915 he accepted the Chairmanship of the statutory committee for dealing with Naval and Military pensions but continued to serve in the army until the end of the war. His younger brother, Prince Albert, was a naval officer, but, after a period of illness, he transferred to the air service, being stationed at Cranwell for a time. He was later stationed at Hastings where he served with the training brigade for Royal Air Force Cadets. In October 1918 he flew to France to take up duties there. Princess Mary eventually became a fully engaged VAD in the Hospital for Sick Children in Great Ormond Street.

From the beginning the Royal family took both a leading part in the raising of funds for the relief of distress and in the visiting of the sick and wounded. Within three days of the outbreak of war, the Prince of Wales appealed for money to help relieve the distress that would inevitably come to those who could least bear it. To this appeal the Queen added her own request, asking ' the women of this country who are ever ready to help

The Prince of Wales in 1918. He later became King Edward VII.

The Prince of Wales (second from left) served towards the end of the war with the Canadian Army. The inscription on the reverse of this photograph states that it shows the Canadians invited to the Thank(s)giving service at Denain (near Valenciennes) on the occasion of their Liberation from the Hun by the Canadian Corps – November 1918.

QUEEN MARY'S NEEDLEWORK GUILD.

BADGE CERTIFICATE.

Miss E. B. Terry

of *48 Combe Park, Bath*

having been engaged in voluntary war work for the Q.M.N.G. has been granted the badge of the Guild, which she is entitled to wear during the war, so long as she continues a voluntary worker.

ST. JAMES'S PALACE.

Date *Sept. 16. 1915.*

Annie Lawley

Hon. Sec.

A certificate for being a member of Queen Mary's Needlework Guild.

F.H. TOWNSEND 1915

FOR THE WOUNDED.

Mr. PUNCH begs to recommend his readers for their own sakes and for the sake of the cause to attend and bid at the remarkable sale which is to take place at Messrs. CHRISTIE'S (8, King Street, St. James's Square) on the first five days of each of the weeks beginning April 12th and 19th, and also on the 26th and 27th. Over 1,500 generous donors (including the KING) have presented art treasures and relics of unique historical interest to be sold for the benefit of the British Red Cross Society and the Order of the Hospital of St. John of Jerusalem. The entire proceeds of the Sale—no charge for their services being made by Messrs. CHRISTIE— will be handed over to these Societies. The exhibits will be on view from April 7th.

An advert from Punch for an auction in aid of the Red Cross and St John's. The King was a generous donor for such occasions.

those in need to give their services and assist in the local administration of the fund.' The King and the Royal family were generous contributors to these funds, whether by direct gifts of money or by sending valuable objects to those Red Cross sales at Christie's which became an annual institution. On 3 April 1916 the King gave the nation £100,000.

The King and Queen began their visits to wounded soldiers in the first week of September when they spent four successive days visiting hospitals in and around London. During the next few months, as well as superintending the vast number of articles of clothing that poured into St James' Palace in answer to her appeal, the Queen worked incessantly in visiting such institutions as the American Women's Hospital, the Indian Hospitals at Brighton and in the New Forest, and the wounded British and

Official portraits of the King and Queen on the occasion of their Silver Wedding Anniversary.

Belgian soldiers in St Bartholomew's Hospital. Or, again, at other times, she would spend an afternoon in visiting various Nurses' Training Colleges in North London, the Union Jack hostel near Waterloo Station and the married quarters adjoining, or the street shrines in memory of fallen soldiers which became a feature in south Hackney and other districts. Both the King and Queen also visited hospitals that specialised in treating soldiers needing artificial limbs.

In order to express the feelings of the women of England for the fighting men, the queen wrote a letter in April 1918:

> *To the men of our Navy, Army and Air Force. Our pride in you is immeasurable, our hope unbounded, our trust absolute. You are*

King George on the top deck of a bus down the Peckham Road, shortly after Armistice..

The King in France in 1918.

fighting in the cause of Righteousness and Freedom, fighting to defend the children and women of our land from the horrors that have overtaken other countries, fighting for our very existence as a People at Home and Across the Seas. You are offering your all. You hold back nothing, and day by day you show a love so great that no man can have greater. We, on our part, send forth, with full hearts and unfaltering will, the lives we hold most dear.

As well as visiting convalescent men, the King and Queen also entertained them at Buckingham Palace on a number of occasions. One recorded instance was on 17 February 1917 when they held a reception for 100 overseas officers who were either on leave or convalescent. In the state ballroom, a stage with a cinematograph screen was erected, and after the show the visitors were given tea in the dining room, served by 'great ladies', while the King, Queen, Princess Mary and the Duke of Connaught walked about chatting with their guests.

Within minutes of the news of the Armistice, a crowd of thousands gathered in front of Buckingham Palace. Several times during the day the King and Queen had to appear on the balcony of the Palace to acknowledge the cheering crowd. Shortly after 1 pm the King gave a short speech: 'With you, I rejoice, and thank God for the victories which the Allied Armies have won, bringing hostilities to an end and peace within sight'. After the King's words the band of the Brigade of Guards played the hymn, 'Now thank we all our God'. The historic scene ended with a round of cheering, in which the musicians and the King joined.

During the war George V had visited France five times, carried out 450 inspections of troops, visited 300 hospitals and personally conferred 50,000 decorations – but the King's war was not yet over. During the remainder of Armistice week, every day, he rode out through some part of London to meet his people. It is generally agreed that, as a result of his work during the war, the position of the Royal family was better secured and stronger than that of any Royal House in Europe.

The Boy Scout Movement

In 1917 Lloyd George, the Prime Minister, wrote

I do not think I am exaggerating when I say that the young boyhood of our country, represented by the Boy Scouts Association, shares the laurels for having been prepared with the old and trusted British Army and Navy... within a month of the outbreak of war (they were) able to give the most energetic and intelligent help in all kinds of service. When the boyhood of a nation can give such practical proofs of its honour, straightness and loyalty, there is not much danger of that nation going under.

How, then, was it possible for a force of mere boys, and as boys, obviously undisciplined, to share laurels with the Army and Navy? The answer lay in their motto 'Be prepared' and in the fact that the structure of the organisation was simple and fluid which would allow it to adapt, very quickly, to fill any gap in public service. Many such gaps appeared as soon as the nation moved quickly from peace to war. One of the first contingencies that should have been provided for was the safeguarding of railways and telegraphs as soon as war was imminent, this would stop any

The dream of many scouts and Special Constables was to find a spy.

interruption to troop mobilisation and the transmission of military despatches. Another obvious requirement was the efficient reinforcement of the coastguards to cope with the extended duties and at the same time fill the places of men called up for the navy. The scouting movement volunteered to help and within twenty-four hours of receipt of intimation that the association's help would be welcome, Scout Troops and Patrols were moving rapidly to fill these gaps across the country.

Led by the Chief Scout, General Sir Robert Baden-Powell, the Scouts prepared to become Britain's second line of defence. That they were prepared for such a mammoth task was a matter of prescience, preparation and good luck. In January 1914 Baden-Powell had told the Scouts that the movement was on the threshold of great developments because the year promised immense national results if the Scouts could rise to the opportunity and 'eclipse all past records in their very very momentous history'.

A Scoutmaster in the early days of the war.

Six years earlier he had predicted, to harsh criticism in both Britain and Germany, that the Germans would bombard undefended towns on the Yorkshire coast when the two nations were eventually at war. Prophetically he repeated this warning to Boy Scouts at Scarborough only four days before the actual bombardment of the town. The utility of the Scouts in assisting in foiling enemy spies was humorously foreshadowed by *Punch* magazine in July 1914. The chief element of good luck, which helped the Scouts fall into line for the defence of the country, was the fact that the war began at the start of the school holidays. As a result many Scouts were already at their annual camp with all their equipment, under their own leaders, waiting for the word from the Chief Constable of each county. When it came, it meant that potential targets like railway bridges, telephone wires, reservoirs, shore-ends of marine cables and other sensitive areas could be guarded. One, probably apocryphal, story from this time illustrates the quality of the average Scout. A passing cyclist decided to find out what they were capable of. As he passed a single young Boy Scout on duty at a lonely railway cutting he dismounted and climbed a telegraph pole and refused to come down. To his horror the boy whipped out a pocketknife and put several slashes in each tyre to make sure that the potential enemy saboteur would not escape!

Little understood before the war, when the organisation was seen as little boys playing at soldiers, it was soon to have a much higher profile by providing valuable service in many different areas of life on the Home Front. As the Scouts would be doing work of a national importance, the government recognised their distinctive clothing as the uniform of a public service, non-military body, and made it an offence for it to be worn by anyone other than an official member of the scouting organisation.

Within days of the start of the war, the Scouts offer had been accepted. The District Commissioner of St Albans reported the process:

1. *A meeting of the Hertfordshire County Commissioners was held at St Albans on Saturday, 8 August, when it was determined to place one thousand Hertfordshire Scouts at the disposal of the Chief Constable.*

2. *A meeting of St Albans Scout Officers was held on Sunday, 9 August, at 10.40 am, when it was resolved to mobilize the six St Albans Troops, as one body, at the Headquarters of the Association at Holywell Hill by 10 am on Monday, 10 August, for the purpose of giving assistance to the local authorities day and night.*

3. *The Scouts were assembled at the commissioner's house by special call at 3 pm on Sunday, 9 August, and, after having the situation explained to them, were asked to volunteer for service. The response was unanimous. Those present, to the number of 130, were divided into three-day watches of four hours each, and one night watch from 8 pm to 6 am.*

4. *Headquarters were opened at 10 am on 10 August, and work at once commenced.*

5. *The first order was received by the Commissioner on Sunday, 9 August, to supply a Scout to take despatches to Clapham.*

6. *The following letter was dispatched to all the Local Authorities,*

Birmingham Scouts building huts for the War Office.

such as Police, Military, the Mayor, Red Cross, etc:

I beg to inform you that the Scout Officials have mustered the local Scouts for the purpose of rendering any possible assistance to the Chief Constable of Herts. So far as their services are not required by him, the Scouts are prepared to give any assistance in their power to the Civil or Military Authorities, day and night, on application being made at the above address.

In every county practically the same things were being done at the same time, and as a result the entire available force of the Boy Scouts was mobilized and came into action over the weekend.

In the first year of the war 100,000 Scouts were employed in public service and in the course of the conflict 80,000 won the War Service Badge, which was initially awarded for twenty-eight days' unpaid service, later being increased to fifty days. At government offices they were constantly employed as orderlies, dispatch riders and motorists. At the start of the war, the War Office applied for 100 Scouts but quickly asked for more. The work consisted of running about all day with messages and telegrams inside the building, while an Assistant Scoutmaster was responsible for most of the outdoor cyclist work. There was no let-up from 9 am to 6 pm every day of the week, but every Sunday one half of the boys would get a half-day rest. After three months' continuous service each boy was given a week's holiday. The work was done so well that the Secretary at the War Office requested that some of them might do duty at St Paul's Cathedral on the day of Lord Robert's funeral. Boy Scouts were also praised for their help with the recruiting campaign.

Many Scouts also worked on the land for extended periods of time in whatever role was required. Their help was rationalised in 1916 by the Ministry of National Service. Standing Scout camps were organised in places where labour was badly needed, and in the locality of each camp the education authorities made arrangements for younger boys to attend and

Scouts helping bring in the flax harvest – pulling and storking flax.

Collecting bottles for sale to raise funds to purchase motor ambulances.

help as far as possible, consistent with the needs of their school work. For example, initially, 100 Scouts over school age went from east London to work in the flax fields around Peterborough where they weeded the crop, but, in total, over 300 scouts from eighty schools in east London alone were eventually employed, being organised in nine camps spread around Peterborough. There were many more involved with the flax harvest. Each Scout was allowed 14s a head and 11d a day pay. With typical Scout thriftiness, the catering came in under budget, thus increasing their wage. Each boy worked for six hours a day but with such efficiency that the local farmers compared their work to ten hours of work by local boys. In general, agricultural work of any sort was undertaken, and land camps organised in Middlesex, Suffolk, Dorset and Lincolnshire provided employment for 500 London Scouts in 1918.

Boy Scouts also worked directly with the army. As each new camp was formed Scouts took up a number of roles, such as cyclists, messengers, telephonists, until their educational needs became paramount after the first few months of the war. Many were also involved in assisting at army supply depots.

Household waste was an area that many Scout Troops turned to their financial advantage. The Boy Scouts of Belfast collected and sold old glass bottles, using the money to buy a recreation hut for the use of the armed forces, while a troop in Devon collected waste paper and from the profits bought a sidecar with trailer and transporter for the Red Cross. Many Scouts put their daily wage together to buy huts for use at the front that provided shelter as well as books, games and gramophones, while others purchased motor ambulances.

The war effort was further helped by the collection of items of household waste by the Scouts. Waste commodities such as eggshells, fruit stones and nutshells, along with previously unused items like horse chestnuts became essential war commodities that they helped collect and salvage, from such unlikely places as the King's dustbins, even though their use was not fully explained at the time. *The Times History* explains how whimsical the idea was with its description of the role of a humble cherry stone which was

> '*hardened by the sun in a Kent orchard, which went via the mouth of a King, a dust-bin, a Boy Scout's basket and a manufactory to Flanders, where it saved the life of a British soldier from German gas.*'

The work undertaken by the Scouts was not without risk and this was acknowledged by a three-tiered award for gallant conduct. This award graduated upwards through the Gilt Cross for exceptionally good conduct in an emergency, the Silver Cross for gallantry with risk, to the Bronze Cross for acts that were heroic. In 1917 alone twenty-four of the latter were awarded even though the conditions for its award were very stringent. There was also a medal for life saving and again in 1917 this medal was awarded 525 times.

Probably the most prominent work of the Boy Scouts was that undertaken under the control of the police. At the start of an air raid, 'the all-clear boys' would assemble at the police station with their bugles and cycles and wait for the raid to end. When it did, they would cycle off into the dark, whatever the time or weather, to blow the all-clear. However, this was not their only role during air raids. Many were employed as orderlies and messengers, others dealt with the wounded and helped rescue people from wrecked houses and assisted in controlling gas pipe leaks, with many being presented with medals for their work during the raids. The following extract from a report on their behaviour during the bombardment of and east coast town is typical:

Wounded soldiers arriving at hospital with the ever-present Boy Scout ready to lend a hand.

Boy Scout. "SKETCHING THE HARBOUR'S NOT ALLOWED."
Artist. "CONFOUND YOU! MY NAME'S CADMIUM BROWN, AND——"
Boy Scout. "CARRY ON, THEN. WE'VE GOT ORDERS TO TREAT YOU AS HARMLESS."

Any person painting harbours was immediately classed as suspicious.

According to the scheme previously arranged, Scouts attached to the Cyclist section of the Local War Emergency Committee were dispatched with all speed to call up the special constables in different parts of the district. Another section were told off for duty directing the women and children to a place of safety, assisting the infirm, and carrying children and baggage. A patrol of Scouts was dispatched to help the Fire Brigade and perform salvage work, rescuing valuable books, etc., from the flames and ruins caused by the shells... A relay of Scouts is attached to the constabulary and doing other very useful work. They are on duty for the same hours as the police, eight hours' reliefs day and night, and receive weekly pay. The Chief Constable states that they are very intelligent and smart in their various duties.

Hospitals and various other public bodies also benefited from their use of Boy Scout labour.

Although not related to the Home Front, it is of note that in the first four months of the war over 10,000 ex-Scouts and Scoutmasters volunteered for the armed forces, with the great majority of them immediately becoming officers and NCOs. In one territorial battalion, the 5th Highland Light Infantry, a company of 240 men were all ex-Scouts. At one advanced dressing station the detached unit in charge were all ex-Scouts. Also, the training that the ex-Scouts had received meant that they were more likely to be employed in battalion intelligence, signals or scouting sections.

Many Scouts joined the armed forces and were awarded medals for bravery, the most famous being Jack Cornwell who was posthumously awarded the Victoria Cross at the age of sixteen for having served in an exposed position on HMS *Chester*. Although Scouts were forbidden to collect

Sea Scout examining a photographer's permit in a forbidden area.

money from the public they managed to raise £1,487 from their own pockets for the Cornwell Memorial Fund. There were many other former Scouts who won awards for conspicuous gallantry, including Piper Laidlow, VC, Second Lieutenants Craig, Haine and Toye, VC, Sergeant Haine, VC and Private Cruickshank, VC.

Inland, the work of the Scouts helped release men for active service, while on the coast, Sea Scouts also released large numbers of Naval Reserve men. Here they were quickly employed as coast watchers, and as signallers, cooks and so on, aboard auxiliary vessels, with many helping on mercantile marine ships whenever possible. For the great service rendered by the Sea Scouts they became known as 'Men of the Second Line'.

Coast watching released thousands of men for the navy and as each man was recalled for service, his place was taken by a Sea Scout. Eventually the whole coast from Land's End to John o'Groats was covered, throughout the war, by a force of 1,400 young coastguards under the command of veteran coastguard officers. Whereas land Scouts had to provide their services for free, Sea Scouts involved in coast watching were granted an allowance of 18s a week, without rations. In return the boys did their own catering and cooking, looked after their own quarters and patrolled their own stretch of coast day and night, watch-keeping, signalling, telephoning and cyclist despatch-riding, under the orders of the petty officers in charge of stations.

While much of the work undertaken would have been generally uneventful, it was not without interest as is shown by the following logbook entries:

Warned a destroyer off the rocks in a fog.

Sighted and reported airship going SSE five miles distant.

Provided night guard over damaged seaplane, which was towed ashore by drifter.

Light shown near... at 3.15 am for seven minutes, and again from apparently the same spot at 4.35 am.

Trawler No. ... came ashore. Permits all in order except J M, who had none. Took his name and address to police superintendent at... .

Floating mine reported by fishing boat... .

Proceeded with the patrol boat which located and blew up the mine.

Provided guard over wreck and stores three days and nights in... .

At the same time the Sea Scouts also helped the farmers and fishermen around them.

The quality of their work was never in doubt as is shown by this typical extract from the reports of the officers in charge:

They are doing excellent work, entirely by themselves... they have never failed to patrol the coast and railway line and to carry their dispatches through by night since August 4, 1914, although, as you can well understand, the weather conditions in these parts are very bad.

And these were boys of fourteen to eighteen years of age, many of whom did not possess the right clothing for continuous exposure to wet and cold, and who had to patrol four or five miles of lonely road on a dark night for four hours at a time until the Patrol was relieved after its full month of duty.

That they were often as good as, if not better than, many of the men they replaced is shown by the following incident. At one station, when Scouts arrived to take up the duties of the five men who had been drafted off to the fleet, they found that the coastguard petty officer in charge had procured some meat which he thought would be enough for the boys for that day; he was, however, puzzled how to get it cooked. To his confessed surprise the boys quickly settled the matter. The leader told him that the meat was sufficient for two and a half days and the cook of the patrol would at once cook the day's ration. Two other boys paraded for duty and the other two formed camp. A further example of the life of a Sea Scout at this time, is shown by a letter written by one of the boys of the 1st Withington (89th Manchester) Troop, who proceeded by train to provide a patrol for duty at Newbiggin in Northumberland in January 1915 for a six month period:

A typical Sea Scout of the period.

*Learning knots and helping
wounded soldiers.*

*A scout employed as typist to a
coast-watching officer.*

> *Two Zeppelins, most distinctly seen, were, of course, speedily reported. We witnessed a torpedoed steamer gradually settling in the stern and finally, with her bow perpendicular in the air, sink like a shot. We also saw many derelicts, ships which had been damaged by mines or torpedoes. Amongst the wreckage found on patrol could be enumerated almost every conceivable thing – including a battered piano, bicycle, mangling machine, mincing machine, and furniture of all kinds and eatables, sacks of flour, candles, and any amount of new timber. In the storm one ship was wrecked near us; a fishing boat was capsized, but the crew was rescued by lifeboats and we helped to keep back the crowd when the half-drowned men were brought ashore; two cobles went down in a blizzard, one in our view, with a loss of seven lives. During this blizzard we were unable to get fresh water from the usual place, owing to the terrific gale, so we melted snow and washed and cooked in the resultant water. We were inspected by Lieutenant Commander Hordern, who said everything was most creditable.*

It was never the purpose of the Scouting Association to help produce a citizen army. However, the demands of the war and the idea that there was no harm in helping the older boys to prepare themselves for the defence of their homes if need should arise, resulted in the formation of the Scouts' Defence Corps which gave actual military training to some of the older boys. However, the introduction of conscription stopped the need for such an organisation. Just as they were approaching military age, War Office-appointed instructors and examiners in aeroplane fitting and preliminary knowledge of air work service trained a number of Scouts in these fields.

For the period of the war the Boy Scouts served their country well. Lord Rosebery summed up their contribution:

> *If I were to form the highest ideal for my country, it would be this – that it should be a nation of which the manhood was exclusively composed of men who have been, or were, Boy Scouts and were trained in the Boy Scout theory. Such a nation would be the honour of mankind. It would be the greatest moral force the world has ever known.*

3

Fishermen and the War

A t the outbreak of the war the fishing industry consisted of four fleets of steam trawlers working the North Sea: the Red Cross, the Great Northern, the Gamecock, and Messrs Hellyers, with a multitude of separately owned boats. Very quickly this vast fleet disappeared to become auxiliaries of the Royal Navy, forming the trawler section that contributed to the safety of the bigger boats by helping to remove the danger of mines.

The Germans were quick to appreciate the potential of the trawler fleets and they tried hard to seize or destroy such vessels. In one swoop in August 1914, they captured a number of steam trawlers that were fishing in the North Sea and made their crews prisoners. Subsequently many steam trawlers were lost – many by submarine attack but more by mines. Many fishermen lost their lives, and some were taken prisoner. After eighteen months, there were nearly 300 fishermen prisoners in Germany for whom help was provided by a special fund maintained by the Royal National Mission to Deep Sea Fishermen. The level of losses is shown by the figures for Grimsby in 1915: 57 steam trawlers lost with a death roll of 287 men.

When the war broke out, the majority of the 3,000 first class steam fishing vessels were drifters and trawlers. In 1913 there were more than 1,600 steam drifters at work, in addition to motor and sailing craft. The total number of full-time fishermen was in excess of 125,000, and it was calculated that the entire industry supported one-twentieth of the population, with an invested capital of £200,000,000. Within nine months of the outbreak of war 14,000 men were engaged in minesweeping, using a thousand trawlers.

Sweeping for mines required two trawlers, steaming abreast at a certain

Women working on the fish dock cleaning mackerel.

Trawler converted into a minesweeper.

Many fishermen were captured and taken to Germany as prisoners of war.

distance, dragging a weighted steel hawser which, striking the mooring of a mine, brought it to the surface where it was exploded by gun-fire from an accompanying destroyer or armed trawler, or by rifle fire. Minesweeping work was dangerous for those on deck, particularly for those controlling the towing warps, and at all times they were threatened by the presence of unseen mines. It was not uncommon for fishing trawlers, to unwittingly become minesweepers when their nets caught a mine. In some cases these detonated on contact when they hauled their catch in. To this could be added the dangers of German fire. One fisherman recorded how while sweeping in a North Sea gale they were fired upon by German cruisers – 'They must have taken us for dreadnoughts', he recorded sarcastically.

A further danger was of course the weather. During the first winter of the war, Admiral Jellicoe's secretary, writing from the *Iron Duke*, the flagship of the Grand Fleet, to a little blind girl who had sent the Admiral a knitted scarf, wrote:

> *We often pass German mines floating about in the water, and we know that if we did not see them, but ran into them, the* Iron Duke *would be blown up... It is very cold on the North Sea, and very stormy, too, and sometimes the snow falls so heavily that we cannot see at all where we are going, and very often the great seas sweep right over the ship.*

If it was this dangerous for a battleship, how much more so for a very small trawler?

Losses, although not as great as on the Western Front, were a constant drain on manpower. The level of danger involved is illustrated by this one example: on 19 December 1914, in the space of ten minutes, in one small minesweeping flotilla, two trawlers were damaged by mines and another one blown up.

As well as protecting the navy and mercantile marine, the fishermen of the minesweepers also made the seas safe for other fishermen. Admiralty arrangements made it possible for a small composite fleet of steam trawlers to work in a comparatively safe area at a considerable profit. Record after record was made, and the share system employed on board provided a good living for skippers and mates. In April 1916, a few days before Good Friday, when fish was scarce, the Hull trawler *Elf King* landed a catch worth £3,670 (the previous record had been £3,480 held by the same trawler). This gave the skipper a wage of £300 a trip or around £5,000 a year, making him a wealthy man.

While those still fishing were making money, the reduction in the number of vessels meant a corresponding decrease in wealth for fisher-girls who lost their traditional occupations of 'gipping' and packing. They moved into munitions, postal work and other employment, but most of them found it hard to match the standard of living they had been used to.

It was not only those involved in minesweeping that experienced the war firsthand. The war also came to the fishing fleet, not just in the form of mines, enemy vessels and submarines, but also from the air. On the night of 31 January 1916, a squadron of German airships raided some of the Eastern and Midland Counties, killing a number of civilians and damaging property. The airships escaped, but one of them (the L15), that was believed to have taken part in the raid, was found a helpless wreck, floating on the North Sea. It was discovered by the skipper and crew of the Grimsby steam trawler, the *King Stephen*, and was found to contain twenty-two living Germans. Carrying no weapons and having a crew of only nine men, the skipper declined to believe the word of the airship commander not to overcome his men, and sailed off to inform the first Naval vessel he came to. Consequently, the skipper and crew were accused by the German government of cowardice, brutality and inhumanity towards their airmen. An auxiliary patrol trawler later discovered the wrecked L15 off the mouth of the Thames.

Further danger came from the air when the Germans declared their intention of using all means within their power to destroy British fishing vessels. If they could not be mined, shelled or torpedoed, then they were to be bombed or blown up in any way possible. A possibly apocryphal story was told of a wooden box floating in the sea which, when opened, was found to contain a tin box with a fish inside. The fish suddenly began to burn and emit a sulphurous smell at which point it was thrown into the sea. Upon contact with the water it exploded, nearly capsizing the fishing boat and destroying the small boat and lanterns. One man was nearly killed.

By 1917 100,000 fishermen were serving with the Royal Navy and about seventy-five per cent of the first-class fishing boats were on admiralty service across the globe. Yet in spite of this massive loss of manpower and ships, the total catch only fell by about thirty per cent. The shortage of trawlers had an effect on their value: a wooden smack built in 1866, which before the war was only fit for scrapping, was suddenly worth £400. With so many men involved with the navy there was also a shortage of fishermen; a shortage that was solved by elderly crews manning old-time smacks – 'from decaying fishing ports old men once more adventured with fresh life and hope'. A not untypical example was the crew of the Lowestoft drifter *Success* that was

A successful catch.

manned by seven hands with a total age of 478 years; the 'boy' was 62, the skipper was 69 and the rest of the crew were 64, 68, 69, 72 and 75 years of age. And then there were the very young, those men not yet old enough to legally join the armed forces.

Many fishing vessels were lost from enemy action. Submarine raids on trawler fleets were a constant danger as is illustrated by the attack on the Brixham fishing fleet on 28 November 1916. At 2 pm, in broad daylight, a submarine rose to the surface among the trawlers and attacked the defenceless ships. The submarine opened fire on the *Provident*, whose skipper, William Pillar, had helped rescue men from the torpedoed battleship HMS *Formidable* earlier in the war. The shells from the submarine brought down the jib of the *Provident*, and also parted her topsail halyards. After the first shot the crew took to their boat, and the submarine then came in close enough to put a bomb in her that caused her to sink. Then the raider opened up on the *Amphitrite*, skippered by William Norris, who reported that the Germans had fired two shots at the small boat as they were escaping but, having missed, resumed their shelling of the trawler. The third vessel to be attacked was the *Lynx*; her crew immediately took to their boat, were likewise shelled from a range of not more than 200 yards, but fortunately escaped. For some reason the *Lynx* was not sunk but later found derelict and brought back to Brixham. This group of trawlers were lucky; no fatalities were sustained.

Usually there was little warning so the trawlermen had little time to react. Earlier in the year on 3 August, a calm and peaceful night was disturbed by the sudden appearance of a German submarine among a group of small motor herring drifters. The boats had their nets out, their lights were showing and they were keeping a good watch. At about midnight an explosion was heard, and it was instantly suspected that a submarine was at work. A second explosion followed, and a fishing vessel was seen to disappear. A number of drifters had already cut their nets adrift and were making a rush for port and safety. The German submarine surfaced rapidly by the side of one of the escaping boats and the skipper was ordered to stop. Two tall men carrying bombs boarded the drifter.

The drifter was destroyed and her crew taken on board the submarine; in all there were twenty fishermen on the submarine deck. When the submarine got underway, the commander persistently questioned one of the skippers about the lights that were seen and whether any of the fishing vessels carried guns. A stop was made to destroy another drifter and then put the rescued seamen out on the submarine deck. Fortunately for the prisoners no naval vessel was seen, for they were all certain that the submarine would submerge leaving them in the water. After about seventy-five minutes the captives were put aboard a small drifter with strict instructions to keep their lights burning and to not move until daylight; if they did not obey they would be destroyed. Having issued his directions the commander resumed his work of sinking drifters.

The skipper of one of the sunken vessels later described the destruction as very deliberate and well organised, and he calculated that on average one vessel was sunk every sixteen minutes. In some cases, crews of destroyed craft were set adrift in their own little boats; in others refuge was sought on board vessels that had escaped destruction. Finally a patrol boat picked up some of the men and took them into port. The time of the year and the calmness of the weather prevented much suffering and loss of life.

Some fishermen seemed to lead charmed lives. None was better known than 'Submarine Billy' who was blown up three times on three different fishing smacks. The second time he was sunk, he was shot through the thigh while in the 'little boat' (the emergency boat carried by the fishing smack). Helpless on the water the boat was deliberately fired upon by the submarine. The crew of each smack was given five minutes' notice to quit and take to the boat before the smack was blown up. He stated that,

> ...about a quarter of an hour after we left the smack there was a terrific explosion... The deck split up, there was a lot of fire and smoke, she began to sink, and in about eight minutes she had gone altogether. Our floating home and everything in it went to the bottom.

Shortly afterwards he was 'gassed' by the fumes of a bomb dropped from a Zeppelin which was hovering low in a thick haze.

As the war grew longer, so too did the casualty lists for the fishermen. To take a typical example: on 6 December 1916 the Admiralty List, published in *The Times*, showed that 27 fishermen, second hands, deck-hands, enginemen, trimmers, etc had been killed; a further 21 were missing, believed killed and 11 were missing. Three days later, 7 skippers were listed as killed and an official publication of January 1917 gave the names of 80 skippers who had been killed in action.

Much bravery was shown but unfortunately most of it was not recorded. One incident that was, however, is the story of an un-named Grimsby fishing vessel. The vessel's hull was holed; the damaged boiler filled the little cramped engine-room with scalding steam, while the sea rushed in and almost overwhelmed her. This extremely perilous situation called for prompt action. The chief engineer, F P Wilson and the second engineer, C E East set to work to save both life and ship. Wilson, reckless of the scalding steam and rush of sea, forced his way into the engine room and plugged, as best he could, the hole caused by the explosion. East, although violently thrown against the boiler by the motion of the vessel, made his way to the bunker to save his fireman;

> *...he struggled in the blinding, scalding, darkening atmosphere of what was nothing more than a large steel box, crawled and dragged himself to the appalling little hole which was called the bunker, and saved the imprisoned stoker whose chance of salvation seemed hopeless.*

While this was going on, another trawler near at hand, which had been mined as well, was sinking and her crew were in danger of drowning. The second hand on Wilson's vessel, E R Gooderham, launched the small boat and went over to the other trawler, arriving just as it started to capsize. Gooderham fought his way into the vortex, and though the sinking vessel was almost turning completely over onto his own boat he somehow managed to save the seven men of the sinking ship and returned to his own trawler. For their heroism the engineers were awarded the Distinguished Service Medal and the second hand was highly commended for exceptional bravery in emergencies.

Of course, not all trawlermen were angels; many of them found themselves on the wrong side of the law when they returned to port. As today, deep-sea fisherman work and play hard. Most cases were inconsequential but one made the news through the Honours List for the Police:

> *Albert Edward Bell, constable, Isle of Man Constabulary. A drunken skipper of a patrol boat came ashore at Ramsey Harbour with two revolvers, and landed four of his crew as armed sentries. He threatened various people, fired two shots, and then aimed at one of his crew. The revolver missed fire, and while he was raising it again Bell rushed at him and took the revolver away.*

Despite the losses in men and vessels, and although annual catches were below pre-war levels, there was still a good supply on the market. The weather at the start of 1917 was the worst in the North Sea for twenty-two years, covering ships in ice, but even so 7,348 tons were landed at Billingsgate market in January, nearly 600 tons more than the same month the previous year. The *Board of Trade Labour Gazette*, in a review of food prices in 1916, stated:

> *In July 1916, fish averaged about 80 per cent above the level of two years earlier, this being the lowest point reached during the year and representing a drop from 105 per cent at the beginning of February. At the end of 1916 the price of fish was about one-third higher than a year earlier.*

The work of the fishermen was a very valuable contribution to the Allied cause's eventual success as it helped other more glamorous units gain final victory. By keeping sea lanes open and relatively safe they helped the Royal Navy perform its main role of protecting the British Isles and its shipping, allowing the passage of essential raw materials to Britain. It also directly contributed to the health and diet of the Home Front. Fish and chips were never off the menu!

3

Looking after the Troops

At the start of the war, regular battalions had the safety net of a regimental association to look after cases of extreme need, general creature comforts when on active service and their prisoners of war; likewise the territorial battalions also had their own Territorial Force associations. With the massive increase in the size of the armed forces, these organisations were insufficient to deal with all the demands made on them, and other voluntary organisations stepped in to assist. Each area in the country has its own story to tell; this is the story of the Hull and East Riding Fund for the needs of local units and Prisoners of War during the last year of the war. The information that follows is taken from the final report in 1919 when the organisation was wound up.

The Hull and East Riding Fund for the needs of Local Units and Prisoners of War was approved by the War Office and registered under the *War Charities Act* of 1916. Its headquarters was Peel House, 28 Beverley Road, Hull. The Presidents were The Lord Nunburnholme, The Lady Nunburnholme, The Lord Mayor of Hull, Major General Sir Coleridge and Colonel Stacey-Clitherow. Mr W F Harris was the chairman of the central committee, assisted by ninety-two trustees. The organisation began its activities, just before the war, on 2 August 1914 when Peel House was opened by the Presidents, Lord and Lady Nunburnholme, and these were extended from time to time as necessity arose and were continued without stopping until 31 January 1919 when the last boat-load of repatriated prisoners arrived at the Riverside Quay. During this period, local support

A Christmas card from the Central Prisoners of War Committee showing the typical contents of a POW box.

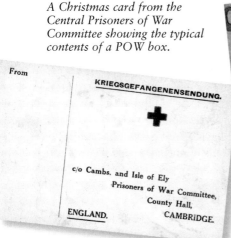

A postcard to let the senders know that the parcel had reached its destination.

Wounded soldiers collecting for the Red Cross.

was very generous and the fund finished in profit. At the cessation of its role, this excess was given to the Central Prisoners of War Committee.

Buildings for the work were provided at 28 and 30 Beverley Road by W Cussons Limited and, when storage space ran out in 1918, Mr Witherwick loaned the organisation the use of 15 Beverley Road and Blundell, Spence and Company, on the corner of Beverley Road also provided floor space. The executors of George Winn also loaned the committee the shop at the corner of Prospect Street.

The final report also thanked the many ladies and gentlemen who organised concerts and other entertainments for the benefit of the fund, especially the 2/4th East Yorkshire Regiment that was serving in Bermuda for its regular contributions. The Khaki Magazine Fund supplied generous gifts of food throughout the final year and the local press had helped the fund in all possible ways. As the prisoners were repatriated the local food control committee disposed of excess food.

PRÉCIS OF WORK DONE 1914-1918

	1914/15	1915/16	1916/17	1917/19	Total
No. of articles despatched to East Riding troops	24,854	38,221	34,389	12,436	109,000
No. of parcels (food and clothing) sent to POWs	147	7,200	54,000	69,994	131,341
No. of men passed through rest station (day and night)	27,840	108,741	302,800	326,225	765,606
No. of hospital supplies despatched	4,729	9,100	22,426	115,784	152,039
St. John VAD hospital: out-patients attended and in-patients treated, 1917 to 1919	Out patient (1917) 2,739	In patient (1917) 1,620	Out patient (1918) 41,940	In patient (1918) 2,774	In/out patients 4,394 44,679

MONIES COLLECTED 1914-1918

	1914/15 £	1915/16 £	1916/17 £	1917/18 £	1918/19 £	Total £
Collected for 'Comforts fund'	1,837	5,477	2,516	132	171	10,133
Collected for Prisoners of War fund	-	1,960	10,862	27,951	14,855	55,628
Receipts, &c. at 'Rest Station'	117	109	900	2,196	923	4,245
Collected for hospital supplies fund	-	776	686	786	-	2,248
Collected for St John VAD hospital	-	-	14,935	7,686	-	22,621
Collected for Christmas funds	-	1,421	1,435	1,230	-	4,136
Totals	1,954	9,743	31,384	39,981	15,949	99,011

Since the 1917-18 report was issued the work of Peel House had increased enormously and many changes had been made. The report continued:

The number of prisoners having mounted up to over 2,000, Mrs Eyre kindly undertook to form a committee of ladies, with Mrs Conran as Secretary, to pack and despatch from Beverley all clothing for men of the East Yorkshire Regiment other than the Territorial Battalions. The East Riding Territorial Force Association became responsible for the issue of clothing to their men. In spite of this great assistance, it became necessary to pack food parcels six days a week. The Central Committee authorized the packing of one 15lb parcel a week instead of three 10lb parcels a fortnight in October 1918, which alone made it possible during the last few weeks of the war to continue the supply of food to our men with unfailing regularity.

Funds to cover the cost of these parcels were raised from a number of sources. One unusual contribution came from the residents of Freehold Street, Hull, who had a Bread Fund that raised money to provide bread for the prisoners of war.

Economy leaflet printed on transparent paper advising how to send cigarettes to active service personnel.

The packing room of the Hull Prisoner of War Committee.

Another way of making money was the sale of postcards and stickers.

The shop of the Hull Prisoner of War Committee building where relatives and friends could buy articles to include in a soldier or sailor's parcel.

The Committee wish to express their hearty thanks to the ladies who, by dint of constant hard work, kept Peel House going through an exceedingly heavy year. The work entailed in the various departments was enormous: Firstly, in the Storekeeper's Department, where the parcels were evolved and arranged for the packing; then in the Bond Department, where the Bonded goods had to be checked and specially entered as they were issued; then in the Label Department (under the supervision of Mrs Merryweather, where lists of names and addresses had to be kept daily up-to-date), where the labels and boxes and postcards had to be addressed and checked. This was all constant work which had to be kept up day by day. In addition to this continuous work of preparation, there were of course stock-books and ledgers to be entered up regularly, and returned acknowledgement cards had to be checked, and forwarded on to relatives and

Many were the causes for which 'flags' were sold. The top one was to raise money for the Wounded Soldiers & Sailors Fag Day Fund. Underneath is a flag for Queen Alexandra's Field Force Fund.

adopters. This was a ceaseless routine which increased day by day, as, of course, did the interminable correspondence with relatives who wanted information on all sorts of subjects. Interviews with relatives were also incessant, and the shop-work grew so heavily that it was necessary only to open at stated times; to which, however, the relatives agreed very amiably. Coupons for personal parcels also were much appreciated.

In the early part of 1918, when the last Report was issued, it was noted that the number of prisoners was increasing at an alarming rate, while the funds were remaining more or less stationary. After this had been made known at a public meeting, Mrs Hide (from the Packing Department) suggested that the various works in Hull should be canvassed with a view to obtaining regular subscriptions from the employees, who would be only too glad, no doubt, to help their comrades in this way. She expressed her willingness to start this campaign, and the Committee gratefully accepted. The immediate result of Mrs. Hide's efforts was astounding. The employees of Messrs. Amos and Smith were the first to set the ball rolling, and they agreed to adopt twenty men at a cost of £42 a month. Soon after the employees of Messrs. Earle's shipbuilding and Engineering Co. adopted eighty men (£168 per month). Both these contributions were increased later on. As will be seen from the Adopter's List, a large number of the prisoners were soon adopted by the employees of various large firms in Hull and the district. Mrs. Hide also canvassed the employers and private individuals, who also responded generously, with the result that through *her efforts alone the fund was richer by over £10,000 per year...*

Whilst Mrs. Hide was collecting in Hull, Mr. Eyre was being equally enterprising in the Riding. Through his energetic labours, villages and parishes began to send in regular subscriptions. At the same time, the Lord Lieutenant issued an eloquent appeal, so that the fund was also materially increased through the generosity of inhabitants all over the Riding. The prisoners continued to increase, but so did the adopters, and we have no doubt the Hull and East Riding Fund compares well with other similar funds all over the country. The Committee is most grateful to all the ladies and gentlemen who worked so earnestly in this direction. To their efforts also is owing the fact that this year it was not necessary to hold a Prisoners of War Flag Day in Hull and the district – a welcome relief to many people.

In June, 1918, it was decided to amalgamate more closely with the East Yorkshire Regimentals Comforts Fund, and for this Committee to take over the care of the prisoners of the 1st and 2nd Battalions.

This amalgamation took place in order to reduce any duplication of work, especially correspondence, improve efficiency and provide a higher level of benefits for the prisoners. The regimental 'Comforts Fund' for the two regular battalions was to be unaffected by this change.

The packing of parcels was stopped on Wednesday, 13 November, and very soon afterwards it was announced that many of the prisoners would return home, via Hull. General Sir Stanley von Donop, commanding the Humber Garrison, asked Lady Nunburnholme to get together a group of ladies to welcome the men on their arrival at the Riverside Quay. Peel House workers all volunteered to help, and from 17 November, when the first boat arrived, to the 31 January, when the last boat delivered its load, the ladies attended regularly, in shifts of twelve to meet the men. They helped the Navy and Army Canteen

A postcard from the recipient of the gift, Private Baillie of the 1/5th Seaforth Highlanders, to the sender, thanking them for the cigarettes.

Board by distributing their 'Luxury Parcels' for them, and they also distributed newspapers, postcards and pencils. The newspapers were supplied free by the London Daily Mail, The Daily Chronicle, and the local Hull News and the Daily Mail, and they were much appreciated by officers and men alike. The postcards were collected again before the trains left the station, and posted for the men. Sometimes, in the case of officers, telegrams were taken to the G.P.O. and despatched for them.

A more unusual way of collecting money – a collecting cat.

Later, when the 'Luxury Parcels' were put on board the ships at the other side, Peel House distributed cigarettes, and also gave each man a card of instructions from the Central Prisoners of War Committee.

The Central Prisoners of War Committee having passed a resolution that no further Subscriptions should be received by local Committees since the date of the Armistice; all expenses in connection with the welcome of the Prisoners were met by the Repatriation Fund, although several voluntary gifts were received as well.

...after three and a half year's solid work in connection with the Prisoners of War it was both a privilege and a pleasure that the Hull Committee should be the first to welcome the prisoners on their return home.

As well as providing the necessaries of life for local Prisoners of War there was also a 'Comforts Fund' for Hull and East Riding troops that was independent from the fund run by the East Yorkshire Regiment for its two regular battalions. The fund controlled two War Depots, Number 1 at the Guildhall, of which the Lady Mayoress was president and Number 2 at Beverley, with Mrs Eyre as the president.

'Comforts Fund' depots were set up to provide extras to local men serving at home and abroad and also to aid the VAD Hospital in Hull. Volunteer helpers, often over 70 years of age, undertook the cutting out, machining and fixing of shirts, the packaging of warm clothing and socks for the troops. When military demand was not high they made hospital garments such as flannel under-vests and pants, and also repaired clothing and bed and table linen, for the VAD hospital. Wool was distributed to home workers to make items such as socks and mufflers. Between 1 January and 31 October 1918 the depot received 4,129 articles from sources as

THE CHARGE OF THE LOYAL NORTH LANCS.

Written in aid of Winter Comforts for our Local Lads.

Most of them lads who, before the war, had never held a gun,
Most of them, too, had never dreamed that they would face the Hun;
They went when their country needed them to take an active part,
And the charge they made on June 15th is impressed on every heart.

Most of the lads were from Preston, and the neighbouring places around,
Yet the bravest of our British lads among the 1/4th were found
In the gallant charge on June 15th, when they faced the German Hun,
They showed they were from Lancashire, and made the German's run.

No need to give an order twice, the 1/4th were staunch and true;
They thought of fallen comrades, of England, home, and you,
And indignation filled their hearts, as they entered in the fight
Prepared to conquer or to die, that long-remembered night.

All battalions of the Loyal North Lanc.'s have taken a fore-most part,
Their bravery all throughout the war has stirred each British heart;
But our local lads, the gallant 1/4th, in the brilliant charge they made,
To England's history added a page that shall not fade.

You read about that gallant charge, about that noble deed,
Then let us all together strive to help their present need;
A long, dreary winter's near at hand, the local lads away
Need comforts we at home can give, then let us start to-day.

GOD SAVE THE KING.

M. WILDING, Oct. 25, 1915.

As well as national charities, each regiment had its own aid fund that raised money by subscriptions or from the sale of items like this postcard.

diverse as the Guildhall working party, the Hornsea working party, Canon England, Mrs Savory and Friends, and the Craven Street Girls' School. During this same period they despatched 3,452 articles to destinations as diverse as the VAD hospital on Cottingham Road, the Military hospital in Middlesborough, Reckitt's hospital, Colonel Wilkinson (500 pairs of socks), Mr Rippon (two pairs of socks) and a soldier's wife (one pair of socks). Twenty-two different types of goods were despatched, the most numerous being socks (1,760 pairs); the other articles sent out were 367 shirts, 69 pants, 16 cardigans, 235 comfort bags, 281 pairs of mitts, 7 pairs of gloves, 198 mufflers, 214 helmets, 55 operation stockings, 4 belts, 56 vests, 1 pair of boots, 6 handkerchiefs, 38 bed jackets, 1 dish cloth, 2 chest protectors, 1 tin cover, 125 face washers, 12 cushions, 2 bandages and 2 Housewifes. Over roughly the same period (1 January to 30 September), the Beverley War Depot and the East Riding War Depot received 3,492 articles and despatched 4,650. Like the Hull depot, the most common article to be despatched were socks (4,600 pairs). During the same period the Beverley depot also sent out 1,430 articles to hospitals. Sub-depots at Rise, Bridlington, Cottingham, Welton, Norton and Settrington contributed articles to the main Beverley depot.

To finance this work the War depot received money from the Hull and East Riding War Needs Fund, donations and self-generated income from the sale

of teas. From 14 November 1917 to 31 October 1918, including bank interest, this amounted to £216 17s 8d; outgoings during the same period left just over £95 in the bank. The Beverley depot received £414 19s 3d over roughly the same period (September 1917 to September 1918) with just over £157 in the bank. The East Riding War Depot had over £142 in the bank when it was closed on 31 May 1919; this was paid over to the Red Cross Convalescent Home for

Prominent people also used their image to aid the troops. This card, of Miss Mabel Sealby (a singer), was sold to raise money for 'The Performer' Tobacco Fund.

For Christmas 1916, The Daily Telegraph *helped raise money to purchase Christmas puddings for men at the front.*

Discharged and Disabled Soldiers at Bridlington. To further aid its finances, the Bridlington sub-depot held a flag day, a whist drive and a sale of work, while one of its members made 600 ironholders and two local churches held a collection for it. When its local prisoners were repatriated they were welcomed back with tea and entertainment and a gift of 15 shillings each.

The Beverley depot, which opened in December 1915, recorded that in September 1918, they sent out 3,000 pairs of socks alone and that since May of that year they had become responsible for sending clothing to East Yorkshire Prisoners of War, despatching between 21 May and 1 July over 400 parcels of clothing. When all the prisoner's details had been fully transferred from Peel House they were able to increase their output and from the middle of July to the end of September they despatched 1,215 parcels of which 807 went to new prisoners. The hospital department sent out nearly 2,000 hospital requisites during the period January to September 1918. These went to the St John Ambulance Brigade hospital at Etaples and to the York Hospital Supply Depot. The Etaples hospital was bombed into ruins in July 1918 and re-started in Trouville. As a result of a public collection in Beverley and around the East Riding, £200 was collected to provide a Beverley Bed and an East Riding Bed in the new hospital.

REQUISITIONS SUPPLIED FROM THE WAR DEPOTS
from January 1918 to 1919

Unit	Socks	Shirts	Helmets	Mufflers	Pants & Vests	Miscellaneous
4th East Yorks, 1st line	500					
7th East Yorks	500					
10th East Yorks	1,000					Hockey sticks and balls for 92 Bde
11th East Yorks	1,000					Sewing machine and typewriter
12th East Yorks	1,000					
13th East Yorks	1,000					
East Riding Yeomanry						Gramophone, records, tobacco
140th (Hull) Heavy Battery						Song and dance music
1/3rd Northumberland	100	35			20	
St John VAD Hospital, Hull	300			50		
Sir Edward Ward, DGVO	1,316	926	526	125	20	250 pairs of mittens, 50 comfort bags and 18 handkerchiefs
Total	6,716	961	526	175	40	

Tobacco and cigarettes were sent to local units by the *Hull News* tobacco fund.

Christmas Comforts Funds (1916, 1917 and 1918)

Towards the end of 1916 Lord and Lady Nunburnholme issued an appeal to the public for funds to provide Christmas comforts for the officers and men associated with Hull and East Riding units serving overseas. The response was immediate and in one day over £1,000 was collected. For the remaining Christmases of the war the fund was taken over by the Lord Mayor.

Children were encouraged to help the soldiers and sailors by sending them gifts.

The level of contribution in military terms that Hull made to the war effort, without taking into account the men in the navy and air force, is shown by the length of the list of gifts the Lord Mayor sent at Christmas 1918.

Unit	Amount £	Unit	Amount £
1st Bn. East Yorks	100	146th (Hull) Heavy Battery RGA	25
2nd Bn. East Yorks	100	77th Siege Battery RGA	25
6th Bn. East Yorks	100	164th Siege Battery RGA	25
7th Bn. East Yorks	125	32nd Divisional Ammun.	
10th Bn. East Yorks	125	Column RFA	50
Bn. East Yorks	100	251st Brigade RFA	25
2/4th Bn. East Yorks	100	102nd Bn MGC	50
1st Garrison Bn. East Yorks	100	1/1st East Riding Field Coy RE	25
31st Machine Gun Bn.	25	1/3rd Northumb. RAMC	20
1/3rd Coy Northumbrian RE	25	545th Heavy Battery RGA	25
2/3rd Coy Northumbrian RE	20	47th Brigade RFA	10
124th (Hull) Heavy Battery RGA	25	256th Siege Battery RGA	10
		Total	£1,230 0s 0d

Most cities and towns with major railway connections set up a soldiers' hut for transient soldiers and sailors. This is the Reading Room of the Hull soldiers' club.

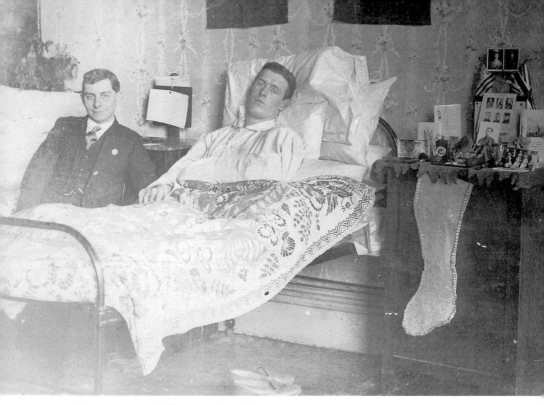

Christmas in a VAD hospital in Paignton.

Paragon Rest Station

As a major port and railway terminal, Hull had large numbers of military personnel passing through in transit to their destination. This put a strain on local resources even when facilities were open, and it was soon realised that the best way to deal with this transient population was a dedicated facility which was opened on 1 September 1914. From the commencement of its service, Paragon Rest Station was open twenty-four hours a day, providing shelter and refreshment to tens of thousands of men. Initially, everything was provided free of charge but as the cost of food rapidly increased, the sub-committee of the rest station were compelled to make the small charge of a penny, later rising to two-pence; expecting a decrease in use, the committee were pleased to find that the converse occurred.

After two years' work, the committee provided sleeping accommodation for stranded men. Thirty-four bunks were provided and fully equipped with bedding, through the kindness of the Ellerman-Wilson line, and for these a small charge of two-pence was made, while the North Eastern Railway Company provided the room, the heat and the light gratuitously. A buffet, at which sandwiches, pies and a variety of cake could be obtained, was also run. The station was exclusively staffed, night and day, for the first two years, by nursing members of the VADs of the St John Ambulance. After that time they were assisted by voluntary female helpers.

A bedroom at the Church Army Soldiers' Hostel in London.

Year	Number catered for
1914 & 1915	27,840
1916	108,741
1917	302,800
1918	322,950
1919	3,275
Total	765,606

Beds were found for 42,132 men during the war.

Reckitt's Hospital

This hospital was organised and financed by Mr and Mrs P Reckitt and was staffed by VAD nurses. It closed in January 1919.

Brooklands Officers' Hospital

In the early part of 1917 there was an urgent need for sick accommodation for officers connected with the Humber Garrison. As a

The Church Army Soldiers' Hostel canteen at Buckingham Palace Hotel, London.

consequence Brooklands came into being under the auspices of the East Riding branch of the Red Cross with Mrs Strickland-Constable as Commandant.

Lady Sykes' Hospital

This was equipped by the late Sir Mark and Lady Sykes in the Metropole Hall, Hull, being staffed by trained and VAD helpers. It was decided later it was not needed and was transferred to France where it stayed until its return to Hull in January 1919.

The Voluntary Aid Detachment Hospital and Depot

Most towns and cities set up VAD hospitals, indeed many such hospitals were set up in hotels, stately homes and any other large buildings that suited the task, and even schools were used. As well as a hospital it was also necessary to set up a hospital supplies depot that dealt not only with the voluntary hospital but also with military hospitals and army hospitals abroad. The following account, based upon the experiences of Hull during the period 1918/19 is not atypical and gives a flavour of the work done all

A building commandeered to act as a war hospital supply depot.

A boat trip for wounded soldiers lucky enough to be in hospital at the coast.

over the country during this period.

During the year the work of the Hospital increased steadily, and the total number of 4,933 were treated – in addition to the important work of the Out-patient Department – the average number of in-patients being 287, compared with 190 in 1917. The largest number in one day was 432.

In the Out-patients' Department great developments have taken place, and surgical, massage, several kinds of electrical and Dowsing radiant heat treatment are now available. An electric switchboard was

The Plains VAD hospital for the lightly wounded in a country house at Elland.

presented by the officers of the 5th (Reserve) Durham Light Infantry, and an electrical vibrator by the officers of the East Yorkshire Regimental Depot at Beverley, and a considerable amount of other apparatus has been purchased. Seven masseurs are now employed, and the total number of out-patient attendances for the year has been 4,390.

The influenza epidemics of July and October put a severe strain upon the resources of the hospital, and upon the staff, many of whom were themselves ill; and it is greatly to their credit that the work was carried on efficiently in the face of such difficulties.

During the autumn there were a number of repatriated prisoners (of war) who required hospital treatment before being sent to their home(s), and everything possible was done for them – the usual restrictions as to food, etc., being entirely relaxed.

The hospital received many gifts during the year – too numerous to mention... but which have been of the most essential value in carrying on its work. As will be seen from the balance sheet, £6,032 9s. 9d. was received in donations, of which about £5,000 was given in response to a special appeal from the County Director for the General Maintenance Account, and it is desired also to acknowledge generous subscriptions to special funds. The 'Compassionate Fund' was established by a grant from the Lord Lieutenant's Fund, for the assistance of relatives of men seriously ill who were unable to afford the expenses of visiting them, and has been a great help.

The 'Comforts Fund' originated in a scheme of the Hull fruit Merchants, to sell by auction some fine specimens of vegetables grown at the hospital. This sale took place on 24 September, and was splendidly assisted by Mr Fred Terry and Miss Julia Neilson, with the very gratifying result that £172 2s 6d was realised. Other subscriptions have been received, and the fund has provided special wheel chairs, cigarettes, tobacco, music, and other things for the pleasure and

A Huddersfield based charity fund-raising postcard.

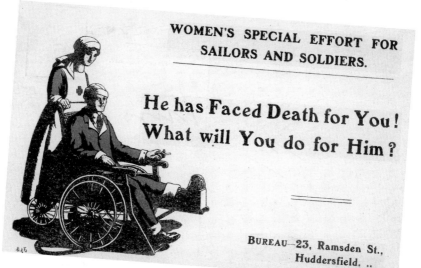

WOMEN'S SPECIAL EFFORT FOR SAILORS AND SOLDIERS.

He has Faced Death for You! What will You do for Him?

BUREAU—23, Ramsden St., Huddersfield. ..

comfort of the patients, which have been greatly appreciated by them.

Our special thanks are also due to the Artistes from the Hull Theatres and Music Halls, and to the many excellent Amateur Companies, who since the opening of the Hospital have given so many splendid entertainments, and to Mr S Whitby for organising these functions. Great hospitality was also shown to patients (who were able to get out) by Messrs Earle's Distress Committee, the Commercial Travellers' Association, several Hull Firms and Parishes, and Mrs Hide, and other kind friends.

The Ladies' Committee (Secretary the late Mrs Bilson) undertook the supply of flowers to the wards, and also taught handicrafts to the patients. The regular visits of the ladies were greatly appreciated by the men, and thousands of specimens of beautiful embroidery and other work were executed in the Hospital.

Christmas 1918 was felt to be an event of special celebration, and Major and Mrs Atkinson collected £226 5s 2d for presents and general festivities. Everyone who spent Christmas in hospital is likely to remember it as a thoroughly enjoyable and happy time...

For their services to the hospital Mrs Arthur Atkinson (Deputy Commandant), Sister Fanny Pease and Sister Lucy Brooks were awarded the Royal Red Cross, 2nd Class.

As well as a hospital, St John's Ambulance also ran a hospital supplies depot from September 1916 until the end of hostilities. The depot was formed by amalgamating two similar organisations and was placed under the control of Peel House that also dealt with Prisoners of War and locally raised army units. All the work of the depot was carried out in the Banquet Hall of the Guildhall and an adjoining room.

When the VAD hospital was opened the depot was able to substantially contribute to its initial needs. The needs of the hospital now took priority and so made it impossible for many of the VADs to continue working at the depot. However, other workers came forward, and the activities of the depot increased. During the two years and four months 138,210 articles were sent out – 24,206 to France, large numbers to Hull hospitals, St John's Headquarters, and to Sir Edward Ward, Director-General of Voluntary Organisations. St George's War Relief Committee in New York sent large consignments of garments, many of which were used to re-equip a bombed hospital in Boulogne. The depot was an expert manufacturer of a special dressing for the Carrel-Deakin treatment; the dressings were sent to Red Cross Hospital No. 9 in France.

The depot officially closed on 20 December 1918 but in response to an appeal by Sir Edward Ward to help the devastated areas of France, the depot collected and sent out just under 4,000 new garments of one type or another. In just over twenty-eight months, the depot had sent out 142,000 articles.

Belgian Refugees

The onslaught of the German army in the early days of the war created large numbers of refugees, particularly in Belgium. With virtually none of their country left to migrate to, many thousands of them sought shelter in Britain. The exodus began in the latter days of August 1914, rapidly increased through the autumn and winter, and by the middle of June 1915 it was estimated that there were over 265,000 Belgian refugees in the country; an unprecedented migration.

Although there were some wealthy families and many professional men among the refugees, the majority of the migrants were from the working classes. Every trade was represented, from the peasant in his wooden sabots and the dock labourer of Antwerp, to the postal employee, the railway servant and the skilled mechanic. Whether true or not, *The Times History* recounts that 'some had left behind them their burned village or the flaming streets of Louvain. Some had seen husband or wife or child butchered before their eyes.' The majority simply fled from the reputation that the Germans had quickly made for themselves.

The level of preparedness for the exodus varied and must surely, in many cases, have shown the speed at which the decision to flee had been taken and or the situation in which they had found themselves. Some, recorded *The Times History* 'came in haste, the women with a shawl on their heads and their working aprons round their waists, carrying nothing but their babies in their arms', while others set out with as many possessions as they could carry, and one sometimes saw a father struggling under the burden of a mattress, while the mother carried a bundle and the little children had each a pot or pan.

They arrived at Folkestone, Tilbury, Hull and many ports in between, in

Belgian refugees retiring towards the Allied rear areas. Many thousands of such people were soon to arrive in Britain.

From Antwerp to England by barge.

every kind of ship, from the yacht and the smack to the mail-packet and tramp steamer. Ernest Cooper, solicitor and Town Clerk of Southwold recorded the event in the journal he wrote up after the war from the diary he kept at the time:

> *We hardly realised what war really meant until the 15 Oct. when the Ostend smack* Anna Williams 028 *arrived in the Harbour with Belgian Refugees and we saw numbers of other smacks making for Lowestoft. I boarded her with a pilot at the Harbour mouth and found her crowded with men, women and children from seventy years to an infant, who had fled just as they were with pitiful little bundles and boxes, leaving everything else to the Germans who were reported just outside Ostend. These people were well looked after by the Southwold folks but were ordered to London and left the next day in a special motor bus for Halesworth where they joined the Lowestoft refugees about 1,000 in number. There was great excitement about these poor people and we thought it might be our fate later.*

Their journey from Ostend to England had not been easy, recorded *The Times History*:

> *The shutters were up in the shops, the hotels abandoned, and even when they had money in their pockets there was neither food nor rest to be had. They waited with their bundles on the quays through a night or a day, until at last a boat bore them to safety.*

Nor was their condition good:

> *They landed in the last extremity of mental depression and physical exhaustion. Babies were born during the flight. Some families had brought with them an aged and almost bedridden grandparent. The children, who began soon after to regard their experiences as an exciting and delightful adventure, were at this stage perhaps the worst sufferers of all.*

218

An unknown Belgian refugee family safely placed in an English home.

The size of the migration arriving on the east coast was to be a severe test of English hospitality.

The first comers were chiefly people who paid their own way, and landed with enough money to last at least a few days. Later arrivals, the destitute, as *The Times History* calls them, started to arrive just before the end of August, arriving in London at the start of September, at the rate of 500 a day. The fall of Antwerp rapidly increased the numbers arriving. One steamer alone was reported to have carried over 2,000 refugees. In one day 11,000 of them reached Folkestone harbour and, in the week that followed the fall of Ostend, over 26,000 arrived at Folkestone; among them were many wounded Belgian soldiers. By the end of November 45,000 penniless refugees had arrived, with a further 12,000 more in December. Each month after this date the number of refugees dwindled until by April 1915 it was down to 4,642. Later arrivals all came from Holland, and the migration, which fell in the summer of 1915 to about 2,000 per month, was carefully controlled and confined to workmen who were certain to find a job.

A detailed census of the refugees was carried out after they arrived, in order to provide statistical data for the Local Government Board that controlled the new arrivals, to assist the Labour Exchanges in finding suitable employment and to allow the Belgian government to trace men who were eligible for military service. As an after-thought, it was placed at the disposal of the refugees so that they could trace lost friends and missing relatives. Somerset House,

A souvenir postcard sold to raise funds for the Belgian and British Relief Funds.

Stanley's Press Agency.

GENERAL JOFFRE.

Pierre Petit Copyright

ONE PENNY.

BRITISH & BELGIAN RELIEF FUNDS.

FIVE SHILLINGS ON EVERY HUNDRED CARDS SOLD GO TO THESE FUNDS,

Official

by arrangement with the Belgian Authorities.

which dealt with the work, calculated that by June 1915, 265,000 refugees had arrived in Britain from Belgium, of whom 40,000 had been wounded soldiers and 15,000 were Russian Jews who had worked in the diamond-cutting industry of Antwerp. Of these, 6,000 were cared for entirely by the Jewish population of London without cost to the taxpayer. Around 10,000 of the refugees (mostly men) returned to Belgium as a result of the tax that the municipalities under German control levied on the property of absentees.

CENSUS RETURN OF JUNE 1915

Age and gender breakdown of refugees	Number in group
Men over military age of 25	51,000
Men of military age (18 to 25) who were married, about to enlist or unfit for service	8,000
Women and girls over 16	80,000
Boys between 16 and 18	6,000
Boys and girls under 16 but over 5	46,000
Children under 5	20,000
Total	211,000

Prior to the war, the Ulster organisation had prepared for a potential civil war if it had to physically resist the Home Rule Bill. The women's organisation of Ulster had quietly arranged for many of the non-combatants to be provided with safe accommodation in England. When approached by Lady Lugard, the organisers quickly gave permission for the accommodation to be used by the Belgian refugees. At the same time, the Earl of Lytton started a relief fund. The first public appeal from the War Refugees Committee appeared in the newspapers of 24 August, asking for hospitality, money, clothes, food and personal service. On the first day, more than a thousand letters arrived, each offering hospitality; within a fortnight offers of hospitality for 100,00 refugees had been received. The offers came from all over the United Kingdom.

> Many a working-man offered a share of his cottage to a comrade from Belgium, and groups of neighbours combined to share the responsibility of feeding and housing one of the families.

The immediate problem was not how to organise this hospitality but what to do initially do with thousands of hungry, tired and sometimes ill refugees, many of who were also in need of clothing. To overcome this initial difficulty required a system of temporary receiving depots. The next problem was to decide in a very short period of time with only a few scant details which refugees could be placed with which host; matching occupations and social levels was to prove very difficult. All of the work initially done to help the refugees was voluntary; in all, over 2,000

Dinner time at Alexandra Palace.

voluntary local committees were involved.

Folkestone bore the brunt of the first migration. Here the local committee met the refugees as they landed, provided them with a hot meal, attended the sick and the wounded, housed as many as the local area could accommodate and then supplied the wants of those who were going onto London. Here, the first task was to provide temporary accommodation, often very quickly. In the Borough of Camberwell a hundred Belgians

A notice from the National Committee for Relief in Belgium to be read out in schools to help raise money for the Belgian children left behind.

Wounded Belgian soldiers at a VAD hospital.

were housed in Dulwich baths, while in the space of fifteen hours the War Refugees Committee took over an empty shirt factory near Victoria Station and converted it into housing. The empty but clean building was lent free of charge by the Army and Navy Stores who supplied all the beds at cost price while the crockery and linen were lent by the Rowton Houses. Work started at 8 pm and by 3 pm the next day the beds were made up, a kitchen installed with eight big stoves, the tables were laid and a hot dinner awaited the first batch of 250 refugees.

As the numbers of refugees passed the 100,000 mark, it became obvious that there would have to be some form of government intervention. Such a deluge of immigrants could cause public health problems and could have a severe effect on employment. There was also the possibility that some of the refugees could be German spies. On 10 September 1914, Mr Herbert Samuel on behalf of the government offered the Belgians the hospitality of the nation. The Local Government Board was given the responsibility of dealing with the problem.

Many hosts and a large number of committees provided entirely for the maintenance of their refugees but, where the government committee paid, the flat rate was 10s a week for adults and children. As well as paying some of the costs, the government also had to arrange an education for between two and three thousand children using French or Flemish-speaking teachers. Grants were also necessary to provide health care for the sick.

Middle-class refugees who had arrived without any means of support were a major problem because they were less likely to find suitable work in Great Britain. For their needs, flats were taken in 'model' dwellings in Battersea and Brixton, with rents varying from 6s 6d to 15s 6d a week. Suites of furniture for each flat were purchased at discount prices and hired to the refugees at charges that quickly covered their costs; in this way families were kept together. About 1,100 people were housed in London under this scheme. Alternative arrangements were made for other middle-class Belgian families in the form of eleven hostels, conducted like private hotels. Food was organised by the National Food Fund which received

The dormitory at Alexandra Palace.

generous gifts of food from Colonial governments and from English firms; purchasing in large quantities at low rates, it passed on its savings to the refugees. The Committee's clothing department, under Lady Emmott, distributed over a million garments and boots to the refugees, mostly supplied by free gifts.

For the majority of the new arrivals their reception was in temporary shelters provided by the Local Government board, acting through the Metropolitan Asylums Board, first at the Alexandra Palace and afterwards in the Exhibitions buildings at Earl's Court; together they held about 12,000 people. Here they were provided with a clean bed and warm shelter. Earl's Court was converted into airy dormitories with hundreds of beds in orderly rows; the big central hall was a dining room and in the kitchens Belgian chefs and bakers were at work using food provided by the

Programme of music at the Chatsworth Hydro for Christmas 1914 signed inside by resident Belgian refugees.

colonies. A spacious reading room and a big sewing room occupied the refugees in their spare time, while the children were provided with a well-equipped schoolroom and the babies an up-to-date crèche. There was a laundry and the small theatre had been converted into a chapel.

After three or four days the refugees were sent to other quarters, initially found by private individuals. They entered private houses as guests, sometimes permanently but generally only staying for a few months. Local committees lent or hired houses and in some areas locals clubbed together to maintain a Belgian family among them. Generally these arrangements catered for small numbers of refugees, it was up to the big cities to take the majority of the temporary residents. Glasgow, with financial aid from the rest of Scotland, took in 10,000 refugees, as well as subscribing £130,000 to the Belgian Relief Fund. However, in many areas it was not possible to accommodate refugees because of the needs of the new armies.

With the continued influx of refugees it was necessary to find even more accommodation. Britain's seaside resorts were to provide the answer. The outbreak of the war in the middle of the holiday season had meant a considerable amount of lost business, and the arrival of thousands of refugees paying 10 shillings (eventually 11 shillings) a week was a boost to many a local economy, especially as the accommodation would be occupied during the normally quiet period of winter. The seaside resorts of Devon, North Wales and Blackpool provided the refugees with pleasant and healthy surroundings.

However, there was one major drawback: such resorts had no industry

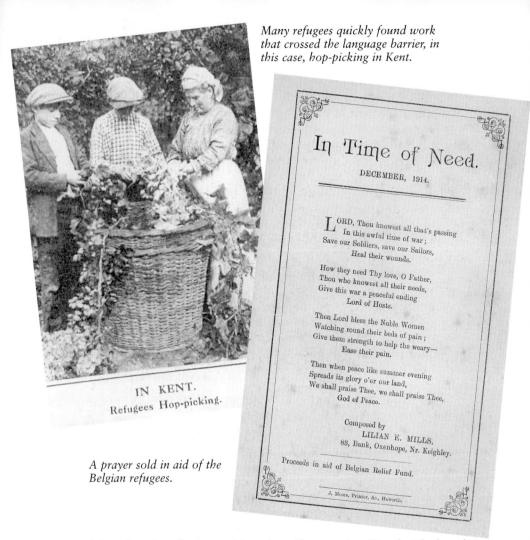

Many refugees quickly found work that crossed the language barrier, in this case, hop-picking in Kent.

IN KENT.
Refugees Hop-picking.

A prayer sold in aid of the Belgian refugees.

In Time of Need.

DECEMBER, 1914.

LORD, Thou knowest all that's passing
    In this awful time of war ;
Save our Soldiers, save our Sailors,
    Heal their wounds.

How they need Thy love, O Father,
Thou who knowest all their needs,
Give this war a peaceful ending
    Lord of Hosts.

Then Lord bless the Noble Women
Watching round their beds of pain ;
Give them strength to help the weary—
    Ease their pain.

Then when peace like summer evening
Spreads its glory o'er our land,
We shall praise Thee, we shall praise Thee,
    God of Peace.

Composed by
LILIAN E. MILLS,
83, Bank, Oxenhope, Nr. Keighley.

Proceeds in aid of Belgian Relief Fund.

J. Moore, Printer, &c., Haworth.

and therefore the refugees could not be self-supporting. To take Blackpool as an example: it had 2,090 refugees, of whom, by June 1915, only 200 had found employment on the railways, as military tailors or with the council. This meant, for the majority of the refugees who were sent to such resorts, enforced idleness and no money. Such conditions could easily have led to social problems but the Blackpool police, in the first four months of this 'friendly occupation' reported only half a dozen minor misdemeanours among the 2,000 refugees.

The children benefited most from the healthy and interesting environment. They learned English much more quickly than their parents and were generally able to converse freely in their new language. Two elementary schools were provided for their sole use where Belgian sisters taught them in Flemish. Around fifty went to an ordinary Blackpool elementary school where they did well. Twenty middle-class children received free scholarships to attend the secondary school.

A PLAIN DUTY.

Britannia (*to Holland*). "MY RESOURCES AND MY OBLIGATIONS ARE GREATER THAN YOURS; LET THIS SERVICE FALL UPON ME."

[The number of Belgian refugees in Holland is probably ten times as great as the number in England.]

A large number of Belgian refugees crossed into Holland and then sailed to England.

With British industrial manpower on the decline because of the demands of the armed forces, the refugees might well have provided a potential pool of extra labour. However, the urgency of housing them had dispersed potential workers away from possible employment. The Committee divided the refugees into three categories:

1) those qualified for industries in which labour was short – armamemts, glass, wool, coal, motor works and agriculture;
2) other manual workers;
3) professional men, civil servants, teachers, clerks and artists.

Even with a shortage of labour many of the refugees could not or would not work. Many refugees in Blackpool were offered unskilled work in the Lancashire chemical industry at 25-30s a week, a wage that would not provide for the basic needs of a family. Coal miners refused to allow Belgian miners to work underground because their lack of English could affect safety; some, however, were given jobs on the surface. Belgian dockers could not find equivalent work because they were not allowed into the restricted areas around the coast due to espionage worries. The Belgian fishing fleet went to Milford Haven, releasing British trawlers for mine clearance and patrol work. It was even more difficult for the middle classes to find suitable work – what sort of employment could be found for the 105 wine merchants among the refugees? However, some of the lawyers found employment of one sort or another and one university lecturer found work in the local tramway sheds. By the end of June 1915, 20,000 Belgians had found work through Labour Exchanges while another 50,000 had found their own employment. This left around 50,000 who were still unemployed, one of whom refused any offers of work on the grounds that he was the King of England's guest!

Many non-commercial schemes were put into place to provide some form of employment for the refugees. One scheme in Hammersmith took a group of carpenters and boot makers and taught them cabinet making, wood carving and leatherwork; using the knowledge gained they made English and Belgian style furniture and copies of chests and lamp-stands from Ypres. In Bradford the local refugee committee ran classes and workshops in dressmaking, millinery, boot repairing and carpentry and taught the workers English. After successfully finishing the classes they graduated to the workshops where they made articles of clothing or furniture that would be of use on their return to Belgium, or repaired their own clothes and boots. Among the men trained we find an architect, a lawyer and a schoolteacher. All the workers received skilled worker rates of pay, of which half was deducted for their board and lodging, fifteen per cent was given as spending money and the remainder was put aside, at their own request, for when they returned to Belgium.

3

The Special Constables

According to *The Times History of the War*, 'no men were called upon to discharge more thankless and unprofitable work than that which was done by special constables' specially as they were bound by terms of service which only ill health or other urgent reason could nullify. In some parts of the country the service was easy, but in London and other areas subject to air raids the task of the Special was both trying and dangerous.

At the beginning of the war, men flocked to their local police station to join the Specials; their names and addresses were taken, and they were told which police station would swear them in. And with little in the way of age restriction, one London Special had previously served as a special constable back in the 1880s. Another special constable, Chief Inspector Maynard-Taylor completed three years of service at the age of seventy. During that period, working for an average of $4^{1}/_{2}$ hours a day for 1,096 days, he had missed only one day of duty. As long as a man was healthy he could join the Specials.

Most urgently needed were motor and ordinary cyclists. These men proved their value in patrolling scattered areas, in carrying dispatches, and in giving warnings of air raids and announcing the all clear. Prominent actors formed their own group that was used for patrol work between midnight and 4 am, while Lord Goschen undertook to organise bankers in the city into a unit for the special constabulary. One particularly volatile and dangerous area was the East End of London where it was estimated that there were over 100,000 aliens resident, and for service in this area a knowledge of German or Yiddish was considered useful.

Enthusiastically they went forth to do jobs for which they had neither the training nor equipment. Their uniform consisted of their own clothes.

Colonel Sir Edward Grey inspecting Special Constables at the start of the war.

Armed with only a whistle, a notebook and a truncheon, the 'Specials' were given the same roles as the regular police force.

GUARDING THE WATER WORKS.

One of the many places
Specials were given to guard
were water treatment plants.

If they were lucky they had a truncheon – a weapon that had to be hidden from view lest it created alarm in the public mind; this resulted in the construction of secret pockets in their clothes where a truncheon was not visible, but could be easily pulled out. The use of a lead core in the truncheon was expressly forbidden. Thus equipped, they were detailed off to guard what were classed as potential danger spots, places which were likely to be attacked by organised gangs of aliens. The numerous locks, bridges, wharves and waterworks between Deptford and Teddington had to be guarded and for this duty men with motorboats were asked to form river patrols. Throughout the war, fortunately, no such attacks materialised but the special constables won the respect of the population in other ways.

As well as guard duties, early duties included the conveyance of enemy aliens to internment camps and the protection of anti-aircraft gun sites. While some were also involved in air raid duties, many just assisted the local police and kept the numbers on the beat at pre-war levels. One London constable calculated that he had walked nearly 4,000 miles during his nightly beat.

The Home Office controlled the Special Constabulary, but the supervision of its formation was carried out by George Cave, MP, on behalf of the Home Secretary. In the beginning each member was called upon to take duty for four hours every day, being provided with – in theory – a truncheon (the only permissible weapon, except under special authorisation), a whistle, a notebook and an armlet, (to be worn only during his tour of duty), and a warrant card bearing the number by which he would be known. Members came within the scope of the Police Act and were required to obey all orders from superior officers.

It was arranged that they should be, as far as possible, employed near their homes. Companies were allotted to divisions according to each area's requirements, each company consisting of one inspector, three sub-inspectors, ten sergeants and ninety constables. Members above the rank of constable were appointed by the members of the company, subject to the approval of the divisional commander. In London the headquarters were at Scotland House, New Scotland Yard, with district commandants at district headquarters at the Vine Street, Kentish Town, Kensington Lane and Old Street police stations. The same pattern was followed across the country. By the end of September 1914, there were around 30,000 special constables patrolling and guarding London's streets alone. While this was to be the main role of the majority of the Specials, there was also, for the very few, a secret service section known as the Central Specials.

In London formal enrolments took place at eighty-four separate buildings: police stations, public libraries, Town Halls, petty sessional courts, the Kingston Assize Court and the Royal Opera House in Covent Garden. Professional, business and working men of every sort joined, amongst them a former judge of the King's Bench, Sir Thomas Bucknill. More Specials came from the members of the Whitechapel and Spitalfields Costermongers' and Street Sellers' Union. Each enrolled man took an oath to uphold the law without favour, which in some cases later proved hard to do. One very early London special constable proved to be a German who was sentenced to six months' imprisonment and recommended for deportation.

Many had joined in the hope of catching spies. The first duty assigned to the London Specials, the guarding of railway arches, canal banks near tunnels, and bridges, electricity works and reservoirs, stimulated such expectations. German desperadoes provided with bombs for the railway arch or poison for the reservoir might come along any night – or day (at the

Special Constables called out for air raid service.

The Automobile Association's section of the Central Division Motor Police.

beginning of the war the watch on vulnerable points was a twenty-four hour job). As most of the Specials worked during the day it was often difficult to man these points fully during normal working hours. Disappointment quickly set in when the regular flashing lights turned out to be tram flashes or, often, actual signals being exchanged between London's own protecting forces. One minor success was achieved by a Special on Parliament Hill Fields when he observed two German-looking men. On sitting down near them, he heard enough to discover that they were from south London, and was able to secure their conviction as uninterned enemy aliens transgressing their geographical limit.

For most there were only the normal police experiences, stopping a runaway horse or tackling a drunk and disorderly, helping round up a burglar, helping at a fire or finding a suicide's corpse in the canal. There were also tragic incidents. A north London Special was found dead in a reservoir; the death was recorded as misadventure caused through age and one-man duty in the dark. However, at most vulnerable points duty proved disappointingly tame. With the approach of the winter months, each Special was issued with a waterproof cape and braziers were provided to keep them warm during the winter nights. Later in the war vulnerable points duty had virtually disappeared and the normal job of a Special was to relieve the regular police by patrolling in couples. The duration of the patrol was also gradually reduced to three and then two hours. After the Armistice, patrolling ceased early in the small hours, then it stopped altogether.

Pounding the streets night after night exhausted shoe-leather rapidly and originally the men had to provide their own. An original suggestion was that those who could afford it paid for their own repairs. However, this idea was dropped and each was provided with an issue pair of boots. The question of a distinctive uniform would not occur until later in the war and was a bone of contention for many Specials, who felt that the armband alone did not make them into 'real' policemen. For some time they were the butt of many jokes. One supposedly true story shows how contemptuous some people were about their role:

A professional man who, being called to a suburban house by a smart maid, was asked by the lady of the establishment if he was a Special,

and upon saying, 'I am, madam. Why have you sent for me?' was told,
'I want you to take my two little dogs out for an airing!' And before
the dignified constable could recover, there had been thrust into his
hands a lead, attached to which were 'two poisonous-looking pugs'.

Providing the men with a metal special constable badge did nothing to remove the problem. The official argument was economic but there were also problems of supply. As if to emphasise the danger as well as to protect them, the final piece of uniform to be issued was a steel helmet.

The first serious incident that the Specials had to deal with in London and in many other towns and cities across the nation, were the problems caused by the explosion of anti-German feeling after the sinking of the *Lusitania*. In London they were called out in force to protect the bakers' windows and to prevent the spread of trouble. Although bound by an oath, many of them found it difficult to protect Germans against their fellow countrymen, especially as in some cases the Germans had been offensive in tone and action.

Similar service was done in cities like Manchester and Leeds whenever there were disturbances caused by aliens. At one period there was a deeply hostile attitude towards Jews in connection with military service and serious disturbances seemed likely. In London it was common practice to use mounted police to control crowds but in the provinces these were not available and a different form of crowd control was needed. The plan was to make use of Specials who owned their own cars and organise them into 'storm' constables who drove their cars into and around the crowds using the same techniques as the mounted police. On such duties the police provided the petrol.

Some Divisions did detective work in plain clothes. In the autumn of 1915, many public houses were kept under observation to ascertain how many women customers entered the selected premises during the last two hours before closing time on Saturday nights (8 pm to 10 pm). This head count was part of the research for wartime regulation of the liquor traffic.

The most important work undertaken by the majority of the Specials was in connection with air raids. In London, the calling out of the Specials

Edmonton Special Constables' motor ambulance built by one of themselves.

OUR LONG-SUFFERING SPECIALS.

1. "'ANG THE BATON UPON THE RIGHT THUMB—SO."

2. "SPIN IT ROUND SHARPLY, AND THE BATON COMES NATURALLY INTO THE 'AND."

3. "SO —— AS YOU WERE!"

Teaching the 'Specials' to move their truncheons into place.

became the universal sign that a first warning had been received and was the signal for the underground and other shelters to fill. Often the Specials were called out to wait for long hours for a raid that did not materialise, and this when they had done a day's work, or were coming off patrol duty and had to go out on duty again afterwards. Some London districts had terrible experiences of death, fire and destruction from the first raid on. The Specials won the praise of the regular police for their coolness and organisation during the raids. First came the call, carried out mainly by cyclist messengers, in many cases while the guns were firing and the bombs exploding. Specials were distributed as needed, with a reserve being kept at the station for emergencies. The first Special to die was killed in the Strand while going to his duty.

A particularly trying duty was the regulation of food queues in the larger cities and towns, and more especially in the Metropolitan area, where difficulties had to be overcome that were far more acute than in the provinces. What made the duty so difficult was that the Specials shared the population's problems and so had great sympathy for those with whom they were dealing. Food queue control helped the people in the queue, the hard-pressed shopkeepers, and the police whose manpower was insufficient for the demands made on them.

By the end of the war the Special Constabulary had been fully uniformed. Here a sergeant is controlling traffic during the London police strike.

One special duty performed by the Specials was the guarding of Buckingham Palace. The men picked for this duty were of professional and business importance and were formed into the Headquarters Central Detachment of Special Constabulary. Formed in November 1917 from volunteers belonging to the principal London clubs, it took the place of the Yeomen of the Guard and the regular police who had patrolled the Palace gardens from sunset to sunrise. Each section's turn was one night in eight. The members were called out at every air raid on London; they lined the roads during processions and public ceremonies, and were on street duty during the police strike and later during the influenza epidemic that followed. Most of the members of this section, who provided their own uniform, were well over military age.

For the majority of the Specials, the most distasteful task they had to undertake was replacing the regular police in London when the latter went on strike in the autumn of 1918. The relations between the two forces had been very good and in many areas it took great persuasion to get the Specials out on the street. When they did go out on the streets, they were met with insults and violence against them by the police. A letter in *The Times* of 10 September 1918 made it clear how one particular Special felt.

I do not know whether you are aware of the bitterness and resentment which obtain amongst the great majority of Specials at the treatment they received at the hands of the regular police during the strike, and I venture to believe that if the public were aware of the insults and

A late war photograph of some of the Birmingham Special Constabulary.

Sergeant Weir of the Metropolitan Special Constabulary.

violence given to the London Specials their anger would be equal to the disquietude and loss of confidence which, I fear, they feel at the present moment in regard to a force they have looked up to and trusted.

Official appreciation of the work done by the Specials was expressed at the beginning of June 1919, when on being 'stood down', Sir Edward Ward, Chief Staff officer of the Metropolitan Special Constabulary, thanked them for the steady, loyal and devoted service by which they had earned the esteem and admiration of their fellow citizens by their patriotic unselfishness. At the same time, King George approved the issue of a long service medal for special constables who had served during the war. Although they had been officially 'stood down', their service had been so useful that in London a Metropolitan Special Constabulary Reserve was formed for use in any future civil or military emergency. In Shropshire the Specials were not even disbanded but increased in number from 300 to 547.

The London Specials officially ceased to exist at noon on 16 June 1919. On the preceding Saturday afternoon, more than 17,000 of them made their last public appearance when they marched past the King and Queen at Buckingham Palace. On a brilliantly fine day they marched, headed by the massed bands of the Brigade of Guards, taking an hour to pass the Royal couple. At the end of the procession each man received a copy of a message from the King thanking him for his devoted service.

The final parade of the Metropolitan 'Specials' past King George on 14 June 1919.

3

The Volunteer Force

Chaotic conditions prevailed in the earlier stages of the war Volunteer movement (initially men over military age and those unable to serve because of health or occupation). There was no organisation or acknowledged plan of training; discipline was almost a matter of choice. A Volunteer corps was fortunate if it had an ex-Guardsman as drill instructor; most units had no one with experience, and as a result had to make do with well-meaning but incompetent men showing other equally ignorant men how to use a bayonet or some other similar military task. In the early days of the war, 'the Volunteers were cold-shouldered at every turn and left to work out their own salvation' even though they existed for home defence.

Each Volunteer paid his subscription, hired or bought his Martini rifle, paid for his uniform, and, if he went to camp or firing practice at a range, bore all the expense himself, unless the Corps had been able to raise the money by public subscription. Even though they were well intentioned, they were ridiculed in public places during their training, as a result of which many of them resigned.

At an early stage Volunteers were provided with a brassard – a red armlet bearing the letters G R in black. The letters, which represented the Latin words *Georgius Rex*, gave rise to the nickname of 'Gorgeous Wrecks' for men who had passed their prime. There were no definite

The Volunteers, like the Special Constables, were given the job of guarding important places.

Initially many of the 'Volunteers' formed rifle clubs in order to promote military preparedness.

City of London National Guards on a route march (note that some are in uniform and others in civilian clothes).

rules for the remainder of the uniform, and, for many poorer members, it would remain the only article of uniform for some considerable time. An unattractive greenish-grey uniform was common at the start of the war among the Volunteer movement, but, as the organisation came under the control of the military, the uniform changed to the standard khaki of the regular army. Throughout the war the original uniform continued to be worn by older members and such bodies as the National Guard. In the early part of the war, many of the Volunteers were young men, but as time went on and conscription was introduced, the average age of the Volunteer force increased considerably.

A considerable number of what were known as 'special units' were quickly formed at the start of the war: units like the Businessmen's 'Friends' Battalion, the Athletes' Volunteer Force, the National Association of Local Government Officers' Special Battalion and various reserve regiments of Yeomanry, Artillery and Infantry, as well as Public School and other corps. The London Volunteer Defence Force, that had existed to encourage recruiting to the army and to induce men disqualified from service in the ranks to drill and learn musketry, and to co-ordinate existing organisations with similar objects, became the Central Volunteer Training Force. The War Office authorised a Colonial Infantry Battalion for men who were or had been associated with the Overseas Dominions and Colonies, with its headquarters at White City. All over the country, small Volunteer forces were formed, so many that the government had to call a temporary halt.

The Volunteers trained hard and in most cases became proficient soldiers

Motor Volunteers at Golder's Green. They are carrying a force of Volunteers to Potter's Bar for field day exercises.

with many of them becoming marksmen. Route marching and physical exercise helped many of the middle-aged men to regain much of the suppleness of youth.

Easter 1916 was the great turning point in the history of the war Volunteers. From this point onwards the War Office officially recognised them as soldiers; no longer was there a need to wear an armband to show who they were. However, after the initial announcement it was to be some time before they were fully assimilated into the military framework. One problem they posed was that, after a period of military discipline, they could become civilians again; another was their ability to resign at any time.

Slowly, however, the independent corps that had been formed coalesced into recognised army regiments – for instance, the City of London Volunteer Corps, the National Guard and other London-based units became Volunteer battalions of the City of London Regiment; the same procedure was applied across the country. Rules were laid down to secure efficiency and discipline as conditions of recognition, and the Volunteers were divided into four categories, A, B, C and D:

J Ford of the Eastbourne Volunteer Corps, September 1914.

'A' *category men* – undertook to serve as Volunteers until the end of the war and to make themselves efficient by attending the authorised number of drills and passing the recognised tests. These men were fully recognised by the government and provided with equipment and eventually with uniform.

'B' *category men* – mostly men of military age but exempted from service for the time being as munitions workers, miners, or for other reasons. These men were liable to be withdrawn from the Volunteer Force and sent abroad when their tribunal exemption was withdrawn.

A First Aid section of the Volunteer Training Corps.

Many men who managed to gain exemption from the military were told to join the Volunteers, even though they did not want to.

V.T.C. Recruit (who has joined under Tribunal compulsion). " OH, I SAY, SERGEANT, IF I COME TO THE PLATOON WHIST-DRIVE WILL IT COUNT AS A DRILL?"

'C' *category men* – boys under military age.

'D' *category men* – no obligation at all and could leave the force at two days' notice.

Of these groups it was obvious that the only ones that could be realistically counted upon for home defence were the category 'A' men, and Lord French, the C-in-C Home Forces, made a strong appeal to any man who was physically fit and over the age limit – for military service – to join this group. The purpose of this acknowledgement by the government was solely to provide an efficient home defence in case of invasion; there was to be no possibility of them being used out of the country.

A further problem to maintaining an efficient home defence was posed by the regulations governing tribunal exemptions. While they could grant a man an exemption simply on the condition that he joined the Volunteers, the exempted man was under no compulsion to sign the agreement and the officer commanding had no power of punishment if the man failed to attend

Learning trench digging on the site of the old Post Office, St Martin's-Le-Grand.

drills. An example of this is shown by the case of the Mayor of Daventry, who was ordered by the tribunal to join the Volunteers as a condition of exemption. The Mayor failed to join and, when asked why, stated that he could not join during his year in office. He complained that the position of Mayor in Daventry was not respected; if it were, he would not have been subjected to such annoyance and insult. This annoyance and insult amounted to the fact that the Town Clerk had reported him for not joining the Volunteers; unfortunately for the Mayor, the Town Clerk was both the clerk to the tribunal and the commanding officer of the local Volunteers.

According to *The Times History of the War*, the National Guard did excellent work. The members did twenty-four hour turns of duty, two hours on guard, four hours off, first at the Thames Tunnel and afterwards at the central telephone office of the General Post Office. This latter

City of London National Guard marching to Buckingham Palace to be inspected by the King.

The most widely worn uniform of the Volunteer Training Corps. The badge on the right cuff signifies proficient marksmanship.

Inspection of the National Motor Volunteers by General Sir Francis Lloyd at Wellington Barracks.

position suffered severely during an air raid. The National Guard also provided men to attend at St Bartholemew's Hospital during the air raid period, ready to help to remove the patients to the lower storeys when necessary. The City of London Volunteer Corps for some months provided a nightly and all-day Sunday guard for certain valuable barges at the West India Docks, supplementing the work of the Royal Engineers who were there on weekdays.

Other invaluable services were provided by the Motor Volunteers, who drove around the East End after air raids helping wherever needed. Another special section were the signallers of the Post Office who mended the damaged wires after air raids. Two of these Volunteers met their death when out for air-line practice one Sunday. The heavy Post Office van went down an embankment while attempting to avoid a collision with a tricycle, with the result that the men were crushed to death.

One special, non-military service that was discharged by the National Guard in London was to host those men who were returning home or going to the Continent. This work was done at railway stations that were extensively used by the troops, and particularly at Victoria. Tired soldiers, bewildered and ignorant of London, had the help of Volunteers, who directed them to their proper stations and told them the best way to get to their destination. These duties continued long after the Armistice was signed.

With the Armistice, the Volunteer Force was rapidly disbanded but in recognition of their services, officers who had served for an aggregate period of six months, and whose service had been 'good and satisfactory', were given an honorary rank equal to the one they had held with the Volunteers.

By the end of the war the Volunteers had become attached to regular army units and had been equipped with full army uniform.

3

A City At War

The following is taken directly, without correction, from the *Peace Souvenir* book produced by Hull Corporation in 1919. It detailed Hull's history from its origins to the end of the war and was a display of civic pride intended to show the importance of Hull through the centuries with a slant on Hull's importance to the overall war effort and as such is certainly biased. However, it does reflect the feelings of the times.

Probably the complete story of Hull's part in the Great War will never be known, so extensive and so diverse were the ways in which its thousands of workers toiled. In the actual output of certain classes of shells and other munitions the millions that were made may be fairly correctly estimated, but the figures are so vast that it is impossible to grasp their full significance. In repairs and alterations to the hundreds of vessels used in the Navy, and in the actual construction of ships of war, the amount of work is more difficult to put on paper, albeit the total number of ships dealt with is very great indeed. Our vast engineering works were quickly transformed from shops making all manner of articles for use in peaceful occupations, to furnaces and whirring lathes and steam punches, producing shells and grenades and bombs and various forms of weapons of war, which only became useful when blown to smithereens. Thus, while their production has unquestionably assisted in the successful termination of the war, it is sad to think that the result of all this expenditure of labour, wages and material, is so much scrap iron, and that lost! Whereas had the same expenditure resulted in the production of machinery or ships or articles used by civilised nations in peace times, how much richer might the world have been by the result!

Quite apart from the amazing record of munition-making, much was accomplished which, for various reasons, it is not possible to record. It is likewise difficult to estimate the large extent to which our Oil, Paint and Colour trades helped; the various factors and manufacturers of food stuffs and many smaller trades; in fact it would be difficult to find many which had not, in some way or other, assisted.

This tremendous result is all the more remarkable when it is borne in mind that nearly all the youngest and strongest of our workers, thousands of them, were over the seas fighting. Yet as a result of masterly organisation, long days of work by men and women, backed up by the ever present feeling that this country was on the side of right,

City Hall on Victoria Square. After initial recruiting offices proved to be too small to cope with the numbers, the City Hall became the main recruiting office.

The loss of light caused by the dimming of street lighting was partly alleviated by kerbstones being whitewashed.

Young munitions workers – the 'Somme' Munitions Boys.

Women war workers.

this miracle was achieved. Many of the men were those who had retired from business after many active years of hard work, hundreds of women and girls volunteered for duties which before the war even they themselves would have deemed impossible, and numbers of the best of our business men have certainly shortened their lives by the long hours and incessant worries and duties which were theirs. And now it's all over and we think of the hardships and the toils that have been, the grievous losses we have had, and the altered conditions of life of so many, we pause and ask ourselves – Was it worth while? Then we think of the future outlook of Belgium, of France, and of Britain – now the war is won – and try to imagine the conditions which would have obtained, not only for these countries but for civilisation generally, had the war been lost.

There is only one conclusion. It was worthwhile.

Recruiting

At the outbreak of the war when it was found necessary to raise, at the earliest possible moment, a huge army, Lord Nunburnholme was requested to obtain voluntarily as many men as possible from the City of Hull and the East Riding of Yorkshire.

He made strong appeals to the patriotism of the public, and the recruits came forward in large numbers.

The recruiting office in Pryme Street was found to be totally inadequate to cope with the number of men coming forward for enlistment. The Lord Lieutenant aroused interest and enthusiasm by the formation of local battalions, obtaining official consent to do this from the War Office.

The first of these Battalions was known as the 1st Hull Battalion ("Commercials"), and it was composed almost entirely of men drawn from commercial life. It was recruited in a few days at the Wenlock Barracks, Colonel George Easton being in charge.

This local battalion was one of the most successful raised in the country. Largely composed of intelligent and able men, it was soon found to contain a large number of men admirably suited to hold commissions in His Majesty's Forces.

The urgent need for Commissioned and Non-commissioned Officers in the newly-created army was as great as the need for men. Large numbers of men from this Battalion were granted commissions and many were promoted to Non-commissioned rank. This Battalion, which fought with such great distinction in various theatres of war, holds a meritorious record.

The Lord Lieutenant soon came to the conclusion that a more central Recruiting Office was necessary. He approached the City Corporation. The late Alderman George Hall dealt with the Lord Lieutenant's request in a sympathetic and patriotic manner, and largely due to his advocacy the use

Even with the war on, carnivals still took place. This one is a hospital parade float in Ecclesfield during the summer of 1916.

Soldiers on active service were issued with a postcard on which only words or phrases could be altered. Punch *suggested a similar sort of card for people in the Zeppelin zone.*

An advertising poster for war savings.

LEND YOUR FIVE SHILLINGS TO YOUR COUNTRY AND

CRUSH THE GERMANS

Words or phrases not required may be erased.

At the Front—Somewhere in England.

I am quite { well. / ill.

My windows are { smashed. / intact.

I have { a / no } crater in my { front / back } garden.

I { saw / missed seeing } the Zeppelin.

I { slept / did not sleep a wink } the whole night.

Grandmother behaved { like / unlike } a brick.

Letter { follows. / does not follow.

Signature only }

Date _____

MR. PUNCH'S SUGGESTION FOR A ZEPPELIN POST CARD FOR SENDING TO ANXIOUS FRIENDS AT ONE THE OTHER FRONTS.

Lighting regulations meant that all vehicles had to carry lights after dark, even prams.

of the City Hall for a considerable period was generously granted free of charge.

The Lord Lieutenant, together with the chief Recruiting Officers of the Northern Command, approached Mr. Douglas Boyd, Rating Surveyor and Superintendent Assistant Overseer of the Hull Corporation, with a view to his accepting the position as Recruiting Officer at the City Hall. The necessary consent being obtained, Mr. Boyd was granted a commission in His Majesty's Forces for this purpose, and opened the City Hall for recruiting on the 6th September, 1914, the special feature being the formation of the 2nd Hull Battalion.

A male Red Cross worker most of whom were too old or unfit for active service.

Within three days the 2nd Hull battalion was raised.

The success attending the formation of the 1st and 2nd Hull Battalions prompted the Lord Lieutenant to raise two further Battalions. As a consequence the 3rd and 4th Hull Battalions were subsequently enlisted, and the 'Hull' Brigade thus completed. Brigadier-General Sir Henry Dixon was appointed to the command.

The number of men raised for each Battalion at that time was 1050.

The 5th, or 'Reserve' Battalion raised was largely composed of men of smaller stature. These men were known as 'Bantams', little men with big hearts! This fine Battalion was also known as 'Lord Roberts' ('Bobs') Battalion.

During the whole of the time that the local Battalions were being raised, severe losses were taking place in connection with the various East Yorkshire units employed in the Expeditionary Force in France. The wastage in these regular units had to be made up, and men were recruited as quickly as possible as reinforcements. Recruits were also enlisted for all the different branches of the service, and whilst the raising of the local Battalions was a special feature, it did not in any way represent the large number of recruits who attested.

The great success of recruiting in Hull was attributable in no small degree to the central position of the City Hall, the unique accommodation which it provided for recruiting purposes, and to its exceptional adaptability for advertising, full advantage of all being taken. In the early stages of the war recruits were drilled in the main hall, the front of the building was extensively used for advertising purposes, whilst the balcony provided excellent accommodation for the various military bands drawn from the various Depots and Units stationed in the district.

Much time and effort was spent in raising funds to buy tobacco for the troops. This is an acknowledgement card for the Evening Express *(Cardiff) Tobacco Fund.*

If convenient, will you please write on these two postcards. You will notice one postcard is addressed to the donor, who would be glad to hear of the safe arrival of the parcel. The other postcard is addressed to the Editor of the Paper who collected the money.

POST CARD.

PASSED BY CENSOR
Nº 2071

The Editor,
"EVENING EXPRESS,"
CARDIFF,
S WALES.

ARE WE DOWNHEARTED ?

There was insufficient hospital space for all the returning wounded so many large houses were converted into temporary war hospitals most of which were run by volunteers.

A fancy dress costume of the period.

Great excitement prevailed, speeches were continuously being made from the balcony and the City Square, and hundreds and hundreds of men, moved to a sense of their national responsibility, streamed into the City Hall and offered their services to the country.

The necessity for raising more and more Units of Artillery soon became apparent, and the Lord Lieutenant obtained permission to raise various local Artillery Units. In succession three Heavy Batteries were formed and recruiting for these was very popular. Only specially selected men were taken, and the result was that three of the finest batteries in the kingdom were raised under the City's auspices.

The next Unit to be raised was the Divisional Ammunition Column, subsequently known as the 32nd Divisional Ammunition Column. This also stood out as one of the finest columns in the army. It was largely recruited from members of the City Police Force and the Tramways, and was commanded by Lt.-Col. James Walker.

Special attention was always given to the raising of reinforcements for the various Territorial units serving abroad, several of which suffered severely, particularly the 4th East Yorks. Battalion (Territorial Force) commanded in the early stages by Colonel Shaw who fell at the head of his men during their first engagement in France, in April 1915.

The losses in connection with the 4th East Yorks. Battalion (Territorial Force) necessitated special efforts being made for the raising of reinforcements. Lieutenant Colonel Arthur Easton heartily co-operated with the Recruiting Authorities in this direction.

Mercantile Marine

The example set by the Mercantile Marine was of such an exemplary character that large numbers of men in civil employment were induced to join the colours. But for the great courage displayed by the Mercantile Marine, in risking their lives in order that the necessary produce and goods should be brought (from) overseas, the war would have been certainly lost.

Fishing industry

Large numbers of men were recruited within the City from the Fishing Industry for the purposes of mine-sweeping and hunting submarines. The response in this respect was magnificent, and the citizens of Hull and the East Riding owe a deep debt of gratitude to the men who took the great risks associated with this service.

Humber Garrison

Great assistance was at all times rendered by the Humber Garrison. The various Officers Commanding, viz., Major-General Nugent, Major-General Ferrier, and Major-General Sir S.B. von Donop, K.C.B., at all times co-operated in obtaining men for any branch of the service. The sympathetic help extended to the Recruiting Authorities, especially during the period of voluntary recruiting, when route marches were arranged and military bands provided, was invaluable.

Soldiers' Club, etc
The various organisations within the City especially raised for the comfort of the men who were serving, also contributed very largely to the success of recruiting. Special mention should be made of the Soldiers' Club, Beverley Road, the welfare of which was presided over by Major A. J. Atkinson, assisted by his indefatigable wife.

'The Soldiers' and Sailors' Wives' Club, Mason Street, presided over by Mrs. Hubert Johnson, also deserve mention. This club proved how much could be done by those devoted to the cause to find relaxation for the wives of soldiers and sailors absent from home.

Tramways Committee
The Recruiting Authorities were indebted to the Tramways Committee for placing at their disposal special cars during the voluntary period of recruiting, and for allowing the use of cars for advertising purposes.

Very large numbers of men were raised locally for the Royal Flying Corps, Motor Transport Services and the Inland Water Transport Service.

All this took place during the period of voluntary recruiting.

Towards the middle of the year 1915, it was found that voluntary recruiting was not providing sufficient numbers of men to meet the requirements of the army. At the same time it was obvious to the government that the production of munitions of war was of equal importance to the production of men for the army. Men were being taken into the army from various industries, the maintaining of which was of vital war importance.

It was decided that a scheme of registration should be put into operation that the actual man power of the country could be ascertained, and the employment followed by each man noted.

It was determined that the work of registration should be carried out by the various local authorities. The actual registration took place on the 15th August, 1915.

The Local Authorities handed to the Recruiting Authorities forms containing the names of all men of military age, together with their occupations and other necessary particulars. The Recruiting Authorities then compiled registers of all men of military age.

The appeal for voluntary help within the City of Hull and the East Riding of Yorkshire was one of the most pleasant features associated with recruiting. Relays of helpers of both sexes attended morning, noon and night, in order that this work could be completed at the earliest possible moment. From four hundred to five hundred voluntary clerks were in continuous attendance at the City Hall for a considerable period. After a time it was found necessary to organise a permanent staff to carry on the work.

Major Douglas Boyd approached the Education Authority, which agreed to one hundred mistresses and lady teachers being accommodated at the City Hall for the work. The great help rendered by these ladies was invaluable.

As sufficient numbers of men under voluntary recruiting were not forthcoming it necessitated the introduction of what was known as the "Derby" scheme. This met with a great response within the City, many thousands of men enlisting.

The accommodation provided by the City Hall again proved its value, as Hull was one of the very few recruiting offices within the kingdom which was able to cope with the huge stream of volunteers. Over 12,000 men were dealt with in three days at this period.

The various groups were called up on Proclamation, but it was found that more men were required, and the Conscription Acts came into force. In this way men were called up in class order, particular consideration being given to those engaged in important occupations. Local and Appeal Tribunals met daily for the purpose of adjudicating on the claims for exemption put forward by the men called up for

A motorcycle ambulance of the St John's Ambulance Brigade in Nottingham. These were used to ferry the injured or wounded around the city upon their arrival.

VAD officers at Northwood House, a war hospital.

Most towns and cities provided soldiers' recreation rooms. Rather bizarrely, this one is in a Friends Meeting House. (The Friends were Conscientious Objectors).

Patriotic fancy dress.

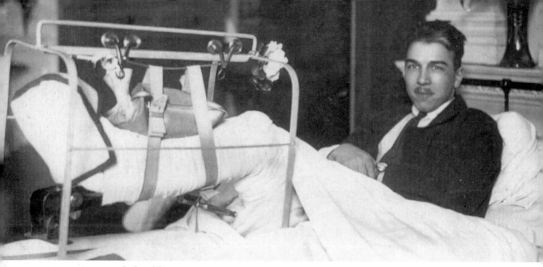

A wounded soldier.

service. This work was very strenuous and severely taxed the tribunals. Praise is due to the large number of gentlemen who voluntarily acted as Military Representatives during this period.

In the early stages of the war, particularly during the period of voluntary recruiting, much work fell upon the local Recruiting Committee, presided over by Sir Erik Ohlson, who, with the Secretary, Dr. T. C. Jackson, devoted much time to the work.

They were in attendance at the City Hall daily during the whole of the period.

Much important work was also done by the Advisory Committee, presided over by Mr. Walter Fred Harris. This Committee sat several hours daily to advise the Recruiting Officer in all cases where applications for exemption from military service were lodged.

The Port Labour Committee, which was appointed to consider claims for exemption from military service made by dock workers and others, did its work remarkably well under the chairmanship of Mr. C. S. Page.

An advert from Punch *magazine for a summer fund-raiser.*

A flag-day pin for the same event.

Packing a requisition in the warehouse in a hospital supply depot, in this case at St John's Gate.

A 1918 photograph of two boys emulating their elders.

Medical Boards

Recruiting in Hull could not have been carried on with such success but for the self-sacrifice and devotion of the medical men of the City, almost all of whom were over military age. Most were already doing double duty, having undertaken to look after the patients of younger medical men who had volunteered for service abroad with the Royal Army Medical Corps.

Rotas were formed and several Boards were in constant attendance at the City Hall, from the outbreak of war until the armistice.

A deep debt of gratitude is due to the medical profession for their untiring labours under most trying conditions.

Schools for Officers

The Hull Recruiting Office was looked upon by the War Office as one of the most successful and efficient recruiting offices within the kingdom. It was selected by the Northern Command as a centre for training Officers for recruiting work.

When the work of recruiting was taken over by the Ministry of National Service, the Hull Office was selected as a Provincial centre for training officers for the Ministry.

Letters of congratulation were received from Sir Auckland Geddes in appreciation of the excellent work done and the results attained.

Theatres and Cinemas

Great assistance was rendered by the various proprietors of Theatres, Music Halls and Cinemas within the City, by allowing their premises to be used during performances for the purpose of making recruiting *speeches to the audiences assembled. They also undertook nightly to throw upon their various screens recruiting slides of a patriotic and inspiring character.*

The total number of men raised within the City of Hull for all branches of His Majesty's Service was over 75,000. This is a magnificent record.

Territorial Force Association

During the whole period of the war the help rendered to recruiting by the Territorial Force Association was unlimited. In this respect the name of Colonel George Easton, D.L., T.D., should be associated.

Yeomanry

The East Riding Yorkshire Imperial Yeomanry (Territorial Force), commanded by Colonel Guy Wilson, D.S.O., earned for itself a meritorious record for services rendered in Egypt and elsewhere.

2nd Northumbrian Brigade Royal Field Artillery (Territorial Force)

Raised in the City, this unit served overseas with great distinction.

Northumbrian Field Ambulance Royal Army Medical Corps (Territorial Force)

Commanded by Colonel Faulkner, this unit, which was raised in the City, served with the 50th Division on the Western Front.

Fortress Engineers

From time to time considerable numbers of men were enlisted for the East Riding Fortress Royal Engineers (Territorial Force). This unit, originally commanded by Brevet-Lieutenant-Colonel E. M. Newell, distinguished itself in no small degree overseas.

5th East Yorkshire (Cyclists) (Territorial Force)

This was a home defence battalion used for coastal defence. All the 'A' category men were sent overseas as infantry after the introduction of conscription. It was commanded by Sir Robert Aske.

East Riding Royal Garrison Artillery

Commanded by Lieutenant Colonel Robert Hall, this battery was tasked with the defence of the City and County whilst stationed at Spurn and elsewhere.

Private Mennell volunteered for service with the 5th (Cyclists) Battalion of the East Yorkshire Regiment. With the introduction of conscription, all the able bodied territorials were sent overseas as reinforcements. Private Mennell was killed in action on 2 November 1916 while serving with the 10th West Yorkshire Regiment.

Five Hull Pals who volunteered at the start of the war. Of the five, only Private Hirst (top right) was not wounded after the attack on Oppy Wood on 3 May 1917.

Volunteer Battalions

The raising of the four Volunteer Battalions, two for the City and two for the County, caused much work for the Lord Lieutenant and Colonel W. Lambert-White.

These Volunteer Battalions, which were among the most proficient in the country, made it possible to release a considerable number of regular soldiers for service abroad.

Shortly after the declaration of war several bodies of men who, owing to their age, or for other reasons, were unable to enlist for service overseas, formed themselves into Rifle Clubs, with the object of defence in the event of invasion. These Clubs approached the Lord Lieutenant with the object of enrolling as Volunteers. His Lordship, however, deprecated the introduction of anything which might compete with recruiting for the New Army Units, to which he was devoting much energy and enthusiasm.

Immediately the last service Unit was raised, however, Lord Nunburnholme convened a meeting of those interested, and the two Hull Volunteer Battalions were speedily formed. The Second Battalion was largely raised from members of the Hull Golf Club, who had already enrolled themselves as Special Constables. In the formation of this Battalion considerable assistance was rendered by Mr. G. Morley, the Chief Constable.

The 3rd or County Battalion quickly came into being, and these three Battalions were grouped together under the original style of the East Yorkshire Volunteer Brigade.

The raising of the Brigade was entirely centred round the Lord Lieutenant, through whose initiative the Corps, at an early date, was ahead of any other in the kingdom. His lordship, recognising the liability of this coast to attack, appealed for subscriptions, which amounted in the aggregate to £17,600, and was devoted to the purchase of arms, equipment and clothing. Among the donors who should be specially recognised were the Corporation of Hull, and the East Riding County Council, both of which subscribed £1000 each. The Hull Corporation at a later date gave a similar amount to the funds of the 2nd Battalion in recognition of the service of its members as Special Constables. Among the generous supporters was Admiral Walker, of Beverley.

The Bridlington Corporation also purchased the arms and equipment of the Unit raised in that Borough...

Within a short period the Brigade was armed with 2800 Martini-Henry Rifles and 100,000 rounds of ammunition, and clothed in serviceable grey-green cloth, at a time when other regiments in the Kingdom were drilling with wooden rifles and clad in thin cotton drill uniforms...

Quite early in 1915, the Army Service Corps, then styled the Brigade Transport, was raised. This Unit was the only one in the kingdom. Its horses and vehicles were lent by patriotic merchants and others in the City, and its likelihood of practical utility and the magnificent stamp of horses were especially commented upon by Lord French at his inspection of the Corps in April, 1917. The Field Marshal's gratifying report on this inspection was much appreciated.

A study of the Official Volunteer List shows that out of 88 counties providing volunteers, the East Riding alone furnished as many as five specialist Units. The large counties of Northumberland and Durham and the cities of Edinburgh and Dundee come next, with four each – eight others only have three.

Flag days were a simple and inexpensive way of raising funds. This is just a small selection.

The Tank Bank was a popular method of getting the public to invest in the war after 1916. Tanks such as this did regular tours around the country.

The East Riding was the first to raise Volunteer Royal Garrison Artillery Companies. There were three companies of Royal Engineers formed – Works, Electric Lights and Signal. The Corps also raised the Motor Transport Volunteers, Army Service Corps. Members of this corps placed their cars at the disposal of Headquarters and Battalion Staffs for visiting and inspecting the various units in the region. Colonel Easton raised a Royal Army Medical Corps unit and in 1918 there was an anti-aircraft unit formed. This was as a result of a shortage of replacements for gunners sent overseas. In 1916 six Volunteer officers, over active service age, were given commissions in the regular army to assist with anti-aircraft work.

Like every city and town in the country, the role of policeman was taken on by the man in the street. In Hull over 3,000 special constables assisted the police in whatever way they were needed. As a port, Hull had considerable numbers of aliens living in the city, and an even greater number passing through on the ships that docked, resulting in much escort work which was continuously provided for the safe conduct of undesirable aliens while they were in port. Being close to the coast, the Specials were also involved in assisting, should there be an invasion. Hull's docklands covered a vast area that had to be guarded by the specialist Dock Guard Patrol. Other duties performed were controlling traffic coming into the city; during the King's visit in

WAR LOAN

LEND YOUR SAVINGS
TO THE NATION
TO-DAY

Apply for particulars at the nearest Post Office

War loan poster. Saving money in this way kept it out of circulation and reduced inflation.

1917, they were responsible for the control of street traffic and for keeping order. As in other towns subjected to air raids, the special constables had designated roles to perform and posts to man. Unlike London, no special constable was killed during the raids, but, several were injured, some seriously.

Further details of Hull's contribution to the war effort are covered in the section 'Looking after the troops'. What is detailed above was reflected in the war histories of numerous cities and towns across the kingdom, with each knowing its part was important and each vying to be more prominent in some respect than any other community. *A City at War* shows the story of the home front in a microcosm, a story that is largely forgotten or ignored.

Select Bibliography and Further Reading

Barnett, L M. *British Food Policy during the First World War*. George Allen & Unwin. London. 1985.

Bilton, D. *The Hull Pals (10th, 11th, 12th and 13th Battalions East Yorkshire Regiment)*. Pen & Sword. Barnsley. 1999.

Bilton, D. *The Trench, The full story of the 1st Hull Pals*. Pen & Sword. Barnsley. 2002.

Bishop, J. *The Illustrated London News Social History of the First World War*. Angus & Robertson. London. 1982.

Brown, M. *The Imperial War Museum Book of the First World War*. Sidgwick & Jackson. London. 1993.

Castle, H G. *Fire over England*. Leo Cooper. London. 1982.

Condell, D & Liddiard, J. *Working for Victory?* RKP. London. 1987.

DeGroot, G. *A Lost Generation?* Modern History Review. Volume 11, Number 1. Philip Allan. Deddington. 1999.

Gleichen, Major General Lord Edward. *Chronology of the War, Volumes I, II & III*. Constable & Co. Ltd., London. 1918, 1919 & 1920.

Horn, P. *Rural Life in England in the First World War*. Gill & Macmillan, Ireland. 1984.

Liddle, P. *Conscientious Objection*. Longman. London. 1977.

Liddle, P. *The Worst Ordeal*. Leo Cooper. London. 1994

Markham, J. *Keep the Home Fires Burning*. Highgate Publications. Beverley. 1988.

Martin, C. *English Life in the First World War*. Wayland. London. 1974.

Marwick, A. *The Deluge*. Bodley Head. London. 1965.

Marwick, A. *Women at War 1914-1918*. Fontana. London. 1977.

Mould, D. *Remember Scarborough 1914!* Hendon Publishing. Nelson. 1978.

Moynihan, M. *People at War 1914-1918*. David & Charles, Newton Abbott. 1973.

Munson, J. *Echoes of the Great War*. Oxford University Press. Oxford. 1985.

Pankhurst, E.S. *The Home Front*. Hutchinson. London. 1932.

Rickards, M & Moody, M. *The First World War - ephemera, mementoes & documents*. Jupiter Books. London. 1975

Robb, G. *British Culture and the First World War*. Palgrave, Basingstoke. 2002.

Robottom, J. *Britain and the Great War*. Longman. Harlow. 1996.

Sellers, L. *Shot in the Tower*. Leo Cooper. Barnsley. 1997.

Sheppard, T. MSc *Kingston-upon-Hull Before, During and After the Great War*. A. Brown & Sons, Ltd. Hull. 1919.

Southall, R. *Take me back to Old Blighty*. Milestone Publications. Horndean. 1982.

Strachan, H (Ed.) *The Oxford illustrated history of the First World War*. Oxford University Press. Oxford. 1998.

Simpkins, P. *Kitchener's Army*. Manchester University Press. Manchester. 1988.

Swinton, Major General Sir E. *Twenty years after*. George Newnes. London. 1938.

The Times. *The Times History of the War*. London. 1915, 1916, 1917, 1918, 1919.

Turner, E S. *Dear Old Blighty*. Michael Joseph. London. 1980.

Walsh, C. *Mud, Songs & Blighty*. Hutchinson. London. 1975.

War Office. *Statistics of the Military Effort of the British Empire during the Great War*. HMSO. London. 1922.

Williams, J. *The Home Fronts*. Constable & Co Ltd., London. 1972.

Wilson, T. *The Myriad Faces of War*. Polity Press. Cambridge. 1986.

Winter, J M. *The Experience of World War I*. Macmillan. London. 1988.